171 91

EXPRESS HOW
MUCH I APPRECIATE
THE INSIGHT &
INSPIRATION INTO
MY WORK, THIS
FINAL SEMESTER.
IT HAS BEEN
GREAT GETTING
TO KNOW YOU.
I HOPE YOU ENJOY
THIS BOOK AS
MUCH AS I DO —
BEST WISHES
IN YOUR WORK
THIS SEMESTER
AND ALWAYS.
    THANKS AGAIN
        ANNE

The Century of Artists' Books

The Century of Artists' Books

Johanna Drucker

Granary Books

New York City

This book is dedicated to Betsy Davids in affectionate appreciation of her contributions as a teacher, book artist, and friend.

Johanna Drucker is associate professor of contemporary art at Yale University. A writer and printer since 1972, she has produced some twenty letterpress artist's books, many using experimental typographic design.

Granary Books, 568 Broadway, Suite 403, New York, NY, 10012, USA
© 1995 Johanna Drucker and Granary Books
All rights reserved. Published 1995
Printed in the United States of America

ISBN: 1-887123-01-6

Library of Congress catalog card number 95-79670

The paper used in this publication meets the minimum requirements of the American National Standard for Information Sciences-Permanence of Paper for Printed Library Materials, ANSI Z39.48-1984

Contents

Preliminaries and a Personal Note

Artists' books have come of age in the 20th century. **The Century of Artists' Books** provides an overview of the development of this artform by mapping a history of major areas of activity in artists' books over the last hundred years and offering a critical structure for looking at work in this field.

The enormous amount of activity in the realm of artists' books in recent decades builds on the outpouring of creative production which has developed in the 20th century. Given the role which artists' books have played in most aspects of modern and contemporary art, it is particularly important to recognize them as a form in their own right, not an incidental spin-off of other concerns. To do this requires looking at the many kinds of work which are now known by the term artists' books, interweaving conceptual and critical issues with materials spanning the full range of the historical dimensions pertinent to this artform. Artists' books continue to proliferate rapidly.[1] It would be hard to find a moment in time when there was more interest in the field or more artists contributing their own work and vision to its development. Given all of this, it is remarkable how little comprehensive critical work has been done in the field of artists' books. I hope that this book will provide the impetus for further writing and research with historical and theoretical dimensions.

In any book which undertakes to chart a field of such scope and complexity, there are bound to be omissions. There are many artists, publishers, institutions, critics, and other professionals involved with the field who have been included in this work. But there are also some who have been left out. Generally this was because I chose an example which I knew better in order to make a critical point. This has not posed any obstacle to carrying through my highest priority: to make a survey of artists' books and to discuss their many varied concerns. I only wanted to write about books I had actually seen and handled myself. Since availability and familiarity were determining criteria many unique books were eliminated. Later editions of this work — or that of others — will no doubt expand beyond the names and titles featured here. In the meantime, I extend sincere apologies to anyone who finds themselves not listed in the index, not discussed in the text, or not mentioned in the footnotes who feels that they should have been included. In almost every case where that occurs, the omission is incidental, not intentional.

I have made a conscientious effort to include at least one book by every major book artist that I know of even if it is not the one by which he or she is best known. Major book artists are defined in terms of their status in the field and the critical contribution their work makes to investigating the book as an artistic form. I also mention many books by less well known artists, some of whom may have produced only a single, sometimes minor, work. If a work could demonstrate some element of structure, sequence, dynamics, or metaphysics of the artist's book, then it was included to show the diversity of approaches to the investigation of the book as an artistic form. There is a geographic bias towards the work of American artists, with Europeans taking second place; the artists of Asia, Africa, Australia, and South America are distinctly underrepresented. All of these are shortcomings which, hopefully will be forgiven by the reader and later corrected by myself and other writers.

The choices about how to structure this work conceptually and where to draw its boundaries were quite fully thought out — choices about what does and doesn't constitute an artist's book, where publishing interests overshadow artistic creativity, or where the concept of a book becomes lost or subsumed under another artistic definition such as installation, sculpture, or performance. My major focus is on showing the range of works which fall indisputably into the category of artists' books — and in engaging with the tremendous diversity, specificity, and varied character of these works.

My interest in books is as old as my consciousness of them — I cannot remember a time in my life when I wasn't interested in writing and in turning writing into book form. Like many writers I saw books as a form of legitimation — printed, published, bound texts had an air of authority no manuscript could approach. But I was also interested, early on, in formal structures and the relations between format and layout and the production of meaning in a literary text. It was not until later that I started to think about books which were not concerned exclusively or entirely with language.

Though I had made handmade books as an adolescent, clumsy, awkward works of much passion and little skill, it wasn't until 1972 that I first had an opportunity to learn to print. Betsy Davids, at that time my creative writing and printmaking teacher at the California College of Arts and Crafts, initiated a course which combined these two interests in a facility that contained that wonder of wonders — a Vandercook proofing press. I printed my first book in her course in the fall of that year, **Dark, the Bat-elf**, a work of repressed and rather labile sexuality which was vaguely late 19th century in form (red velvet covers, stone lithographed images, hand-set type). From that point onward, I was hooked. One book led to another and when I didn't have a press available, I went back to making hand-made, one-of-a-kind works. I had never heard the term "artists' books" — I just thought of myself as a writer whose interest in typography, printing, and experimentation made my work impossible for anybody but myself to publish.

My scholarly interest in books didn't begin until much later. It was during a three-month stint as secretary to the Registrar of the History Department at the Oakland Museum in the fall of 1979 that I came across a work by Gelett Burgess, **Le Petit Journal des Refusées** (1896), a piece of fascinating and little known California Bohemianism.2 Experimental in format, striking in its graphic quality, and utterly intriguing, this work became the basis of my first research project into printing and book arts history. This led me to apply to the Visual Studies program at the University of California at Berkeley, a loophole in the graduate program which was under the auspices of Tony Dubovsky and Marc Treib in the College of Environmental Design. Though my Ph.D. research ultimately was more focussed on the history of writing and theory of representation than on printing or book arts, the foundation laid in the six years course of study I was able to pursue at Berkeley (I graduated in 1986) are evident in every page of this work. During this period, I continued to make books, and though they were created in the context of a poetry not an arts community, I did begin to be aware, finally, of the growing range of activity in artists' books in the Bay Area and elsewhere.

The idea to write this book has been in my head for some time. While it crystallized rather precipitously and compellingly late in the fall of 1994, the materials I am drawing on have been collecting in my brain as well as in filedrawers and notebooks for much longer. There is much which is personal in this account — its biases, judgements, enthusiasms. I have used my objective perspective as an historian to counter my emotionally invested positions as an artist and have integrated my knowledge and experience of making books with my research into the history of artists' books. Most scholarly work has some kernel of an autobiographical sub-text: in this case, this interface is readily apparent at the surface.

In any project which has a diversity of materials and draws on a variety of sources, many acknowledgements are in order. My thanks to those individuals and institutions who allowed access to their collections: Max Marmor and Christine de Vallet in the Art and Architecture Library at Yale; Louis Silverstein in the Arts of the Book Collection at Sterling Memorial Library, and the other Yale collections and curators: Dick Field and Lisa Hodormarsky in the Yale Art Gallery, Prints and Drawings Department, and Elisabeth Fairman and Duncan Robinson in the Yale Center for British Art. A similar thanks to Robert Rainwater, Roberta Waddell, Margaret Glover, and the staff at the New York Public Library, Spencer Collection and Department of Special Collections and Print Room. Objects from the New York Public Library are photographed courtesy of the Spencer Collection, Miriam and Ira D. Wallach Division of Art, Prints and Photographs, the NYPL, Astor, Lennox, and Tilden Foundations. Also thanks to Tony Zwicker and Steve Clay for access to their personal collections. An acknowledgement is also due to those writers and scholars whose work has preceded mine: I have learned much from reading the work of Keith Smith, Judith Hoffberg, Renée Riese Hubert, Germano Celant, Anne Moeglin-Delcroix, Ulises Carrión, Clive Phillpot, Betty Bright, Nancy Princenthal, the authors of the essays in the anthology edited by Joan Lyons, **Artists' Books: A Critical Anthology and Sourcebook**, and many others whose catalogue essays or articles have helped define the issues and ideas relevant to artists' books. Special thanks belong to Susan Bee for expert copy editing and Gino Lee for design and computer consultation.

Finally, my thanks to those individuals who shared their interest, knowledge, and insights so generously in many conversations over the years. Most recently and immediately with respect to this project I owe much to Tony Zwicker, Betsy Davids, Steve Clay, and most of all, to Brad Freeman without whom this project would simply never have come into being.

1 The number of exhibitions, catalogues, articles, reviews and other so-called "ephemeral" publications, as well as the increase in interest in courses, degree pro-

grams, and professional organizations in the area of artist's books is such that it would be almost impossible to give a complete bibliography of the relevant materials, let alone relevant artists, collections, and so forth. Two examples are sufficient to show the proliferation of activity since the 1970s: **Livres D'Artistes, Livres Objets,** (Editions CERPM, Paris, 1985) an exhibition of unique books sponsored by the N.R.A. Shakespeare International in Paris, contained over two hundred works by individual artists, while the "Llibres d'Artista/Artist's Books" exhibition sponsored by the gallery Metrònom in Barcelona in 1981, contained work (multiples and one-of-a-kind books) by over eight hundred different artists including more than twice that number of actual books. The overlap between artists on both of these lists is relatively small, and there are many artists whose work who did not appear in either of these exhibitions, not to mention that there is entire generation of artists who have begun working with books within the last five to ten years.

2 This work is discussed in Chapter 2 at some length.

I

The Artist's Book
as Idea and Form

There is no doubt that the artist's book has become a developed artform in the 20th century. In many ways it could be argued that the artist's book is **the** quintessential 20th-century artform. Artists' books appear in every major movement in art and literature and have provided a unique means of realizing works within all of the many avant-garde, experimental, and independent groups whose contributions have defined the shape of 20th-century artistic activity. At the same time, artists' books have developed as a separate field, with a history which is only partially related to that of mainstream art. This development is particularly marked after 1945, when the artist's book has its own practitioners, theorists, critics, innovators, and visionaries. Among the many individuals to be mentioned here there are literally dozens whose achievements belong almost entirely to the realm of artists' books and whose work could sustain the kind of in-depth discussion accorded major painters, composers, poets, or other artists who work in more familiar forms.

What is unique about artists' books, however, is that with very few exceptions they really did not exist in their current form before the 20th century. However, a single definition of the the term "an artist's book" continues to be highly elusive in spite of its general currency and the proliferation of work which goes by this name. The increased popularity of artists' books can probably be attributed to the flexibility and variation of the book form, rather than to any single aesthetic or material factor. Rather than attempt a rigid or definitive characterization of artists' books, I am going to sketch out a zone of activity which I think of as "artists' books." This zone is made at the intersection of a number of different disciplines, fields, and ideas — rather than at their limits. Instead of trying to account causally for the development of the artist's book in the 20th century, I hope to make a case for the ways in which it is **the** 20th-century artform par excellence.

It's easy enough to state that an artist's book is a book created as an original work of art, rather than a reproduction of a preexisting work. And also, that it is a book which integrates the formal means of its realization and production with its thematic or aesthetic issues. However this definition raises more questions than it answers: What is an "original" work of art? Does it have to be a unique work? Can it be an edition? A multiple? Who is the maker? Is it the artist who has the idea? Or only if she or he does all of the work involved in production — printing, painting, binding, photography, or whatever else is involved? Or do each of these practitioners have to be taken into account, especially when there are complicated transformations involved in going from drawings to print, or photographs to inked plates, or when the binding has a structural form to it which has been designed or codified by someone other than the artist? What production means can be included in this definition — is a Gestetner print as valid as a means of producing art as a litho stone, a silver print, or a linoleum block? What about computer printers and xerox machines? Is a work which is made only of bound set-up sheets or other found paper a book production?ı Or one made of blank paper? Or appropriated images? Most people would agree to a common-sense definition of what is or is not a book. But with the work of artists this obvious definition soon loses its clarity. Is a book restricted to the codex form? Does it include scrolls? Tablets? Decks of cards? A block of wood with one end painted with a title, like a conventional spine? A walk-in space of oversized panels hinged together? A metaphysical concept, disembodied, but invoked in performance or ritual? While these questions address only a few aspects of an artist's book's definition, they show the immediate difficulty of trying to make a single, simple statement about what constitutes an artist's book.

If all the elements or activities which contribute to artists' books as a field are described what emerges is a space made by their intersection, one which is a zone of activity, rather than a category into which to place works by evaluating whether they meet or fail to meet certain rigid criteria. There are many of these activities: fine printing, independent publishing, the craft tradition of book arts, conceptual art, painting and other traditional arts, politically motivated art activity and activist production, performance of both traditional and experimental varieties, concrete poetry, experimental music, computer and electronic arts, and last but not least, the tradition of the illustrated book, the **livre d'artiste**. Since this last term causes the most confusion and difficulty it serves as a useful point of departure for beginning to sketch out this zone at the intersection of, but just beyond the limits of, any of these individual fields of activity.

The **livre d'artiste** came into being as a publishing enterprise initiated by such figures as Parisian art dealer Ambroise Vollard, whose first productions appeared in the mid-1890s, and Daniel-Henry Kahnweiler who began publishing slightly more than a decade later.2 This trend caught on among other editors who saw the opportunity to market deluxe editions which bore the name of a rising or established star in the world of visual arts or poetry (Vollard was associated with Georges Rouault and Kahnweiler with Apollinaire, Picasso, and other Cubists). Deluxe editions predate the existence of the **livre d'artiste** and books with all of the elements of the genre — large sized format, elaborate production values such as hand coloring, virtuoso printing, fine binding, use of rare materials, texts, or images which catered to a sophisticated or elite market — had long been an established part of the publishing industry.3 The **livre d'artiste** took advantage of the expanded market for visual art which had grown in the 19th century, along with other luxury markets expanded by industrial growth, the accumulation of capital, and an educated upper middle class with an appetite for fine consumer goods. The market for these books was developed as an extension of the market for painting, drawing, and sculpture. Kahnweiler was fully aware that he was creating a sideline in books which could be sold on the strength of the popularity and fame of artists whose work he dealt.

But if for editors these books were attractive in part as a new commodity, for artists they often offered the possibility to produce work which they wouldn't or couldn't normally produce themselves. This might include working in a printmaking medium, for example, or pursuing a theme which did not find an easy place in their other work. The artists whose work was featured in early **livres d'artistes** are among the foremost in 20th-century art, their names are the roster known from survey lectures and blockbuster exhibitions: Pierre Bonnard, Henri Matisse, Joan Miro, Max Ernst, and Pablo Picasso.4 These books are finely made works, but they stop short of being artists' books. They stop just at the threshold of the conceptual space in which artists' books operate. First of all, it is rare to find a **livre d'artiste** which interrogates the conceptual or material form of the book as part of its intention, thematic interests, or production activities. This is perhaps one of the most important distinguishing crite-

3

ria of the two forms, since artist's books are almost always self-conscious about the structure and meaning of the book as a form. For instance, the standard distinction between image and text, generally on facing pages, is maintained in most **livres d'artistes**. By contrast to the lively innovations which abound in artists' books, the work of even recent, late 20th-century, **livres d'artistes** tend to be embalmed in excessive production values, burdened by the weight of traditional format and materials.5 The paper wrappers of these books can barely contain their thick paper pages, and the large scale of the typefaces is surrounded by a veritable swath of blank margin. The images and text often face each other like new acquaintances across the gutter, wondering how they came to be bound together for all eternity in the hushed, mute, interior of the ponderous tome.6

Most of the works produced by entrepreneurs such as Kahnweiler were initiated as the vision of an editor. The artist and writer were often contracted independently (in many cases classic texts or authors were used as the basis of a new modern visual interpretation — Ovid, Shakespeare, Dante, and Aesop were favorite staples of the **livre d'artiste** genre). Artist and writer often didn't meet, or met through the arranged connection of the project, as in some loveless mechanical nuptial of convenience. These editorial habits, however, vary considerably from individual to individual, often with positive results. The contrast between the editorial vision of Collectif Génération and that of Andrew Hoyem at Arion Press, two contemporary producers of **livres d'artistes** — both successful on their own very different terms — makes this point dramatically. Gervais Jassaud, the editor of Collectif Génération, only produces works by living writers and artists. These are previously unpublished, often hand-done or hand-written editions for which Jassaud provides the framework (the shape, size, general format of the book). The degree of collaboration and interaction is left to the artists involved. In addition, Jassaud has worked to make his collaborations and his overall program an international one to an unprecedented degree — not merely publishing artists from a wide range of locations, but also facilitating an international process of exchange. Hoyem, in contrast, has used the texts of living and classic writers, and his work in many ways is a clearer continuation of the **livre d'artiste** tradition. Though in general it is the artist's and writer's reputations which sell these books, a rare or unpublished literary text can also be a selling point.

Editors' visions tend to be market oriented — theirs is a vision whose aesthetics are meant to guarantee the value of the product, not necessarily realize an original work. Thus the discrete nature of the elements: text, image, production (including printing, binding, typesetting, design, and so forth) are independent operations, guided by the editor, who engineers their compatibility with the necessary, consummate, taste. This third point is the telling one: the format of these works is perhaps their most characteristic feature, with a standard alternation of word and visual artwork, usually within a single spread or opening.7 This mechanical repetition of the conventional distinction between image and text returns these works to the category of illustrated books, rather than artist's books. This formula is hardly inevitable. It is interesting to note that some of the earliest examples of **livres d'artistes** were more adventurous in blurring the boundaries of image and text than the later ones. The Ambroise Vollard edition of **Parallelèment** (1900) with images by Pierre Bonnard, shows Bonnard's lithographed images weaving into the printed text, uniting the visual and verbal elements on the page. This approach is a continuation of innovations which began with Romantic printers and engravers almost a century earlier, most notably Thomas Bewick, who were intent on merging image and text in their works.8 While many **livres d'artistes** are interesting on their own terms, they are productions rather than creations, products, rather than visions, examples of a form, not interrogations of its conceptual or formal or metaphysical potential.

Any attempt to describe a heterogenous field of activities through particular criteria breaks down in the face of specific books or artists — and this is true with the distinction between artist's books and **livres d'artistes**. The work of Iliazd, a Russian avant-garde artist who became an editor of fine editions after 1945, is often closer to the conceptual form of an artist's book in its originality of vision and investigation of the book form than it is to the deluxe books it resembles through its materials and production means.9 Similarly, there are many inexpensive books whose format reproduces the juxtaposition of word and image as discrete elements in a pattern characteristic of the **livre d'artiste**. Similar problems occur with other definitions of artists' book activities.

Fine printing, for instance, can't really be subsumed under the **livre d'artiste** nor can it be absorbed into the realm of artists' books — though there are many finely printed volumes in both categories. The term "fine printing" is generally associated with letterpress, handset type, and limited editions, but also can be used to describe carefully produced work in any print medium. There is a category of fine printing which invokes the production of limited edition works for bibliophiles concerned with well-made versions of classic texts printed on archival paper, in durable leather bindings, and so forth. These books are produced with close attention to all aspects of printing art, but are not generally innovative in form or concerned with explorations of books as an artistic concept.10 Though artists' books tend to be associated with offset or electrostatic (commonly referred to by its trade name: xerox) processes, they have also been produced through the methods of letterpress, hand binding, and relief images (woodcut, linoleum, or engraving). Widening access to a variety of printing technologies has played a part in the proliferation of artists' books, especially in the first world, where the ready availability of production means increases in every decade.11

But neither the methods nor the quality of production can be used in themselves as criteria for determining a book's identity as an artist's book. Artists use what they have access to and knowledge of. There have been some wonderfully imaginative uses of letterpress from that of the Russian Futurist Vassily Kamensky's **Tango with Cows** (Moscow, 1914), to pieces produced by an obscure pair of California letterpress printers active in the San Francisco Bay Area in the 1970s: Holbrook Teter and Michael Meyers, whose independent productions had an unsurpassed creative vision, critical edge, and originality while participating in production conventions traditionally associated with fine printing. Letterpress, like offset printing or traditional darkroom techniques, requires a significant investment of time and energy and depends upon regular access in order to be acquired as a skill. However, it does not require huge amounts of capital to set up or acquire.12 Artists' books are often (though not always) produced on a shoestring budget by the artists themselves, however, letterpress is now prohibitively expensive in most situations (since it is labor intensive and thus costly when contracted out) — unless one owns and operates the equipment.13 The tactile, dimensional physicality of letterpress tends to be associated with fine printing, and fine printing with a conservative tradition, but an artist's book can certainly be well printed without losing its identity, just as bad printing is often acceptable and successful in the context of artists' books.14

The field of artists' books also has a relation to other forms of printing activity. One of these, more literary and political in its origins, is that of independent publishing. I define independent publishing as any publication effort which is mounted for the sake of bringing an edition into being which cannot find ready sponsorship in the established press or among commercial publishing houses. Largely associated with the literary realms and political activism, independent publishing allocates the power of production to anyone in possession of a press or the means to pay for printing. The term "independent" suggests an independence from commercial motives or constraints. In the 20th century much of the experimental literature which blossomed as part of modernism, the avant-garde, and other innovative aesthetic traditions, failed to find a receptive place in established publishing houses. Often authors have early work published in these venues and then are picked up by larger houses. The efforts of the British writers, Virginia and Leonard Woolf, at the Hogarth Press (established in 1917), or of John Heartfield and his brother, Weiland Herzfelde in the establishment of the Malik Verlag (also 1917), or of Caresse and Harry Crosby's Black Sun Press (begun in Paris, 1925) are a handful of the many classic, historic examples of independent publishing.15 Because such enterprises are launched with the ideal of publishing innovative, creative, or experimental work rather than making money, and are generally staffed by the editor/publishers who often also print the work, these independent publishers serve to make work available to the public which might not appear if profit were the sole publishing motive. The vast majority of creative writing, poetry, and prose is published through independent means by the labors and efforts of editors who barely break even monetarily or who subsidize their publishing work through other sources of income.16 Funding from private or public organizations sometimes provides additional help, but hardly enough to replace the initiative and determination which carry these projects through on a sustained basis. Artist's book publishing — whether by artists or by the publishers dedicated to artists' books, of which there are a significant number — is often in this financial category. This is not to suggest that artists never make money off their books, but to note that the same impetus which gives rise to independent publishing — the desire to make a voice heard, or a vision available, fuels artist's books.

The idea of the independent publisher is closely linked to that of the activist artist. Activist artists often give little thought to financial return or careerist investment (though both publishers and artists sometimes establish a name and a reputation which they can leverage to future successes as a result of these efforts). Much activist work is topical, politically or socially motivated in its thematics, and distributed through inexpensive editions as cheaply and widely as possible. Artists with a social or political motivation for their work have frequently turned to the inexpensive multiple as a means of gaining a wider audience for the work. Books, because they have the capacity to circulate freely, are independent of any specific institutional restraints (one finds them in friends' houses, motel rooms, railroad cars, school desks). They are low maintenance, relatively long-lived, free floating objects with the capacity to convey a great deal of information, and serve as a vehicle to communicate far beyond the limits of an individual life or contacts. The notion of the book as a means of available communication is part of what informs the myth of the book as democratic multiple, in spite of the many paradoxes of production involved in this idea.17 From the Russian Futurists to the Fluxus artists to the Press at the Woman's Building in Los Angeles, to the Lower East Side Print Shop in New York, the idea of making the book a tool of independent, activist thought has been one of the persistent elements of the mystique of the artist's book. That artists' books can facilitate a change of consciousness is clear, as with any other symbolic form be it poetry, visual arts, or music; whether such work can result in a change of political structure and policy opens the door to another set of debates about the role and function of art in the 20th century which cannot be adequately addressed here.

It would be hard to find an art movement in the 20th century which does not have some component of the artist's book attached to it, though in some cases this definition would have to be stretched to include journals, ephemera, or other independent publications.18 For example, Guillaume Apollinaire and Pierre Albert-Birot produced books in the context of Cubist art while Russian and Italian Futurism had many practitioners committed to books as a major part of their work from Velimir Khlebnikov and Natalia Goncharova to Franceso Depero and Filippo Marinetti.19 A path could be traced which would include Expressionism, Surrealism in Western and Eastern Europe, Dada in Europe and the United States, as well as post-war movements such as Lettrism, Fluxus, Pop art, Conceptualism, Minimalism, the Women's Art Movement, and Postmodernism to the present mainstream artworld concern with multiculturalism and identity politics.20 It is clear that books played a part in other movements as well, including the activities of experimental musicians such as John Cage and Henri Chopin, performance artists such as Carolee Schneemann,

Robert Morris, Vito Acconci, artists involved with systemic work, such as Mario Merz, Ed Ruscha, or Sol Lewitt and so on. This list would be exhaustingly long if it were complete and in spite of that fact, artists' books as a genre have not been surveyed, codified, or critically incorporated into the history of 20th-century art.21 These works will appear here but they will be treated as books and as examples of artistic involvement with the book as a form, rather than as attributes or sidelines of the movements with which the artists are associated. The sensibility of Sol Lewitt or Marcel Duchamp or Hanne Darboven is indissoluble from the aesthetic issues which form the mainstream context for their work, but their engagement with the book as a form has been more than incidental. Among mainstream artists, these are people who have looked at the book as a form to interrogate, not merely a vehicle for reproduction.

It is the fact of this engagement as a major feature of art of the 20th century which argues for the identity of artists' books as a unique phenomenon of the era. To an unprecedented degree books have served to express aspects of mainstream art which were not able to find expression in the form of wall pieces, performances, or sculpture. Dick Higgins has even suggested that the book as a form of **intermedia** (to use his term), combines all of these modes of art in a characteristically new way.22 In some cases artists have made use of the documentary potential of the book form, while in others they have engaged with the more subtle and complicated fact of the book's capacity to be a highly malleable, versatile form of expression. Not every book made by an artist is an artist's book, in spite of the old Duchampian adage that art is what an artist says it is. It is also as true in the late part of 20th century as it was in the early decades that books are often produced on the strength of an artist's capacity to generate sales, and books are a cheap sideline for many galleries. A mere compendium of images, a portfolio of prints, an incidental collection of images original or appropriated, is not always an artist's book, though the terms on which the distinction may be sustained are often vague. The final criteria for definition resides in the informed viewer, who has to determine the extent to which a book work makes integral use of the specific features of this form. The desire to engage with the elusive character of what constitutes a book is part of the impetus for my current project: to seek critical terms on which to examine a book's book-ness, its identity as a set of aesthetic functions, cultural operations, formal conceptions, and metaphysical spaces.

9

Just as books have served to extend the possibilities of visual arts, performance, and music, they have also offered a unique conceptual possibility to the poet.23 Concrete poets have engaged with books as a conceptual space, one which by its form and finitude, its structural specificity and visual restraints, has offered a unique means of realizing particular works. While many concrete poets have worked with sculptural elements, sound, or at the level of the single, flat sheet or broadside, there are a substantial number who have used books as the form for their work. Again, not every concrete poet is a book artist, and not every concrete work is an artist's book, but there are works which demonstrate the ways in which concrete poets have been able to extend the parameters of what a book does as a verbal field in a manner which also extends the possibilities of the way an artist's book can function as a poetic text.

The crafts of book arts have also burgeoned in the latter part of the 20th century. Workshops and classes in binding, papermaking, book structures, and so forth are a major staple of centers devoted to book arts.24 Though structure is an important component of a successful book the craft aspect of book production is not sufficient in itself to constitute the substance of an artist's book. Attention to materials, their interactions, and the content bound within the book are an integral feature of a book, but as with other aspects of production, artists' books tend to bend and stretch all the rules and conventions of craft decorum. One can trace the influence of individual practitioners among certain communities of artists involved with books — for instance, the popularization of certain structures included in Keith Smith's texts on book production. The contribution of Smith, and others who have taught extensively such as Hedi Kyle, or Walter Hamady, in their various past and present arenas of influence, is a visible feature of artists' books in their current incarnation. But there are also works produced from far outside this tradition which succeed without its influence, as there are many works produced as an expression of craft which fall short of being artists' books. An artist's book has to be more than a solid craft production or it falls back into the same category as the **livre d'artiste** or fine print work. An artist's book should not be formulaic — it might be generic, of a familiar type or established category of artists' books and make its contribution without innovating formally, and it might be wildly innovative and sloppy and badly made and in many ways fall short of perfection or even good realization — but ultimately an artist's book has to have some conviction, some soul, some reason **to be** and **to be a book** in order to succeed. It is particularly difficult to keep the craft tradition of book arts and the expressive tradition of the artist's book apart — nor is there any need to — but they should not be confused with each other.

Given the above discussion, it is not surprising that the history of the artist's book is mapped in a wide variety of ways by different scholars and critics. Even among those writers whose general sense of what constitutes an artist's book makes a clear distinction between this form and that of, say, the **livre d'artiste**, there is a tendency to make what seems like an arbitrary and too definitive point of origin. Most particularly the book **Twenty-six Gasoline Stations**, by Ed Ruscha has become a cliche in critical works trying to establish a history of artists' books. There is some reason for this — since Ruscha's work arguably breaks new ground in embodying and defining an artist's book. But it seems counterproductive to try to make a single point of demarcation for this complex history. It seems more useful and interesting to recognize that by the time Ruscha's work was produced (the date of the first edition is 1962) there was already a historical precedent in examples from Russian Futurism through Surrealism to the American avant-garde, from both artistic and literary traditions. To state that the artist's book comes into being through the work of Ruscha, and to credit him with the idea, concept, and form, makes an erroneous foundation for this history on two counts. First, the artist's book has to be understood as a highly mutable form, one which cannot be definitively pinned down by formal characteristics (such as the inexpensive printing and small format of Ruscha's work). The book form is always under investigation by artists who reach into the various traditions described above, as well as into new realms of material expression and creative form. More importantly, this approach to history is hopelessly beleaguered by an old-fashioned notion, one in which there are founding fathers who beget whole traditions through their influence. I prefer to think of the artist's book as a field which emerges with many spontaneous points of origin and originality. This is a field in which there are underground, informal, or personal networks which allow growth to surface in a new environment, or moment, or through a chance encounter with a work, or an artist. This is also a field in which there are always inventors and numerous mini-genealogies and clusters, but a field which belies the linear notion of a history with a single point of origin.

That this history has become more complicated since the middle of this century is quite clear. Where the artist's book has to be coaxed from its art or literary context in the early part of the century it becomes so full-blown and prolific a form afterward that only a general overview or alternately an exhaustively detailed description of activity will suffice to describe that development. I have chosen the former model. Briefly, here is the way I see the post-war history: In the late 1940s and early 1950s there are a number of artists who begin to explore books in a serious way. These include the CoBrA artists in Denmark, Belgium, and Holland as well as the French Lettrists, led by Isidore Isou and Maurice Lemaitre, whose major experimental work is produced from 1948 through the 1950s. The Concrete poets in Brazil, particularly Augusto and Haroldo De Campos, and in Germany and France, also begin working actively with books in the 1950s. By the late 1950s, artists working in experimental music, performance, and other non-traditional forms take up book arts within the context of Fluxus soon after its first events in the early 1960s. There were other localized or individual art formations of the same period — the work of the French composer, Henri Chopin, for example, or Bern Porter the American practitioner of found poetry. Dieter Roth, arguably the most significantly imaginative post-war European book artist, began his work with the book in the 1950s. These are scattered points of activity some of which came into being without connections to each other, while others spun off as part of the large loosely interrelated post-war avant-garde.

In the 1960s books as an artist's medium took off in the United States and Europe. They fit the sensibility of the 1960s alternative scene, whether produced independently by artists or by galleries as an extension of an exhibition, also giving rise to the hybrid genre of the catalogue as artist's book. The proliferation of works which use the small format and inexpensive production methods bespeaks the transformation of print technology as much as the transformation of conceptual sensibility which promotes this expansion. Offset printing and later electrostatic reproduction were further complemented by the increasingly available modes of photographic and electronic type setting. The availability of the Multi-lith, a small, affordable offset press, as a standard job shop item, as well as the rapid transformation of the printing industry from high-speed letterpress to offset (many newspapers and magazines, such as the **New York Times** and **Time** magazine, continued using relief printing until the 1970s, only replacing this with offset equipment as electronic typesetting became viable), were all developments which provided the means for artists to produce inexpensive multiples.25 The development of artists' books was not determined by technological advances but these changes did permit easier access to production than had been the case earlier in the century. In the 1970s major centers for the production of artists' books were established, most notably Visual Studies Workshop (in Rochester, New York), Nexus Press (in Atlanta, Georgia), the New York Center for the Book Arts, Pacific Center for the Book Arts (in the San Francisco Bay Area), Printed Matter (in New York City), the Graphic Arts Press in the Woman's Building (in Los Angeles), and The Writers Center (in Bethesda, Maryland). Other institutional sites developed as well within art school and university programs in the arts, museum and library collections, and private collections. By the 1970s, then, the artist's book had come of age.

By the late 1970s, however, another area of book related activity began to develop a highly visible profile: book-like objects or book sculpture. Their proliferation was apparent in the U.S. in both New York and California, and in Europe as well. This development has fewer precedents in the history of 20th-century arts than does the artist's book. One can point to several works by Duchamp (as always) — such as his altered book, **Do Touch**, with the female breast cast on its cover, or even his large **Green Box** as a conceptual book, and the boxes of Joseph Cornell have a formal and conceptual relation to the sculptural "book." In the 1950s, Dieter Roth shredded paper, boiled it, and filled animal intestines to make "literary sausages." Large scale book works which are as much installation and performance as object were a part of 1960s Fluxus and other investigations. But the recent increase in these productions marks an intensifying exchange between artists who make books and the world of mainstream visual art. In the post-war period the arts gradually turn away from traditional media forms and categories so that the synthetic possibilities seen in the domain of artist's books, and this hybridization of book as object, seem completely consistent with its trends.

In the 1980s, following this wave of sculptural work, one begins to see installation pieces which are ambitious in scale and physical complexity, closet size to room size, with video, computers, and any moment now a virtual reality apparatus. Many of these are made by artists who had previously been involved with artists' books, or who use books as an integral aspect of these installations. Here I am thinking of the Buzz Spector's frozen edition of Sigmund Freud's work, Janet Zweig's computer driven kinetic sculptures, Karen Wirth and Robert Lawrence's **How to Make an**

Antique, Marshall Reese and Nora Ligorano's **Bible Belt**, among others. Much of this work poses important questions for the identity of a book and its cultural, social, poetic, or aesthetic functions, but it could not be accomodated here without stretching the parameters of my discussion into an awkward shape. Some of these are compelling and original works, some are one-liners produced at the expense of books as cultural arti-facts, some are fascinating, fetishistic, or conceptual pieces — but for the purposes of this study, I am keeping them just beyond the zone of artists' books. I am concentrating here on understanding what a book is when it functions as a book, when it provides a reading or viewing experience sequenced into a finite space of text and or images. To extend beyond this would dilute the focus of this book.

In addition, I am convinced that many of these works belong more to the world of sculpture or installation art than to the world of books. They may function as icons of book-ness or book identity, but not provide an experience associated with books themselves. Electronic media, however, pose other, equally complex problems. The book as an electronic form — whether in hypertext, CD-ROM, or as an infinite and continually mutating archive of collective memory and space — is already functioning as an extension of the artist's book form. The issues raised by this medium seem too imperative to leave aside, and so will find their, albeit limited, place in this discussion.

In closing, a few final remarks. Most attempts to define an artist's book which I have encountered are hopelessly flawed — they are either too vague ("a book made by an artist"26) or too specific ("it can't be a limited edition"27). Artists' books take every possible form, participate in every possible convention of book making, every possible "ism" of mainstream art and literature, every possible mode of production, every shape, every degree of ephemerality or archival durability. There are no specific crite-ria for defining what an artist's book is, but there are many criteria for defining what it is not, or what it partakes of, or what it distinguishes itself from. In mapping out this initial definition my intention has been to demonstrate the incredible richness of artists' books as a form which draws upon a wide spectrum of artistic activities, and yet, duplicates none of them. Artists' books are a unique genre, ultimately a genre which is as much about itself, its own forms and traditions, as any other artform or activity. But it is a genre as little bound by constraints of medium or form as those more familiar rubrics "painting" and "sculpture." It is an area which needs description, investigation, and critical attention before its specificity will emerge. And that is the point of this project: to engage with books which are artists' books in order to allow that specific space of activity, somewhere at the intersection and boundaries and limits of all of the above activities, to acquire its own particular definition.

1 **Set-up sheets** are the sheets a printer uses to "set-up" the press: to get inking, pressure, position, registration or other elements of the printing process coordinated. Many printers reuse these sheets several times, creating elaborate overprinting effects of random patterns which can be treated as "found art" or poetry, cut up, bound, and made into a book. Dieter Roth used this approach in a number of works, and it is an idea which I have seen occur to many people who see the set-up sheets around a press.

2 There are other, earlier examples as well, but these figures mark the beginning of 20th-century activity and a new clear identity within the artworld, rather than next to or tangential to it.

3 See William Strachan, **The Artist and the Book in France**, as an introduction to this history, or Douglas McMurtrie's **The Book: The Story of Printing and Bookmaking**. Elaborate folio and elephant folio volumes with colored plates were an old concept which found a broader audience in the 19th century. One such publication which is sufficiently well known to serve as an example is the **Birds of America** from drawings of John James Audubon — and the large format and elaborate work in this edition could be found in many other volumes of natural history, catalogues of architectural monuments, classical statuary — even the history of writing merited large-scale publications with high production values. In fact, deluxe editions and bindings were the norm before the small, inexpensive edition was initiated by the Dutch printing house of Elzevir in the 17th century. Daniel Berkeley Updike's **Printing Types** is still the standard reference in typographic history.

4 The misnamed exhibition, **A Century of Artists Books**, curated by Riva Castleman, at the Museum of Modern Art in New York in the winter of 1994-95, is a representative selection of 20th-century **livres d'artiste**. There are a few anomalies in her exhibition, works which are artists' books, which probably found their way down the elevator from the MoMA Library collection of several thousand artists' books.

5 This point is important because the **livre d'artiste** was a radical innovation at the end of the 19th century but has gone brain dead through the codification of its conventions.

6 Binding fashions differ from era to era and place to place: American bindings tend to be excessively heavy, as if to add importance to these works, while English binders make use of lighter board.

7 The term **opening** refers to the space of an open codex-style book, a **spread** is generally an opening of this sort which preserves the continuity of the sheet across the

gutter, so that an image or text could be printed on that sheet without the need to cope with the gutter as a disjunctive break.

8 Henri Zerner and Charles Rosen, **Realism and Romanticism** (Norton, 1984), especially Chapter III, "The Romantic Vignette and Thomas Bewick."

9 Iliazd was born Ilia Zdanevich in Tiflis, Georgia, in 1894. There are other editors of artists' books who produce work which is not merely **livres d'artistes**, such as Hansjörg Mayer, Frances Butler and Alastair Johnston (Poltroon Press), or Simon Cutts and Erica Van Horn (Coracle).

10 I am thinking of books like those generally produced for the Limited Editions Club. These are different from **livres d'artiste** in that though they may be illustrated, they are generally not lavish in size, or focusing on an artist's work, but are reissues of Great Books or Modern Classics, as the case may be. They are marketed to readers or those who like their library shelves to proclaim their literacy rather than to art collectors. The books are not really expensive — they are more costly than the average trade book, but they are far from a fine arts market.

11 The relationships between technology and the industrial base in the first world, including specific relations among capital, labor, markets, and production means is almost never considered as an aspect of the proliferation of artists's books. Simply on the level of transformations of technology these connections are manifest in every aspect of book production — for instance, consider the possibilities which phototypesetting, computer generated type, and desktop publishing have made available for the manipulation of the text on a page, not to mention the ways in which the commercial industry of advertising has pushed design possibilities. There is a tendency to write the history of artists' books — or, even, of related activity like the history of **livres d'artistes** — as if the specific first world context were irrelevant. This is an area where the work of someone like Felipe Ehrenberg would provide a particularly rich study since his artistic activity spans first and third world cultural, social, and economic fields. He has been involved with teaching book arts and printing in a wide variety of circumstances and communities.

12 It's fair to say that letterpress is taken up for a variety of reasons — some people like the elegance of its product, some find it easy enough to learn and not too mechanically intimidating, some merely have access to it and it works. I am not stigmatizing the medium with any particular character here — but it does get characterized because of the association with the tradition of the deluxe edition.

13 Ann Chamberlain passed on some interesting information to me when I was working with her on an essay to accompany an exhibition she curated at Galeria de la Raza in San Francisco in 1992. She made the point that in Mexico City, one can obtain the skills of letterpress job printers very inexpensively since they set up in the arcades of a particular public square and will print on demand, on the spot, so that many book artists avail themselves of this service rather than print their own texts or acquire the means to do so. This is an anecdote which demonstrates the differences in the economics of printing techonology and availability in different cultural locations. There

are also many artists making books who developed access to equipment by working in print shops in a day job and printing their own work in off hours.

14 Clifton Meador has remarked on how great "bad" printing is — or can be in the right situation. Such "bad" printing reveals itself to the knowledgeable eye, often showing effects of the manipulation of the printing process with respect to pressure, water, inking and so forth. **Fine Print**, a journal which was established in San Francisco by Sandra Kirschenbaum in 1975, and ran for about fifteen years, was one relatively contemporary arena for the discussion of the work of fine print presses, as was the short-lived **Bookways**, published by W. Thomas Taylor. Nancy Princenthal has single-handedly brought attention to actual artists' books in her column in **Print Collector's Newsletter** over the years, but more often **PCN** reviews **livres d'artistes** for their audience of print collectors. There are other publications which address this genre in the international market — such as the **Nouvelles de l'Estampe**, of the Bibliothèque Nationale in Paris, not to mention the many catalogues of antiquarian dealers catering to bibliophiles for whom artists' books are still, often, an unknown, uncharted region.

15 Here again there is a link, rather than a causal relation, between changes in the printing industry and artistic activity, in one important respect. It was the mass production of **type**, made possible by breakthroughs in casting and typefounding, which permitted the spread of printing and establishment of small private shops which could acquire standard sized type from commercial foundries.

16 Rosmarie and Keith Waldrop's Burning Deck Press in Providence is a longstanding example of this kind of ongoing committment.

17 I have written about this paradox in the catalogue essay for Brad Freeman's exhibition **Offset: Artists' Books and Prints** (1993), and also in the essay "Artists Books and the Cultural Status of the Book," in **The Journal of Communication**, special issue edited by Sandra Braman, Winter 1994, Vol. 44, No. 1, but I will return to this later, in the section which explores ideas about production.

18 There are, however, exceptions to any such bold statement. I can think of very few artists' books associated with Abstract Expressionism in its first wave, for instance, but these exceptions are few and far between.

19 Pierre Albert-Birot is another forgotten figure, editor of a Parisian journal of the 1910s titled **SIC**, or **Sons Idees Couleurs (Sounds Ideas Colors)**, as well as of numerous books of his own publication which included visual poems, typographic experiments, and theatrical scripts. Susan Compton's **Worldbackwards**, (British Museum, 1978) and her **Russian Avant-Garde Books 1917 to 1934** (MIT University Press, 1992) are a good point of departure for the Russian materials. The Italian work is also well documented in Giovanni Lista's **Futurisme** (L'Age D'Homme, 1973) among other sources, but Marjorie Perloff's **The Futurist Moment**, (University of Chicago Press, 1986) and the 1993 catalogue of a monumental exhibition in Marseille, **Poesure et Peintrie** [sic] and the older Herbert Spencer volumes on experimental and avant-garde typography, **Pioneers of Modern Typography** (Lund Humphries, 1969)and **The**

Liberated Page (Bedford, 1987) are also invaluable indexes to this material; see also my **The Visible Word: Experimental Typography and Modern Art Practice** (University of Chicago, 1994) though it does not deal with books as much as typographic work.

20 In spite of this activity the literature is small. There are many articles, exhibition catalogues, and ephemeral publications, but the number of books devoted to artists' books can be figured on the fingers of both hands. Among these is a major contribution by Renée Riese Hubert, **Surrealism and the Book** (University of California, 1988). But for the post-1945 period, there is no survey text or major work devoted exclusively to artists' books except the Joan Lyons (ed.) **Artists' Books: A Critical Anthology and Sourcebook** (Visual Studies Workshop and Peregine Press, 1984).

21 The reasons for this are not easy to pin down. The fact that books take up less physical space than paintings or sculptures, are less immediately commanding, and also, generally, more complicated and intricate than other forms of art may be part of their having been granted a "minor" status. The equation of large scale art with importance is certainly a feature of post-1945 art, so that the intimate, personal scale of a book is dwarfed in comparison. There is, again, the market aspect — books tend to sell in a different, generally lower price bracket than paintings or sculptures which perpetuates their perception as of lesser value in a somewhat vicious circle. When one realizes that a single book can consist of what are essentially whole suites of prints, painted pages, or photographs it is interesting to note that they often sell for far less than a single piece of wall art in a similar medium.

22 Dick Higgins, "Intermedia" in **foew&ombwhnw**, (Something Else Press, NY, 1969).

23 The literary engagement with the book form is outside my scope. I would have to include every poet who ever put a line of type at a diagonal or used calculated typewriter spacing to be fair to the field. The work of Jerome McGann and Michael Davidson, as well as Marjorie Perloff and Jerome Rothenberg, Emmett Williams, Mary Ellen Solt, and Dick Higgins, are good points of departure for those interested in this area.

24 Visual Studies Workshop, The Minnesota Center for Book Arts, the New York Center for Book Arts, Pacific Center for the Book Arts, and Pyramid Atlantic to name a few.

25 The term "inexpensive" is deceiving — though printing costs in the 1960s and 70s were considerably lower than they are in the 1990s; I have discussed this point at length elsewhere, as in **Offset** (1993), but the basic issue is that books which sell at an affordable price tend to require considerable cash up front, often costs not reclaimable given the problems of distribution, sale, and lack of audience in the artist's book world.

26 Lawrence Weiner, at the Museum of Modern Art panel, "Artists' Books at the End of a Dream" in May 1994, using the Duchampian "if an artist made it it's art" remark. In this case, however, I have to say that if it ain't a book, it ain't a book, no matter what. Though I still prefer Weiner's line to the hopeless muddle of, for instance, Riva Castleman, who seemed unable to distingush artist's books from **livres d'artistes** or just plain old illustrated books.

27 This comes from Anne Moeglin-Delcroix "Qu'est-ce qu'un livre d'artiste?" from the publication of the Actes du Colloque of the 1991 Biennale du Livre d'Artiste, in Uzerche, which has much to recommend it, but her attempt to define an artist's book is very limited and literal. I know of many great artist's books which are in limited editions, and which are most emphatically not **livres d'artistes** in spite of that, to feel that such criteria can be used. They seem objective, empirical, and desirable, but end up being arbitrary markers of distinction among otherwise common objects.

Ilq̃le cũ le tumefacte bucce fonaua due rurale Tibie, & appodiato ad
uno torofo trunco di Dendro cæfo, da uetuftate tuto uacuo, cum peruie
crepature & rami difcoli rarii & folii, Cum il capillaméto incompto &
in frondato. Tra quefti dui faltaua uno puello nudo. Dalaltro lato era
uno, che fopra gli robufti humeri, uno Armillo futile baiulante lo ori-
ficio inuerfo fopra il cornigero capo il mero fpargeua. Achofta egli era
una matrona, cum il capillamento demiffo decapillata, & quefta & il ua
ftafo dilarmillo nudi, & lachrymabonda. Tenendo una facula cum la
parte accenfa in giu. Tra quefti dui appareua uno Satyrulo puero, ilqua
lenelle mano uno ferpe molto inuoluto ftringeua. Sequiua pofcia una
ruricolauetula canifera, fopra il nudo induta di panno uolante, fopra gli fianchi cincta. Del capo inconcinno fopra il caluato, ha-
uea uno cefticillo, & di fopra portaua una uiminea cifta pie
na di fructi & di fronde & nelaltra mano uno uafo te
niua dilorificio oblongo cretaceo. Quefte figure optimamente erano infcalpte & afpe-
ramente. In larula cufi era infcripto. Ex
citato fummo pere da tanta uenu-
ftate di monuméti quæritabon
do, ad me uno elegantiffimo
in uno faxo infcripto epi
taphio Romano tale
iucundiffimo dia-
logo fe offerite. &
tali cũ ornaméti.

※ ※ ※

q   iiii

Francesco Colonna, **Hypnerotomachia Poliphili**, 1499, printed by Aldus Manutius

2

Conceptualizing the Book:
Precedents, Poetics, and Philosophy

The idea of the artist's book which comes to maturity in the latter half of the 20th century is not without precedents. Many printers, typographers, and publishers were acutely aware of the book as a form and displayed this awareness through their productions. Aldus Manutius' **Hypnero-tomachia Poliphili** (1499), Geoffrey Tory's **Champfleury**, (1529), and the Firmin Didot **Virgil** (1798) are examples of highly self-conscious productions of work in book form. These three are each individually remarkable, but even a cursory glance across at the broad history of printing makes it clear that innumerable extremely well-made, well-thought out works have been produced in book form even in trade publications and commercial works. These are all useful sources for informing contemporary artistic work. One can draw on their formal virtues, their innovative or compelling solutions to technical or design problems, and their aesthetic resolution of relations between elements of text, image, printing technology, paper, binding as well as their substantive content. But these works are not, in any real sense, artists' books. A very simple point of distinction can be brought into play here: an artist's book should be a work by an artist self-conscious about book form, rather than merely a highly artistic book. These outstanding examples of book production do not serve as a point of departure for conceptualizing the artist's book, one whose philosophical and poetic legacy is an integral aspect of its identity.

Genuine precedents for the conceptual practice of artists' books can, however, be found in the work of several individuals. The work of two English artists, William Blake in the late 18th century and William Morris in the late 19th, exemplify certain features which later find varied expression in artists' books, while the writings of the Symbolist poet Stéphane Mallarmé, the Realist novelist Gustave Flaubert, and the poet Edmund Jabès, raise philosophical, poetic, and cultural issues germane to understanding the book as a concept. While these individuals don't exhaust the number of references which could be brought to bear upon the legacy of the book as an artistic idea, but they do mark definitive contributions to the intellectual history of the book.1

William Blake and William Morris established unique precedents for making use of the book as an artistic production. Both were highly individual artists with developed, distinctive, visions of the book as a form which could function as a force for spiritual and social transformation. In addition to Blake and Morris, I will discuss briefly the work of a lesser known figure, Gelett Burgess, a writer, artist, and publisher active in the 1890s in San Francisco's Bohemian art and literary circle.

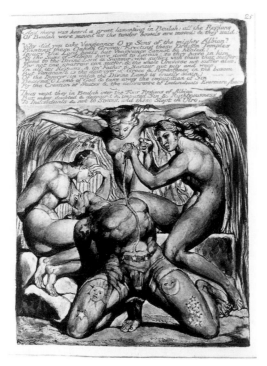

William Blake, **Jerusalem**, 1804

William Blake

William Blake (1757-1827) was an engraver by profession who made numerous books of his own writing and artworks. He printed the first example of what he termed **illuminated printing** in 1788. Titled, **There is No Natural Religion**, the piece was made to express highly personal ideas on the question of religion and faith and as an innovative solution to the problem of publishing on a limited budget. The text detailed Blake's disagreements with the views of the French philosopher Jacques Rousseau with regard to the notion of innate ideas. While Rousseau held the conviction that there were natural ideas held by all human beings — such as the idea of divinity — Blake believed that each individual had their own vision of the world, sense of values, and structure of belief. Any assertion of a unified view of the world, the cosmos, or spiritual life misrepresented the originality and variety of human experience. To realize his edition of this essay, Blake came up with a technical innovation which he called **illuminated printing**. His innovation consisted in part in realizing that the metal plates with which he was familiar with as an engraver could be etched sufficiently to be printed in relief. To solve a major problem — that of writing the entire text in reverse on the surface of the plate with a resistant ground — Blake worked with a transfer process: writing first with the ground on paper and then transferring it by flipping the paper onto the face of the plate. When finished, the etched plate could be used to pull prints as they were needed or ordered, thus allowing him to work with an unlimited edition produced on demand.

Blake obtained the idea for this technique from a vision in which his recently deceased and much beloved younger brother, Robert, appeared and described the process.2 The link between visionary sensibility and the book as a form is thus doubly inscribed in Blake's work — through his engagement with the book as a means of expressing his cosmological beliefs, and through the history of his insight into the form through which this expression could be realized. This revelation solved the problem of funding his publication projects, allowing him to avoid the expense of having his texts set and printed in letterpress. The printed pages were illuminated by means of water-based paint, which Blake ground himself in order to keep the colors vivid and simple. The editions contain considerable variety, not conforming to a single model of painting throughout the full run, but changing over time according to his temperament or disposition.3 Blake's approach to the form of the edition, as something mutable and inconsistent, demonstrates his willingness to transform publishing conventions to suit his personal artistic vision. Significant as these technical and formal aspects of Blake's work are to his conception of the book as a means of publishing independently, what overwhelms these considerations and gives them their fundamental motivation is the compelling symbolic vision he strove to articulate in the works.4

Following the initial publication of his pamphlet on religion, Blake focused his energy on a published work of poetry and painting, **The Songs of Innocence**, which appeared in 1789. Blake, who had little formal schooling (he had refused to submit to the discipline of a pedagogic routine), had been apprenticed to an engraver at age fourteen and subsequently made his living as a commercial artist. Independent of spirit and committed to the expression of the principles of freedom and independence, Blake was not able to transform his vision into a lucrative artistic enterprise through the making of his own editions. However, his commitment to these projects intensified as the process of illuminated printing became more familiar. He then expanded through other technical experiments, particularly a form of color transfer painting he developed in the 1790s.

The tenets of Blake's belief system are apparent in his books, and **The Songs of Innocence** initiate a cycle of investigations which continued through his entire **oeuvre**. For Blake, "Innocence" was a condition of "freedom from Gravity", a condition of enlightenment produced through engagement with the vital energy and spontaneity of life.5 The lightness of the watercoloring in this work fits the expression of immateriality and non-corporeality which is central to Blake's vision of Innocence. The notion of Experience which is the central theme of the **Songs** produced in 1794, was not the opposite of Innocence, but its complement — a more informed and liberated state, conscious, and energized. Innocence was not ignorance, and the enemies of both innocence and experience were rigid constraints of thought or spirit, rote convention, the absence of love, and the coercive forces of oppressive education or law. These are the themes with which Blake is concerned throughout his works. Beginning with a small, modest format (about the size of a contemporary paperback novel), Blake published other volumes in rapid succession — **The Book of Thel** (1789), **The Gates of Paradise** (1793) (one of the only works he did expressly for children), **The Marriage of Heaven and Hell** (1790-93), **The Visions of the Daughters of Albion** (1793), **America: A Prophecy** (1793), **Europe** (1794) and the list goes on. As the work continued, Blake's strength as a draughtsman progressed, and his capacity to make his fluid, graceful line describe forms and forces of profound and terrifying energy expanded his range far beyond the original delicacy of the first works. Successful as they are on their own terms, these early volumes do not display the virtuosity and range of symbolic power of the **Book of Urizen**,

(1794), **Jerusalem** (which he worked on from 1804 to 1820), **Paradise Lost** (1808), or **The Book of Job** (1821).

While it would be a mistake to privilege the later work at the expense of the early expressions of Blake's vision, there is an unmistakable intensification as the visionary theater of the book becomes a familiar form for Blake. His capacity to mobilize the space of the page, the tones of the paper, the colors of ink and paint, to perform a drama of monumental proportions within the relatively small scale of his books demonstrates an understanding of the book's communicative power. The independent spaces of text and image exist in a dialogic relation to each other, often losing their autonomy in the interlacing of border motifs with the letters of the text, the drawn form of the regular, small writing embued with a liveliness of touch which invariably resonates with the sinews of line which inscribe the visual forms of the image. The page is a whole, its divisions interlocked and relational, and each page anticipates and fulfills its place in the sequence of the whole. The effect is one of unity, not monotony, and the repetitive rhythm of Blake's handwriting serves to establish continuity among the variety of visual forms. The intimacy of the situation of reading permits the images to assume amplifications of scale, especially as the forms of the writing establish a normative size line as a more or less consistent measure. Expanding and shrinking against the finite edges of the page, the elements of the whole turn inward for their definition, performing as the basic elements of a replete cosmos of thought.

The kernel of Blake's thought was the valuation of imagination above all, with the corollary belief that each individual's vision was innate and original and that to submit all creatures — human or animal — to uniform laws was oppressive and spirit crushing. A committed radical, despising tyrants, kings, and arbitrary laws, Blake was an artist who believed that the imagination was a liberatory force. In the works of his own literary composition, from the **Songs** through **Jerusalem**, Blake evolved mythic characters who represented his passions and convictions. For instance, the character of Urizen is depicted as the epitome of the spirit struggling to survive in the waters of materialism.6 Blake believed in the power of dynamic energy and spirit — and Urizen's struggle is a further display of the convictions Blake had manifested in earlier work, such as **The Marriage of Heaven and Hell** (1790-93). In that work, the two figures of Heaven and Hell carry values which reverse the conventions — Hell is the positive figure, charged with energy, while passive Heaven carries a more negative stigma. Both aspects were necessary for cosmic harmony, however, they could not be conceived of as positive if they were in static form.7 These symbolic embodiments were not idealizations, but the transformations of symbol into form through visionary imagery. For Blake the book was the one primary form in which the complexities of textual and visual means could sustain a dialogue suitable to his cosmological vision. Blake's work is an entirety, each volume depicts an aspect of the system of values he espoused. He believed in independent imagination and expression, and he developed a means to produce this vision using his own labor with assistance from his wife Catherine. As a precedent for the artist's book, Blake's work serves as the embodiment of independent thought realizing itself through the forms and structures of the book.

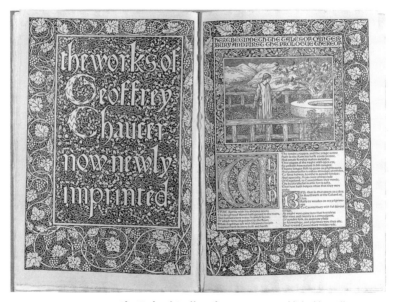

The Works of Geoffrey Chaucer, 1896-8, published by William Morris
Yale Center for British Art, Paul Mellon Collection

William Morris

The books produced by William Morris (1834-1896) nearly a century later, while they have an equal aesthetic intensity and demonstrate a similar commitment to the book as an integral unity, do not have the cosmological convictions which motivated Blake's vision. Morris's vision, though passionate, is more rationalized and less spontaneous. Morris's concern with production was motivated by a different spirit and context from that of Blake, though they shared a distaste for tyranny, oppression, and injustice in the social arena. But where Blake's work was conceived and executed within the artisanal terms of the engraver's trade in the years just prior to the industrial revolution, Morris's work with the Kelmscott Press took its form and agenda from the larger context of his response to the effects of industrialization upon labor.8

Morris was protected by financial circumstances from the task of wage-earning. However, his sympathies with the conditions which industrial technology and mass production imposed upon the working class formed the impetus for his formulation of an aesthetic which symbolized and engaged in labor practices of pre-industrial craft guilds.9 One could debate the issue of whether or not labor practices in a feudal society or within medieval guilds were or were not oppressive and thus question Morris's retrospective romanticization of circumstances of which he had little first-hand knowledge, but that hardly seems useful. Morris's perceptions of the ill effects of industrial production spurred his first commercial enterprise in the 1860s. But it was not until the 1880s that he became an active spokesman within the socialist movement, writing some of his most well-known essays including "Useful Work and Useless Toil." This essay was a response to the idea that work was either virtuous or pleasurable, Morris extolled the value of work which was pleasurable and satisfying as labor, in itself, not merely as a means of generating wages for the worker or excess value for the industrialist. It would be a mistake to see all of Morris's work as an embodiment of a radical political stance. Morris's earliest projects were conceived within the context of fine art, and his first major designs for textiles, furnishings, and glass were motivated by a desire to furnish his own Red House in Upton as much as to embody the teachings of John Ruskin on the virtues of the Gothic spirit in form. Morris and Company, founded in 1861, managed to succeed only through obtaining commissions for private houses and church buildings, and though the labor practices of the firm and the work of artisans in its employ may have followed the lines of Morris's beliefs, the commissions to support them often came from the surplus capital accumulated through industrial practices.

Books were the least and latest aspect of Morris's production. Between the founding of his firm and the establishment of Kelmscott Press in London around 1889-90 lay the nearly thirty years of Morris's mature work in glass, wallpaper, and fabric designs — in many ways a far more enduring legacy than that of the press work.10 He had executed his own illuminated texts, and even designed binding ornaments and page borders in the 1870s, so the Press project was not without precedents in his work. Morris was a poet, as well as designer, and had become intensely interested in medieval manuscripts, which he collected. The integration of elements in the medieval works, particularly the erosion of clear distinctions between borders and letterforms, illuminated initials and actual images, all served to intensify the thematic content of the text. This influenced Morris's mature sense of design. But this maturation took some time. Paul Thompson points out that it took Morris many early efforts and much time to come to terms with the idea of the book as a whole, not merely to see it as an assembly of parts to which he could give his attention as a designer.11 The recovery of a Gothic tradition in architecture, painting, and the decorative arts was not Morris's own invention. His sensibility partook of a broad movement which had begun in literature a century earlier with the work of Horace Walpole, had permeated British architecture throughout the 19th century, and inspired the Pre-Raphaelites while Morris was still an undergraduate at Oxford. But the effects of this interest had not resulted in the transformation of book design until Morris's interventions, and the Kelmscott Press had a striking impact on the fine press movement of the late 19th century and on the look and character of publishing in art periodicals and trade design for books into the early decades of the 20th century. It would be this arts and crafts style which the Italian Futurist Filippo Marinetti would use as the focus of his disdainful attacks in proposing a "modern" transformation of typographic design in 1912.12

Morris's inspiration for the Kelmscott Press was stimulated by contact with Emery Walker, a neighbor of Morris's for some years before Morris heard him speak in November 1888 on the subject of design reform of the printed page.13 Walker's interest in early printed books complemented Morris's passion for manuscripts and helped to clarify the distinction between an interest in the decorative elements of book work and the full, integrated, design of a page and book. Walker's design sensibility, echoed in Morris's essay, "The Ideal Book, " would be realized visually in the Kelmscott Press publications: tight spacing, legibility, blackness of ink, whiteness of paper, an architectural sense of the structure, and a conviction that a book must be designed as a spread or opening of facing pages, not as single sheets. These may seem like obvious points, but they risk both the possibility of being overlooked as fundamental to good design and the pitfall of being followed as formulaic prescriptions for fine printing. These and other guidelines have served as useful points against which to innovate or deviate from the terms of decorum for artists' books. But artists' books are distinguished from fine printing by the disregard for or violation — and sometimes, ignorance — of any such rules. These decisions have to work through either an intuitive or informed understanding of the process of creative production, not merely through ignorance of its basic rules. Morris after all was deviating radically from the prevailing conventions of his time with respect to book design.

Morris went on to produce his own type designs, Golden, Troy, and Chaucer, based on adaptations of the strong, vigorous types of Nicolas Jensen the Italian type designer of the 15th century, whose faces were more robust than the 18th-century modern faces Morris despised. Morris was not dogmatic about the use of traditional craft methods: he allowed the type to be cut by machine and had some images produced using photographic methods. Technology was not demonized by Morris, rather, its effects upon the relation between a person and the conditions or satisfactions of their work.

The great achievement of Morris's book work is his production of **The Works of Geoffrey Chaucer** (Kelmscott, Hammersmith, 1896-8). A work whose pages are dense but even, complex but legible, and expressive of Chaucer's medieval sensibility (though not of his bawdy range or understanding of human experience — this is Chaucer the great author, not Chaucer the rowdy wit), the **Chaucer** united Morris's skills as type designer, book designer, and Edward Burne-Jones's Pre-Raphaelite drawings in a successful harmony of elements.14 To embrace harmony or integration as crucial to artists' books would be to lock them into frigidly classical form and design, and in this sense, Morris's work is more aptly placed within the fine printing and independent press movements for which it was such an inspiration.15 The retrospective, retrograde, aspect of Morris's aesthetic, as well as his highly prescribed rules for fine books, edge toward craft and away from art, since the work becomes so hidebound in its attempts to approach an ideal condition of design that it ceases to engage with Morris's own experience or time. As artistic expression Morris's work is less compelling than Blake's, in spite of its importance as design, since Morris's own romanticization of outmoded forms (prose, verse, decoration) became a confining limit on his imagination.

Morris's place within the history of artists' books is justified by the eccentricity of his work, rather than its success as design. Morris's work embodies, in its enthusiastic recovery of medieval texts and his own imitation of these in poetic works he authored, a vision whose aesthetic was linked to a social agenda through the book as an expressive form. Morris expressed his desire for a cheaper and more accessible book, to be produced in accord with this sensibility, but he realized his works at a monumental scale of production. The paradoxes of this production — the high cost of labor, materials, and the edition — as a vision of labor in an unalienated form is perhaps not so paradoxical if one realizes that the myth of the artist as an individual worker with a personal vision and voice is also embodied in these works. All fifty titles of the Kelmscott Press do not share equally in this idiosyncratic realization, but as an enterprise it is clear that they owe their existence to a passionately artistic vision, not just a commercial or rational engagement with production.

Gelett Burgess

The last of the three artists whose work serves as a precedent to artists' books in terms of production or material investigation is Gelett Burgess (b.1866). Far less programmatic than either Blake or Morris, and of less influence and stature, Burgess may have had more in common with the 20th-century artist's book producer than either of these more monumental figures. Burgess was a member of late 19th-century San Francisco Bay Area Bohemia, an imitation of the Parisian circles of the same and slightly earlier time. Here, cafe and bar society became the refuge and venue for artists, writers, musicians, dancers, and actors. This image of the ideal artist's existence, a cliche of 20th-century literature, film, and adolescent dreaming, served as a model for a tiny but active scene in San Francisco in the 1890s. Gelett Burgess, a character by all accounts, and a multi-talented artist, writer, and wit, was one of its outstanding figures. One of his best-known works survives anonymously as — "A Purple Cow" — a familiar childhood rhyme.16 A graduate of Massachusetts Institute of Technology, Burgess was trained as a designer and even had a brief stint as a professor of topographical drawing at the University of California before his propensity for pranks got him into a public scandal which caused his resignation (he and some friends had destroyed a statue to the American temperance leader Henry Cogswell).17 Burgess and a group of friends who called themselves **les jeunes** ("the young ones") were inspired

Gelett Burgess, **Le Petit Journal des Refusées**, 1896

by such stylish art journals as the **Revue Blanche** and **The Yellow Book** and created a periodical of their own, **The Lark**. 18 The journal ran for a year or two and in its humorous, playful, whimsical tone managed to live up to its name.

But though **The Lark** has its place in the history of letters and arts, Burgess's place in the history of artist's books is based on another project: Le Petit Journal des Refusées. Purported to be the first issue of a journal, the work was in fact conceived as a unique item. Originally meant as a counterpoint to the **The Lark**, which Burgess felt was becoming stale, **Le Petit Journal** was the brainchild of Burgess and one of his close friends, Porter Garnett. He modelled it on the then current "fadazines" or "fad magazines" of the 1890s. "It was in that miraculous Year of our Lord, 1896," Burgess wrote, "and whoever could get possession of a printing press in the United States was helping to burden the news-stands with monthly rubbish, filled with cheap satire and sententious pretension."19 The intention was to "send out a rollicking, whooping gabble of ultra-nonsensical verbiage, eschewing seriousness in any form."

31

Describing the evolution of the work, Burgess detailed with delight the late night after hours sessions at his drafting table spent with Garnett inventing a work which would shock the "Philistines" or "bromides" as he called the safe, dull, middle class. This was the California version of the European "épater le bourgeoisie," ("shock the bourgeoisie") but what is remarkable is the object which resulted. A small format work, about nine inches on its longest side, **Le Petit Journal des Refusées** was printed on outmoded wallpaper, in a trapezoidal format, with all of the images and text produced through woodcuts. The cover of the "journal" displays the characteristic style of the work — an inelegant imitation of Aubrey Beardsley put at the service of broad satire. The work was supposedly a collection of "contributions that had been refused by at least three periodicals of repute, and the articles were all signed by the name of women."20 Burgess later noted that he regretted the gendered aspect of his satire, but saves his strongest regret for the fact that in San Francisco "nothing is strange enough, outrageous enough, or original enough to excite a ripple of interest."21 The originality of the piece, a sixteen-page delirium, filled with patterns of Burgess's "goops" as well as such inventions as plaid hippopotamuses and cubical suns, was evidence of its rapid execution — done in a month of rapid work, in a single burst of energy.

Because of its humor and its innovative play with the forms of publication and the conventions of even the most adventurous of contemporaries, this work seems to participate in the tradition of the artist's book. It is a book, a small, compact, single work and not a journal, since its writer, editor, publisher, and artist are all combined in the collaboration of Burgess and Garnett. Even at the distance of a full century, the work is visually striking — the sinewy lines of its imitation Beardsley drawings combining with innovative patterns — though the thrust of its literary jabs may be blunted by time, their specific targets obscured, the volume functions as a thing unto itself, replete and redolent with spirit, energy, and ideas. **Le Petit Journal** has a spontaneity of expression lacking in the more labored work of Morris or even Blake, it is a topical, even ephemeral work produced in the spirit of a moment, and in this regard, embodies an important aspect of the spirit of artists' books.

Burgess not only represents himself in this discussion but also the work of those inspired, idiosyncratic, and original individuals who no doubt produced books which have fallen into obscurity. I have a conviction, from having worked in printshops myself, that there must have been many instances of typographers, pressmen, or other workers in the printing trade who seized the opportunity to make small, ephemeral works in the course of their careers. If recovered these might bear a striking resemblance to some of the found poems, appropriated assemblages, and or personal pieces which show up with regularity in the rank and file of artists' books. While Burgess's work deserves mention in its own right, it hardly possesses the same conceptual richness as that of Morris or Blake. What it does possess, however, is an ephemeral character, a sense of humor and inventive play — elements which characterize much of what constitutes artists' books as a field — and all features which aren't represented by the more monumental work of the other two artists.

The work of Blake, Morris, and Burgess does not exhaust the possible precedents for the exploration of the book as a direct form of artistic expression. The formal innovations each engaged in certainly pushed the parameters for artists' engagement with the book, one in which books were the objects of inquiry not merely vehicles for presentation. But it is arguable that other innovations — such as the interrogation of the form of the novel in Laurence Sterne's **Tristram Shandy** (1760), the network of relations established in emblem books between image, text, and aphorism, or the elaborate structural features of pattern poetry, also serve as precedents to 20th century artists' books. Nonetheless, these figures each made an outstanding and definitive contribution to the history of books as an art form. What these artists do not do, however, is to self-consciously articulate the metaphysics of the book within the field of either poetics or philosophy. Though they were highly engaged with the idea of the book as a visionary or aesthetic form, they did not produce any discussion of the book as an idea in critical or philosophical terms. Both of these realms, and the more prosaic domain of books more generally considered, allow the book to be investigated according to its conceptual parameters — either in concert with or independent of its formal and physical production.

Stéphane Mallarmé

Following a spiritual crisis he experienced in the late 1860s, the French poet Stéphane Mallarmé began to elucidate an idea of the book as a metaphysical project. He wrote two brief but suggestive essays titled "Action Restricted" and "As For the Book." Metaphoric in tone, poetic in expression, and highly condensed given their profound resonance through the history of poetics, these essays contain potent thoughts on the concept of the book. In "Action Restricted" Mallarmé collapsed his posing of the dilemma of how it is possible **to act** (in the broadest and most philosophical sense of conceiving of action and performing it) with an investigtion of the **act of writing**. For Mallarmé the problem of acting involved the problem of confirmation of existence — how did one know that one did exist without evidence created through the effect of action? That writing might produce evidence of an action and thus an existence was a distinct possibility, but the writer should not be deceived into the belief that mere poetry was sufficient. Writing was an ineffective form of action "as with a cigar in convolutions whose vagueness, at the very least, traced its outline on the raw electric daylight."22

It remained for the poem to become "The Book," as Mallarmé referred to it, always with majuscules (capital letters) to emphasize the distinction between his reference and the banal, quotidian object. The power of this book was that it existed alone, without connection to an author, as a text which "happens all alone; made, being. The hidden meaning stirs, and lays out a choir of pages."23 This book was not the means to counteract the ephemerality of human action, nor was it to be used against the existential fear about identity, adequacy, or existence: it was instead to be recognized as a realm unto itself, capable of containing "certain extreme conclusions about art which can explode, diamontinely, in this forever time, in this integrity of the Book." This idea of "The Book" is not rooted in a psychological function for the artist, nor a cultural function for the writer. Instead, "The Book" functions as a metaphysical investigation which focuses on the possibility that form (in the most abstract and philosophical sense) might be realized through "The Book." For Mallarmé the intangible encounter with the cosmos posed in such propositions was inseparable from his commitment to the poetic expression which he sought. The relations between language and form, ideas and being, were philosophical problems for which he sought poetic solutions.

The idea of "The Book" became a guiding principle for Mallarmé, who used it as the foundation of his poetics. This concept of "The Book" was the basis for imagining a form of representation which would be equal to the full experience of the world and also transcend its limitations. The limitations of an individual experience or perception was not an issue. The limitations of the world as it constituted itself in the most basic sense — as a condition of Being, in fullness and repleteness of all existence —

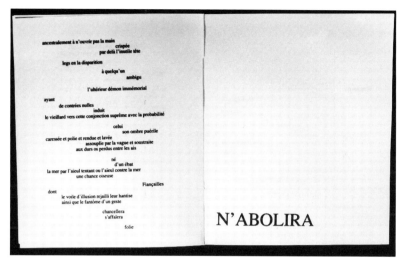

ancestralement à n'ouvrir pas la main
crispée
par delà l'inutile tête

legs en la disparition

à quelqu'un
ambigu

l'ultérieur démon immémorial

ayant
de contrées nulles
induit
le vieillard vers cette conjonction suprême avec la probabilité

celui
son ombre puérile
caressée et polie et rendue et lavée
assouplie par la vague et soustraite
aux durs os perdus entre les ais

né
d'un ébat
la mer par l'aïeul tentant ou l'aïeul contre la mer
une chance oiseuse

Fiançailles

dont
le voile d'illusion rejailli leur hantise
ainsi que le fantôme d'un geste

chancellera
s'affalera

folie

N'ABOLIRA

Stéphane Mallarmé, **Un Coup de Dès**, 1914 edition

was the extreme to which Mallarmé wished to explode and extend the conceptual parameters of "The Book." He expressed this belief at the beginning of "The Book: A Spiritual Instrument:" "All earthly existence must ultimately be contained in a book."24 Denying that he had the power to make such a work, one which would continually enfold the world back into representation, he went on to describe the qualities which such a work would have. It would be: "a hymn, all harmony and joy; an immaculate grouping of universal relationships come together for some miraculous and glittering occasion."25 "The Book" would provide a link between the mere mortal and a divinity through reading, contemplation, and engagement extended the metaphor into the realm of spiritual faith. That "The Book" could be "All" and provide access to divinity through its form was the strongest motivation for Mallarmé's vision.

He described some possible features of this work such as an integration of newspaper typography and the elemental aspects of the bound quires (groups of folded sheets) which formed the book, with all of its "thickness when they are piled together; for then they form a tomb in miniature for our souls."26 Mallarmé disdained the newspaper, it was an open sea, into which "literature flows ... at will" — that is without discretion, form, structure or vision. By contrast a book had the capacity to use its form to "establish some nameless system of relationships" through which its strength could be realized. This could not happen without attention, a self-conscious act by which the text becomes integral with its placement, movement, symphonic orchestration through the space of the book. As far as the ordinary process of reading was concerned, Mallarmé protested that it had a deadly mechanical repetition, a hopelessly mundane "back and forth motion" which caused one to miss the "ecstasy in which we become immortal for a brief hour.... and raise our obsessions to the level of creation."

Mallarmé insisted that the letter was the basic element of the book, which must find mobility and expansion, and used the metaphor of a musical composition as the inspiration for experiments in typography and layout. But Mallarmé's embedding of the concept in metaphor did not end with the possibilities he envisioned for the page. The form of the book as an object was also included in his vision: "The virginal foldings of the book are unfortunately exposed to the kind of sacrifice which caused the crimson-edged tomes of ancient times to bleed. I mean that they invite the paper-knife, which stakes out claims to possession of the book."27 Against this violent image, with its implication of futility in the effort at possession, Mallarmé puts another image, "Yet our consciousness alone gives us a far more intimate possession than such a barbarian symbol; for it joins the book now here, now there, varies its melodies, guesses its riddles, and even re-creates it unaided." Mallarmé's view of the physical violation invited by a book, posed in terms of a gendered metaphor of phallic knife and virginal folds, is in sharp contrast to the process of intellectual engagement which extended his discussion. The literalization of such imagery was hardly Mallarmé's intention, instead he believed his conviction that the spaces of the book could be invested with a far more complex structure and thus become "the divine and intricate organism required by literature." Such an organism must belie the conventional layout of the book with "its eternally unbearable columns" and manifest a constellation of text, with units scattering about the main line in an ornamental but integral fashion. Mallarmé was attempting a synthesis between a philosophical vision of the book as an expansive instrument of the spirit and the capacity of its physical form to reflect and embody thought in new visual arrangements.

While Mallarmé's ideas about the transformation of the layout of the page put at the service of the poetic imagination reached fulfillment only in the posthumous publication of his 1896 poem "Un Coup de Des" ("A Throw of the Dice"), his ideas about the metaphysical extension of "The

Book" were in effect unrealizable. (The first printed edition which attempted to follow his indications appeared in 1914, published by the Nouvelle Revue Française.) Though the structure of poetics might be stretched to the point where it could attempt to be the crystallized form of thought (abstract, mobile, complex, interrelated at numerous levels), the possibility of a book which contained "all earthly existence" was always precluded by its own conceptual parameters. At the point of this limit, the end of the book begins.

Gustave Flaubert, **Bouvard and Pécuchet**, 1896 edition

Gustave Flaubert

The work of Gustave Flaubert (1821-1880) the unsurpassed novelist of 19th-century realism makes an interesting counterpart to that of his more metaphysical contemporary. Prosaic though his imagery is, Flaubert's use of the book as a major point of reference in his last, unfinished novel **Bouvard and Pécuchet**, makes a poignant counterpoint to the infinite space of the Mallarméan vision. In the novel, which he was still working on when he died, Flaubert describes two men who have been clerk-copyists throughout their professional lives who meet in middle age and forge a life together. One of them has come into an unexpected inheritance. Freed from the mundane task of making their living they move into a country house and begin the adventure of their new, unconstrained life. They undertake an endless series of enterprises, and in each new area of endeavor — whether it is aboriculture, agriculture, the collection of antiquities, spiritual enlightenment, or pedagogy — they acquire what they deem to be necessary knowledge through books. Flaubert's ruthless insight is expressed through the terms of textuality, writing, and the pretense to encyclopedic knowledge which the mass production of printed materials permitted to come into book form in the period.

In every field they undertake, Mssrs. Bouvard and Pécuchet are failures. Not mere failures, but complete failures. Their attempts to come to grips with any aspect of experience is always mediated through the work of some purported expert in the field. Refusing, for instance, the expertise of the farmer who rents their property, or the local inhabitants of the district familiar with the character of soil, climate, and vegetation, they consistently prefer the authoritative knowledge provided by a published expert. "They mutually consulted one another, opened a book, then passed on to another, and did not know what to resolve upon when there was so much divergence of opinion."28 The books they require are always ordered from Paris, from their obliging and no doubt satisfied dealer, whose capacity to supply them with tomes on all and any subject seems to have had no limit. Flaubert himself supposedly read some 1500 volumes on various topics as part of his research for the project, and this seems believable given the encyclopedic scope of his characters' investigations. The folly of their undertaking is apparent at every turn and is in every case a reflection of their desire to believe in the book as a source of real knowledge. The escalation of published work, the sheer number of volumes in any field in this period of industrialized printing, became the object of Flaubert's derision. The match between the fatuously totalizing reach of Bouvard and Pécuchet and the dream of the all-encompassing book of Mallarmé is perhaps perverse. They are in some sense opposites — Mallarmé takes the world into the book which becomes significant through its completeness, the books consulted by Bouvard and Pécuchet purport to represent the world, and to be a means to understanding it through their repleteness. In both cases there is a totalizing instinct, but in Flaubert's work this instinct is continually checked, brought to a halt, given another false start, and ultimately, self-destructs in the personal chaos the two men wreak upon themselves. No matter how much they read, they have to reckon with the fact that there is more to read upon any and all subjects: "In order to form an impartial judgement upon it, it would have been necessary to have read all the histories, all the memoirs, and all the manuscript productions, for through the least omission might arise an error, which might lead to others without limit."29 This anxiety about the impossibility of completeness is an aspect of the philosophical extension of theory about the nature of the book in the writing of 20th-century theorists for whom this becomes a philosophical, rather than pragmatic, issue. While the concerns of Edmond Jabès are generated from a different poetic inquiry, his work takes up this issue of the limit of the book.

Edmond Jabès

It was the Mallarméan idea of limit, of space beyond limit, and the space defined by such a limit, which charged the thinking of the 20th century poet Edmond Jabès (1912—1991) and a number of the theoretical writers for whom his work and that of Mallarmé serve as a point of departure. Jabès was concerned with the idea of "The Book" within the cultural legacy of the Jewish religion and its interpretative practices.30 Jabès returns our discussion to a far more ancient tradition than that of French poetics, related though the Symbolist and Realist writers may be to this tradition as an extension of Judeo-Christian thought. Jabès takes the relationship between written text and active, ongoing interpretation which is fundmental to Jewish thought and makes it contemporary, secular, and spiritually charged. It is not Jewish faith which motivates Jabès's writing, but Jewish culture and identity within a 20th-century frame. Within Jewish tradition the Jews have the identity of the people of the Book. The Book is the Bible, most particularly the Torah which is comprised of the five books of Moses. Jews are also the people of the Mosaic law, and writing as an instrument of divine instruction which establishes the basis of a Jewish life through daily interpretation as practice is a theme which Jabès also investigates in terms of the effect of writing as a limit. The idea of limit suggested by Jabès is meant to invoke a sense of taboo, as in the limit of the law, and also a limit of what is representable, the point at which writing leaves off because it cannot extend, by definition, beyond its own capacity to represent. That limit can be interpreted in a positive sense as when Jabès states: "... the Hebrew people gave Moses a crucial lession in reading when they forced him to break the tablets of the law. Because they were not able to accept a word without origins, the word of God. It was necessary for Moses to break the book in order for the book to become human.... This gesture on the part of the Hebrew people was necessary before they could accept the book. This is exactly what we do as well. We destroy the book when we read it in order to make it into another book. The book is always born from a broken book. And the word, too, is born from a broken word...."31

Jabès began his investigation of the book with the 1963 publication of his work, **The Book of Questions**. At that point in his life, Jabès, who had been born to a rich Egyptian Jewish family, was in exile in France, displaced not by events of the Second World War, but by the consequences of the Suez crisis and conflict between Nassar's government and the state of Israel. The theme of the Holocaust is central to Jabès's work since Jabès recognizes the impossibility of writing and continuing past this specific historical limit.32 Jabès does not treat this idea thematically, instead, he attempts to give an account, tell a story, through fragments, aphorisms, bits and pieces, none of which are central or definitive. **The Book of Questions** is not a piecemeal novel, not a "story told" through various perspectives, through evidence, or points of view — it is a book about the impossibility of a narrative as a form.33 It is a book which is incomplete, and is meant to point to the limit of all attempts at narrative completion. Invoking the "question" as the form which shows the impossibility of an answer, Jabès is bringing the Jewish practice of ongoing interpretation, of daily interrogation of sacred text as an approach to divine knowledge, wisdom and being, into the poetic structure of literature. Jabès is a secular writer, but one for whom the image of the book is informed by its spiritual resonance within a hermeneutic inquiry, an ongoing practice of interpretation.

It does an injustice to the work of Jabès to reduce him to these brief notes, but the point is to indicate the rich intellectual literature on the topic of the book as an idea, one which has a very complicated heritage in the history of human culture. Jabès was well-acquainted with the work of Mallarmé. In fact, Jabès and Mallarmé are discussed together in the analyses of Roland Barthes and Maurice Blanchot. For Barthes the idea of the text as a continually changing construction formed through the process of reading is in part derived from the metaphors of these poets, while Blanchot, also a poet, engages both the Mallarméan imagery of the space of the page, the huge "blank" and existentially threatening "nothingness" of

the white surface, and the open structures of Jabès' approach. The elaboration of theoretical discussion in this area becomes entangled in French
Deconstructionist critiques of the concepts of Being as they are linked to
practices of representation and interpretation in critical thought. The
work of Jacques Derrida extends the analysis of writing and the book into
a metaphysical inquiry. In his 1967 essay, "The End of Writing and the
Beginning of the Book," Derrida embraces the idea that the finite nature
to which writing pretends, its definiteness, its capacity to notate with
finality and to exist (philosophically, as a state of **being**) in a condition of
semi-permanence must all be called into question.34 When "writing" is finished through a systematic investigation of its feints, trickeries, and
deceptions, then the "book" as an ongoing open-ended, dynamic operation can begin. Derrida's book in this conception is related to Mallarmé's
— but it gains its totality through its condition of unfinishedness. By being
in a constant state of becoming, the book may be the world, not as its representation or surrogate, but as itself, in all of its unlimited, infinite
entirety — never static and complete, always becoming.

In drawing on historical precedents within the history of book production, the poetic and philosophical investigation of the book as an idea, my
intention has been to open the field of artists' books to a wide horizon
even before I begin to map its many aspects. The imagery of the writers I
have mentioned is in no sense exhaustive and they are but a few repre-
sentatives of a densely populated tradition.

The Concept of the Book

In closing this chapter I want to invoke a few other ideas of the book
in its cultural and metaphoric richness. The book after all is as essential in
its many functional and vernacular aspects and as inspiring in its many
serviceable forms and formats as it is in its more poetic evocations. The
efficient density of the telephone book, for example, which provides a tactile and visual satisfaction through the thin quality of its paper, a paper
which amounts in the bound form to a flexible dense object makes a striking contrast to the pleasures provided by a new notebook, its blank sheets
full of promise and opportunity. In its familiar form the paperback novel,
impressed with the tacky curve of an outrageously molded form, die-cut,
foil stamped, and turning brittle on the same trip on which it is purchased
announces its ephemerality without shame, eschewing all commitment
from the very first, while the heavy black pages of a traditional photo

album absorb memory into their dense field and hold it safe, still, silent and waiting. The inexpensive dimestore diary is of another form altogether, making believe there is a life worth noting as a series of secrets whose value derives from the tiny key which locks them in nightly more than from the childish scribblings in which they are generally, briefly, recorded; while the crossed and criss-crossed palimpsest of the pocket-sized address book provides a whole history of a real life, though none of its narrative fullness. Every book is a metaphor, an object of associations and history, cultural meanings and production values, spiritual possibilities and poetic spaces, and all of these are a part of the field from which the artist's book derives its identity, its shared connections and distinguishing features as a book whose realized forms and thematic intentions are only the most evident aspects of its totality as an idea.

1 There are any number of works in the literature on the history of printing which are relevant here, such as **The Printing Press as an Agent of Social Change**, Elizabeth Eisenman (Cambridge University Press, 1969) the work of Roger Chartier, Lucien Febvre, and even historians of print as a social and cultural form, such as William Ivins, Estelle Jussim and others, all of which are tangentially related to the problem of understanding the book as a cultural and philosophical force; none of these, to my knowledge, actually synthesizes these issues into a basis for artists' involvement with books as a complex and resonant form.

2 Robert Blake, who had worked with William as an assistant, died in 1787. See Kathleen Raine, **William Blake** (Praeger, NY, 1971) p.43.

3 Early editions of **The Songs of Innocence**, for instance, are brighter than those painted later.

4 Joseph Viscomi, **Blake and the Concept of the Book** (Princeton University Press, 1993).

5 See Raine, again, as an introduction, but for more authoritative, recent scholarship, see David Bindman's catalogue, **William Blake: His Art and His Times** (Yale Center for British Art, 1982) as well as Morton Paley's notes to the Princeton edition of the facsimile publication (1991).

6 In **The Book of Urizen** (London, 1794).

7 See William Blake, **The Marriage of Heaven and Hell** (Oxford University Press, 1975) introduction and commentary by Geoffrey Keynes, which details the way this work transforms, comments on, and critiques Swedenborg's **Heaven and Hell**.

8 Some basic sources for this section include Stephen Coote, **William Morris: His Life and Work** (Garamond, 1990), **William Morris and Kelmscott** (The Design Council, 1981), Peter Faulkner, **Against the Age: An Introduction to William Morris** (George

Allen, Unwin, 1980), Paul Thompson, **The Work of William Morris** (Oxford University Press, 1991), and Asa Briggs, ed., **William Morris: Selected Writings and Designs**, (Penguin, 1962).

9 Morris's father had made a considerable sum of money through investment in a copper mine and was able to leave his son a significant guaranteed yearly income upon his demise.

10 The date of Kelmscott Press's establishment could be linked to its first production in 1891, to the establishment of the facility, slightly earlier, or to Morris's first full-scale book productions, printed at the Chiswick Press in 1888, since all of these activities play a part in its evolution.

11 See Paul Thompson, **The Work of William Morris**, Chapter 7, "Book Design," pp.150-165.

12 See below, Chapter 3.

13 Thompson, **The Work of William Morris**, p.159, and through this paragraph.

14 Burne-Jones and Morris met as undergraduates at Oxford and remained close personal friends and professional associates throughout their lives. Burne-Jones is part of a younger generation of Pre-Raphaelites — Dante Gabriel Rossetti was already well-known at the time the two schoolmates made his acquaintance, and the Pre-Raphaelite aesthetic which they took up had already been established.

15 Again, see Thompson, for a mention of Daniel Updike, Frederick Goudy, Bruce Rogers, and William Dwiggins as printer/typographers influenced by Morris — all individuals who brought their skills to bear on both independent publishing and trade design.

16 For those who have forgotten: "I never saw a purple cow, I never hope to see one, but I can tell you this right now, I'd rather see than be one."

17 Details of Burgess's activities are briefly outlined in James Hart's introduction to **Bayside Bohemia**, Gelett Burgess (The Book Club of California, San Francisco, 1954).

18 Among the group were Bruce and Robert Porter, Ernest Peixotto, Porter Garnett, Yone Noguchi, and Willis Polk.

19 Burgess, p.25.

20 Burgess, p.27.

21 Burgess, p.28.

22 Stephane Mallarmé, "Action Restricted," **Selected Writings**, Mary Ann Caws, ed. (New Directions, 1982) p.79.

23 Ibid

24 Stephane Mallarmé, "The Book: A Spiritual Instrument," **Selected Writings**, Mary Ann Caws, ed. op.cit. p.80.

25 Ibid.

26 Through this paragraph all quotes are from "The Book: A Spiritual Instrument."

27 I dread the day I encounter some hideously literal book-sculpture image of these phrases replete with bloodstained paper and sexual imagery.

 28 Gustave Flaubert, **Bouvard and Pécuchet**, (H.S. Nichols, Publisher, 1896, First English edition) p.47.

29 Gustave Flaubert, **Bouvard and Pécuchet**, p.171.

30 There is a substantial amount of critical literature on Jabès, for an introduction see Eric Gould, ed., **The Sin of the Book: Edmond Jabès** (University of Nebraska Press, 1985), as well as Jabès's own writings.

31 Gould, ed., **The Sin of the Book**, p.23.

32 This idea is not unique or original to Jabès. It is found in the work of many post-war writers Adrienne Rich and Max Horkheimer among others, and forms the basis for much critical investigation of art and literature in the post-war period.

33 In this section I have relied on Paul Auster's commentaries in "The Book of the Dead: An Interview with Edmond Jabès," in **The Sin of the Book**, pp.3-25, and the work of other writers in this volume, particularly Richard Stamelman, Maurice Blanchot, and Rosmarie Waldrop.

34 Jacques Derrida, **De La Grammatologie** (Editions de Minuit, 1967).

3

Artists' Books
& the Early 20th-Century Avant-Garde

The history of the book as an early 20th-century artform cannot be separated from the agendas of the artistic factions that comprised the historical avant-garde.1 Political broadsides, artistic poster design, and other forms of graphic activity had been identified with individual artistic expression and political statements well before the 20th century. Throughout the 19th century in England, France, and other parts of Europe, an explosion of periodicals had published exchanges between artists, writers, and other creative thinkers.2 But it is in the early 20th century that books became a major feature of experimental artistic vision, and a unique vehicle for its realization.

The first arena of activity in which this occurs with a high degree of visibility is in the Russian avant-garde. This was due in part to the hybrid nature of the talents possessed by many of the individuals involved — poets had frequently trained as painters or vice versa and often they became involved with experimental theater, music, or dance as well. The influence of French Symbolism, with its emphasis upon the synthaesthetic concept of the arts — the idea that a sensation might be simultaneously represented in a variety of media and translated from one to another — had established the conceptual groundwork for cross-disciplinary work.3

The emphasis which Symbolist aesthetics had placed upon synaesthetic practices, and upon the spiritual and conceptual identity of the book, as in the work of Mallarmé, had an influence in the early 20th century.4 But the aesthetics of that and other late 19th-century movements came under attack. In a similar manner, the ornate pages of the Arts and Crafts movement — as exemplified by William Morris in England, Charles Rennie Mackintosh in Glasgow, and William Matthews in San Francisco — with their sinewy vegetal borders, intertwined floral patterns, and sensual excesses came to epitomize the old-fashioned, retrograde aesthetic against which the early 20th-century artists vigorously rebelled. Nonethe-

45

less, many traits of early 20th-century avant-garde activity betray links to both Symbolist and Arts and Crafts precedents. These include a highly self-conscious attention to materials, the conviction that the form of the book, the layout of the page, and the quality of the image were as much an aspect of communication as was the thematic content of the work. Another carryover was an interest in hybrid forms produced as the result of interrelations among artistic forms.

The transition to modernity can be traced in the Viennese Secession movement which began in the 1890s. Though the most active areas of Viennese productivity were in painting and the applied arts — architecture, textiles, and furnishings — there were also a few notable examples of graphic arts and design. Posters and other ephemera abound, and the journal associated with the Secession, **Ver Sacrum**, exemplifies Secessionist aesthetics. One book from this period, Oskar Kokoschka's **Die Träumenden Knaben** is close to the sensibility of an artist's book. Produced in 1908, the work was Kokoschka's love letter to a young woman he had met and fantasized about as a student. Meant as a children's picture book, the work was conceived by Kokoschka as an expression of a single impulse of communication, and the images (transfer lithographs and linecuts) and text are intricately merged. The work was printed as a project of the Wiener Werkstatt (established in 1903).5 Though it does not have the spontaneity or invention of many later 20th-century books, it reflected Kokoschka's interest in every aspect of book design — binding, typography, illustration. He had become so passionate about the topic of books that he gave lectures on the subject whose sources can be readily traced to his enthusiasm for the work of William Morris. But the book as an artistic form did not find many enthusiasts among the Viennese designers, and Kokoschka's remains a special case. While he did work on other graphic projects, even book projects, Kokoschka did not pursue the innovative use of the form for direct creative expression as his Russian contemporaries did.

The movement of Russian Futurism (which developed independently of the Italian movement of the same name) served as an arena in which the 20th-century art of the book emerged.6 Many features of the Russian Futurist aesthetic in the 1910s were innovative, specifically an interest in traditional Russian folk sources for literary and visual motifs and forms (typical of the neo-primitive wing of the avant-garde) and attempts to discover new symbolic forms of language and images suitable to a contemporary sensibility (an interest of Futurists and **zaumniks** — or inventors of the **zaum** language).7 In addition, Russian artists were well-aware of French Cubism, and though intent upon constructing an aesthetic which did not depend upon the European tradition of fine arts for its identity, the Russian Futurists made a synthesis of cubist analysis and fragmentation and a native folk sensibility.8

There are aspects to the way books are used and produced in the Russian Futurist context, beginning in about 1912, which are very similar to the sensibilities which motivated the creation of artists' books in the 1960s and 70s — most particularly the desire to produce inexpensive works with available means in a format over which the artist or writer had total control.9 In this regard, the works produced by the Russian avant-garde mark the beginning of the 20th-century development of artists' books as a form whose conceptual basis breaks with that of traditional book production. The book becomes a form of artistic expression in the hands of these artists rather than a convention-bound mode of reproduction.

The works produced in the early years of Russian Futurism were done on a very small scale; most were mere pamphlets, of modest dimensions, consisting of a few sheets of cheap paper stapled, or roughly sewn.10 This work continued up until the Russian Revolution, which marked the demise of Futurism and the emergence of Constructivist and Productivist aesthetics, which were more involved in applied design than in fine art or literature. Many Futurist books made use of materials which came from outside the realm of fine arts — burlap covers, wallpaper pages, or other cloth and paper. One unfortunate effect of this eclectic attitude toward materials was the impermanance of the work. Many of these books are now too fragile to handle and crumble or tear if touched. The work was intentionally ephemeral — made for the moment, in order to be circulated among friends and read without regard for preciousness or longevity. This attitude reflected a response to the elaborate productions of fine presses, including those of the Russian World of Art movement from the earlier decade of the 20th century.11

Susan Compton, an expert on Russian avant-garde books, cites various titles (evocative of the irreverent spirit of the early Futurist movement) such as **Worldbackwards** (1912), **A Game in Hell** (1912), **Half-Alive** (1913), and **A Slap in the Face of Public Taste** (1913) as early instances. **Worldbackwards** was printed lithographically, with the text handwritten onto the plates in an uneven, energetic style which interacts with the open,

47

Aleksander Kruchenyk and Velimir Khlebnikov, **A Game in Hell**, 1912, lithographed cover by Natalia Goncharova

sketchy linework of the artist Natalia Goncharova's neo-primitive drawings. The text was the work of Velimir Khlebnikov, a vagrant visionary poet who often kept his poems only as crumbled sheets stuffed into the pockets of a ratty old overcoat. Khlebnikov was a radically innovative poet whose explorations of language as material, as a pattern of rhyme, thought, and image disconnected the traditions of versification from the restraints of narrative or reference.12 Such work — radical in form, execution, and intention — was well-realized in a format which had the appearance of being rapidly and roughly made.13 The collaboration between Goncharova and various poets granted the projects a measure of visibility; she and her husband Mikhail Larionov were two of the most prominent Russian painters of the time, having established their reputations first within a late Impressionistic sensibility, while the poets with whom they collaborated in this period were still largely unknown figures. Goncharova was particularly important in incorporating neo-primitivism into all aspects of her work, painting, drawing, and published imagery, while Larionov created his own visual movement, Rayonism, which had formal resemblances to both Cubist and Futurist fragmentation of forms. These visual innovations combined with equally unprecedented literary work to

48

produce a striking new aesthetic. The impetus for such artistic transformation produced the new vision of the book as an independent artistic expression, one in which there was no obstacle to an integration of image and language, formal experiment, and artistic innovation — all essential features of the early avant-garde.

These were often self-published books and the means employed for their production was lithography, linoleum cutting, potato print, stencil cut, and a now obsolete duplicating form called hectography. It was not uncommon for artists to use rubber stamps, to handwrite a small edition of their work, or to use watercolor and other very accessible means to produce these works. There were also letterpress works among these early editions and these quickly became innovative typographically by making use of the varied sizes and styles of the compositor's case to inflect the printed page with visual emphasis. Compton lists over sixty individual books produced in the years 1912 to 1917 in editions ranging between fifty and a thousand copies. Thus dozens of small books were produced in this period and such outpouring did not stop even in 1917, though shortages brought on by the First World War and the various phases of internal strife and the Revolution limited publishing supplies for several years and disrupted the artistic circles from which they had sprung. The transformation of Russian society into the Soviet Union completely reconfigured the place of art and literature in the culture of the 1920s. The work which grew out of aesthetic debates following the Revolution had long-term effects on 20th-century typographic, photographic, and publication design.14

The remarkable thing about these books is not merely that they existed in such numbers, but that they demonstrated that the book could be rethought to serve new ends. There was no trace in these works of the rules of book arts which had held sway since the invention of printing in the 15th century. The sense that a book was a fresh and vital form for immediate, direct expression, rather than a well-wrought volume which might showcase the finely engraved work of an artist in relation to an expertly printed text, breaks new ground for book production giving it more in common with the pamphleteers of earlier centuries. These artists had little regard for expertise of printing for its own sake. When they made use of letterpress type the result reflected the competence of the commercial printers they hired, but the bulk of these works are intentionally crude in their production. These books did not merely shock and disturb the bourgeoisie — an idea which had been around since the 19th century — but instead sought to create symbolic forms of a new modern experience.

In this moment the book becomes first and foremost a means of direct communication, a multiple which can be readily circulated, given away, or sold for very little money. No established publishers arose from this period (though Ilia Zdanevich did begin his own productions in 1917 under an imprint, 41 Degrees, even his minimal formalization of this activity was the exception rather than the rule). Most of the work reflects the fact that books could be done by artists, with limited means, by making use of the skills and technology at their disposal. This work radically reconceptualizes the book as an artistic form, not a publishing enterprise, not a fine press production, not a portfolio of prints, but a new hybrid form without rules or limits.

While Goncharova, Larionov, Kruchenyk, and Khlebnikov are the major figures in this movement, the three Burliuk brothers, Elena Guro, Kasimir Malevich, Olga Rozanova, and Vladimir Mayakovsky, among others, also made books in this period. Three well-known books from this period, however, were the production of other artists. These are each works which could not have been made without the other projects just discussed, but they are each fully realized works in terms which go beyond the expressionistic spontaneity of these early, small format, pamphlet forms.

The first of these three books is the **La Prose du Transsibérien et de la petite Jehanne de France** (1913), the famous collaboration between Sonia Delaunay-Terk and Blaise Cendrars (the nom de plume of Frédéric-Louis Sauser) who also served as the publisher of the work.15 The book was printed in Paris, letterpress, with various passages of the text printed in different colors. The whole work, comprised of four sheets glued in a four-square grid, is most often shown hung as a wall piece to its full height of over six feet. Around, under, and through the vividly colored passages of type are large, bright, dramatic watercolor decorations, created by pochoir method (painting through a stencil) to provide some unity to the edition. The work has a binary character, the left pair of sheets filled with the dynamic colorful abstract painting of Sonia Delaunay. The passages are composed of large sweeping curved forms, whose play down the sheet moves the eye with a dramatic rhythmic grace which takes the whole work into account. By contrast, the right side of the work is more lightly painted, outlining, floating, and supporting the passages of poetry. The

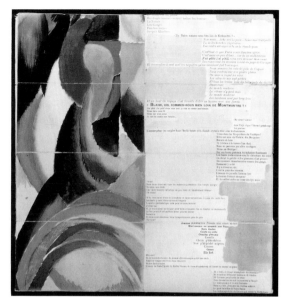

Blaise Cendrars and Sonia Delaunay, **La Prose...**, 1913
The Getty Center for the Humanities

color unites the two realms, the bright ink turning the words into a painted form, and the sheer length of the work mimics the long stretch of the Transsiberian railroad referred to in the title. In its closed form, this work is folded into a parchment wrapper painted by the artist, and it only functions as a readable "book" when it is fully open, defying the codex form by its graphic flatness and large-scale presence.

That Delaunay and Cendrars could conceive of such a work in 1913 is remarkable. Paintings had shrunk from the grandiose history canvases of earlier centuries to a smaller, more domestic scale in the early Cubist period (with a few notable exceptions) and the only precedent for works of this scale in the graphic arts consisted of posters for the opera, theater, or other public events. No private reading experience had ever assumed such dimensions, and the explosion of the book into a piece of this size is a dramatic conceptual as well as formal achievement.

Not all of the work which was important to typographic experiment in the first two decades of the 20th century was done in the form of books. Only a small percentage actually engaged both the idea of the book and the potential for typographic representation to transform the page, which is why the books mentioned here are each so important. The bulk of radi-

51

cal typography was produced in ephemeral forms such as flyers and posters, or in the pages of the many journals spawned by Futurist and Dada activity. Few writers seemed capable of embracing typographic innovation as the basis of a transformed writing practice, and where occasional pages of graphic experiment are reproduced in a volume, they are conspicuous by their visual dynamism rather than integral to the form of a book as a whole. This is the case with the well-known **Calligrammes** of Guillaume Apollinaire, in which his shaped poems are printed as part of a larger collection. Important as they are within the tradition of shaped poetry, and as inspiration for later concrete poetry, such work does not lend itself to a discussion of the book as artistic expression since the book as a form is not a considered aspect of the work.

The first call for typographic innovation in the context of the avant-garde occured in 1909 in the manifestos of Filippo Marinetti, the leader of the Futurist movement in Italy.16 Marinetti desired a completely new aesthetic sensibility in creative work — painting, sculpture, writing, typography. Every aspect of plastic arts was to reflect the new, modern, streamlined world of the "wireless imagination" which Marinetti felt was the spirit pervading the Futurist vision of the 20th century. Though his first manifesto published in the French daily paper, **Figaro**, in April 1909, contained no specific remarks on the form of Futurist typography, later manifestos, such as the "Technical Manifesto of Futurism" published in 1912 and the "Typographic Revolution" of 1913 (appended to the "Futurist Sensibility") were detailed in their exhortation to abandon traditional grammar, syntax, punctuation, and format and to make use of the graphic potential of words on the page to create a vivid "pictorial typographic page."17 Marinetti was also pointed in his criticism of the older aesthetic of the Arts and Crafts movement "with its handmade paper and 17th-century ornamentation of garlands and goddesses, huge initials and mythological vegetation, its missal ribbons and epigraphs and roman numerals" — all details which would aptly describe the pages of Morris's **Chaucer**. In its place, Marinetti wanted fluidity, movement, variety, the freedom to use as many typefaces and colors of ink as were necessary to suit the dynamism of the texts of his "words in liberty."

Though Marinetti was not particularly skilled as a typographer, nor was he gifted with an inspired typographic imagination, his precepts served as a point of reference for work created by Futurist and Dada poets. Some poets knew these manifestos and others simply innovated in what came to be the style of the time. Periodicals were the most important vehicle for publicizing and disseminating stylistic inventions. The pages of Tristan Tzara's **Dada**, which was first published in Zurich in 1916, were highly influential in terms of their graphic impact.18 The same was true of **391**, Francis Picabia's journal, each issue of which had a slightly different format and was produced in various venues as Picabia moved around Europe and the United States in the course of the years of the First World War. Many other journals which appeared for a number or two and then disappeared were dramatic in their incorporation of devices and techniques which had formerly belonged only to advertising graphics.19 These became part of the visual vocabulary of literary writing and were often the inspiration for later work by artists whose careers returned to the realm of applied design such as the DeStijl figures Piet Zwart and Theo Van Doesburg.20

The discussion of the next two books, Ilia Zdanevich's **Ledentu as Beacon** and the collaborative work by Lazar El Lissitzky and Vladimir Mayakovsy, **For the Voice**, both from 1923, have to be understood against this background of typographic innovation.21 It is fair to say that among the handful of outstanding bookworks which made typographic work part of their conception, **Ledentu** and **For the Voice** are particularly striking. In both of them experimental typography reached unprecedented heights of invention, staging formal dynamics which had been technically possible for centuries, but had been inconceivable within standard literary modes of representation. **Ledentu** was the fifth in a series of dramatic texts composed by Ilia Zdanevich (1894-1975), known through most of his later professional life as Iliazd.22 These texts were plays which traced, autobiographically, his development from the image of a "little flea" to that of a full-fledged adult male artist involved in various complex affairs of the heart, issues of identity, and artistic inquiry. Each of the works became a printed text and each of the five books has its own specific typographic treatment. The first four of these, printed in Tiflis, Georgia between 1916 and 1919, had elements in common with the typographically orchestrated and scored pages produced elsewhere in Russian Futurist writing.23 The voices of characters were differentiated spatially or according to boldness or style of face, with overlapping passages designed to be read simultaneously as if they were part of a musical score. Zdanevich not only intended these for performance but also actually had at least one of the works mounted as a small-scale theatrical production. There is a distinct sense that he sees the page as a theatrical environment. By the time Zdanevich printed **Ledentu** he was living in Paris (he had arrived there in 1922), and the Futurist enterprise was rapidly being left behind by the emergence of Surrealism. All of Zdanevich's dramas had been written in an invented language called **zaum**. Other poets, particularly Alexei Kruchenyk and Velimir Khlebnikov had also invented versions of **zaum** — which was an attempt to transcend the limits of conventional languages and express meaning, emotion, and sensation through phonetic means. The term implied a transrational or transmental system of communication. Suggestive, evocative, and rich in phonetic invention, **zaum** was also an essentially unintelligible, highly coded, personal language. Stretching invention to this point hardly netted the poets a wide reading audience, and to this day **zaum** remains a hermetic practice, linguistically difficult and critically inaccessible.24

Ledentu surpassed Zdanevich's earlier printed work in the scope of invention and complexity which he managed to produce from the standard materials of a printer's typecase. Manufacturing large-scale letters out of ornaments, using the widest possible range of contrasting styles to push the communicative effect of typography to its extremes, Zdanevich created a work whose letterpress virtuosity was an apt complement to its linguistic complexity. Across the gutter the pages juxtapose an orchestrated set of simultaneous voices with compositions of wild innovation, and though the horizontality of letterpress is never violated, the linearity and regularity of the page is rarely respected. By 1923 many precedents for such work existed, in the pages of Dada journals, or in the work of the Russian poet, Vassili Kamensky, whose book **Tango With Cows** (Moscow, 1914) had manifested that writer's vision of what he termed "ferro-concrete" poetry. But Zdanevich had a clearer, more thorough understanding of letterpress design than Kamensky. He had apprenticed to a printer for several years in Tiflis and actually set type himself (though whether he set all of the type for **Ledentu** is not clear). He also had a compelling vision of the way in which such work could be sustained throughout an entire book. From the very beginning of his work Zdanevich understood the book form and worked with it, displaying a feel for the relations between paper and page size, elements of binding, and the overall integration of conception and construction of a book.25

Better known by far than **Ledentu**, the Mayakovsky text **For the Voice**, which was rendered into book form in 1923 by El Lissitzky, is a comparable

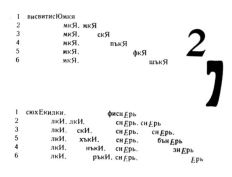

Ilia Zdanevich (Iliazd), **Ledentu as Beacon**, 1923

Ilia Zdanevich (Iliazd), **Ledentu as Beacon**, 1923

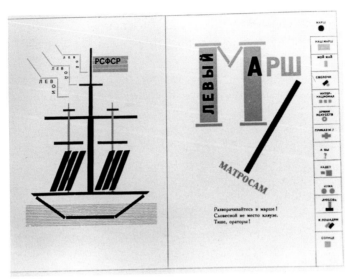

Vladimir Mayakovsky, **For the Voice**, 1923, designed by Lazar El Lissitzky

achievement of integration. This work also made innovative use of the elements of the standard typecase, though Lissitzky limited himself to using pieces of rule or geometric devices to construct pages which were abstract images of highly formal arrangements printed in bright red and black ink. Lissitzky was also borrowing from earlier and contemporary models, some of which he had helped to bring into being through his own design work, other instances of which emerged within the new graphic sensibility of Alexander Rodchenko's Constructivist designs for the pages of **Lef** (in the early 1920s subsequently for **Noyvi Lef**) printed by the radical Soviet artists' group.26 The explosive look of Soviet poster, journal, and advertising design, which later found its way into mainstream Western graphics, had a limited application to book work beyond the cover or title page design.27 Lissitzky, however, used these techniques on the pages which identified individual sections of Mayakovsky's poetic text. The book is cut into index tabs like an address book, and on each of the tabs Lissitzky placed a small motif whose iconic form serves as a reference to the sections of the work. The pages which serve as internal title pages to each section are strikingly designed though the format of the text within the sections is more standard. No literary book had ever been designed with these formal elements, and Lissitzky's capacity to make the visual and graphic decisions serve the scoring of the text so that it became a visual treatment of a text made **For the Voice** a distinct achievement. This is an integrally complete work, in which every element is self-consciously part of the whole and functioning in relation to the bound parameters of the book form.

While **Ledentu** and **For the Voice** are two outstanding works, they are not alone as successful explorations of the newly reconceptualized idea of the book as a medium for direct artistic expression and of the innovative techniques of avant-garde experiments in typographic or visual form. Other such works would include Kurt Schwitters' **Die Kathedrale**, produced in 1920, one of the few expressions of Dada collage sensibility in book form. Collages were featured on the covers of Russian and Soviet books in the late 1910s and early 1920s, with contributions by Rodchenko as well as Gustav Klutsis, Alexei Gan, and others, and also became a characteristic of the German Dada artists centered in Berlin, John Heartfield and Hannah Hoch. Heartfield's graphic work quickly returned to the realm of reproduction, functioning as effective imagery in the pages of **AIZ** (**Arbeiter Illustriete Zeitung**) and in the cover designs he did for the radical publishing company Malik Verlag.28 In addition, many collages appear in books where they serve to illustrate, complement, or extend the full text of the work, but they do not comprise the work in its entirety save in exceptional instances.

Filippo Marinetti's own books also deserve mention. Of these **Zang Tumb Tuuum** (1914) was the most completely worked: in it Marinetti made conspicuous use of mathematical signs in place of punctuation and subdivided the text into blocks and columns to order the pages according to his precepts of Futurist typography. There are individual poems by Marinetti which make more innovative use of the page than any which appear in **Zang Tumb Tuuum**, but they are isolated instances such as "Battle at Nine Levels," printed in the anthology **Words in Liberty** which appeared in 1919. As a collection of different pieces, this later publication contains a handful of striking examples but was not conceived as a book in its totality. The Futurist book which most clearly achieves these aims, aside from **Zang Tumb Tuuum**, is a much later work. Designed by Tullio Albisola, **Parole in liberta futuriste** has been worked out at every level of production and conception. This 1934 book was lithographed onto tin with the stylized geometry of its layouts integrating powerfully with the hard-edged metal of its pages.

Typographic experimentation became a synthetic element of graphic

Filippo Marinetti, **Zang Tumb Tuuum**, 1914

design through the institutionalization of avant-garde typography in the curriculum of the German Bauhaus in the 1920s and early 1930s, through the work of Herbert Bayer who also brought this aesthetic sensibility into an American context, through the independent work of Jan Tschichold with his influential essays on "New Typography," and through the teachings of Soviet, Dutch, and Eastern European designers.29 In a similar way, the techniques of photomontage which emerged from the crucible of avant-garde experiment also found their place in mainstream design. But there were other developments within the art world and in commercial or trade publishing which took up and extended earlier experiments in new forms. Among these were the publications which came from Surrealist art and literature as well as those which extended early experiments into a more mainstream venue.

There was nothing mainstream about Surrealism at the time of its origin. The Surrealist commitment to infusing the character of everyday life with the contents and attitudes of the unconscious, dream life, and eroticism was not likely to find ready acceptance among the French bourgeoisie. In Paris of the 1920s, a group of artists and writers who found their most prominent spokesperson in the poet Andre Breton, took the conventional materials of language and image and reinvigorated them with an imaginative charge equal to that of the Futurist and Dada artists, but characterized by a different sensibility. Surrealist work in book form was often the result of collaboration, and early productions of dreamlike image and hallucinatory verse demonstrate the fluidity with which imagery could be produced at the intersection of these media. Renée Riese Hubert, in her crucial study of Surrealist books, makes some fundamental points about the way this work is distinguished from its precedents.30 Hubert points out that a mimetic or imitative relation between text and image had been typical of 19th-century illustrated books — the pictures fulfilled expectations made in the reader by the story, fleshing out an imaginary idea. But in Surrealist work, by contrast, each element extends the other so that the finished whole is not a predictable aspect of either part, but a new synthesis. As Hubert makes clear, the principles of surprise and disorientation fundamental to Surrealist aethestics play themselves out in these works. Many of these volumes, however, were produced by publishers for whom the conventional format of image next to text remained intact; and despite the rich interrelations produced at the level of content in such works, at the formal level they participate in the tradition of the **livre d'artiste** and illustrated book rather than the artist's book.

There are, of course, exceptions. Most notably there are the elaborate collage narratives of Max Ernst (1891-1976). Almost impossible to see with fresh eyes at this point because they have served as the model for so many imitations, these were the original works to take Victorian engravings from novels, scientific sources, and other texts, and combine them to display a sinister narrative synthesized from this collage technique. Ernst's works have a quality which continues to disturb even at this distance. Page after page shows women (luckless heroines) being constrained, tortured, and subjected to all forms of terror by bird headed, mechanical, or towering oppressors. The quaint engravings still have the capacity to function as symbols of an aberrant dream life, recombining to express the darkest visions of the psyche. Ernst produced many such collages in the late 1920s and 1930s (indeed, throughout his productive life collage remained a central part of his work), and many of these were displayed independently or were produced as part of collaborative projects, such as those undertaken with the Surrealist poet Paul Eluard. But Ernst also produced several book-length projects in which this collage method reaches a pinnacle of narrative and visual form.

Max Ernst, **Une Semaine de Bonté**, 1934

The Hundred Headed Woman and Une Semaine de Bonté (A Week of Kindness) are the two best known of Ernst's collage books. The second of these, produced in 1934, is particularly striking in its overall construction and internal manipulation of parts. The book incorporates the structure of the week, originally grouping the pages into seven discrete sections each of which is housed in a different colored covering. Ernst did not follow through on this division, and the final section incorporates Friday, Saturday, and Sunday into a single unit. The collages recount the hazards and horrors encountered in the sequence of days, and the condensed theater of the page contains the psychic tensions generated through the fragmented, recombined visual elements. Ernst keeps his images more or less within the realm of legibility and standard scale, while paying keen attention to the narrative aspects which move the work forward. There is little visual "noise" in these pages, and within the overall greyness of the recycled engravings, Ernst manages to articulate both a sense of pictorial space and a convincing sense of psychic space. The book becomes a world from which there is no escape, a world whose physical boundaries seem to function as the limits of containment of the hapless victims of his

Max Ernst, **Une Semaine de Bonté**, 1934

explicit images. The claustrophobic aspect of a book's finitude becomes a feature of the narrative, refusing exit to the characters whose plight becomes increasingly tragic as a result. Ernst's books work as a clear instance of the integration of experimental concept and content, quite perfectly realized Surrealist expressions in book form.

While the works of Futurist, Dada, and Surrealist artists clearly participate in the evolution of the artist's book, there are also commercial publications, particularly photographic books, which also serve to establish the formal vocabulary later expanded on by artists. These are not artists' books — they are works by photographers which take into account the concept of a book as a specific form. Some of this work reflects developments in an avant-garde milieu which found their way into mainstream venues through the influence of such figures as Laszlo Moholy-Nagy. It is also important to acknowledge as background to these 20th century books the ways in which the photograph was used in 19th-century albums of travel images, family portraits, and other grouped prints linked by subject, implied narrative, or other affinities. Francis Frith's four-volume work based on his journeys to Palestine (of which **Sinai and Palestine** was the first) were published in the late 1850s and early 1860s by James S. Virtue. These were large, ornate books, printed letterpress, with tipped in photographic images detailing in monumental (if somewhat static) fashion a voyage to the Near East.31 In the 20th-century the photographic book becomes a crossover form, which gains its original impetus from artistic experiment but finds its realization in trade publication.

The Soviet and German avant-gardes thoroughly explored photographic persuasion, montage, and display in posters, periodicals, and other reproduced imagery. The work of Alexander Rodchenko, and his theories of photographic or "factographic" representation were particularly influential both inside and outside of the Soviet environment. The political aspects of much of his early work did not have the same impact as his stylistic innovations — the abrupt montage techniques he developed were widely copied in venues whose ideological agenda was a far cry from that supported by Rodchenko. These photographic works were frequently integrated into books. El Lissitzky, for instance, made photomontages which were part of an early 1920s German publication of short stories by Ilya Ehrenburg. Laszlo Moholy-Nagy's **Painting, Photography, Film**, published in 1925 as the eighth in the Bauhaus Press series, laid the ground rules for making a photographic sequence function beyond the level of mere collection.32 Arguably this book makes its contribution directly to the field of graphic design and trade book publication, rather than to the arena of pure creative activity, but it is an unsurpassed example of the use of structure and format as part of the content, rather than merely as instruments for delivering meaning in an effective or eye-catching way. The photographic section of this book is considered a landmark in its successful manipulation of sequence to produce meaning.33

But the first fully photographic books conceived of as works for publication emerged from the realm of Neue Sachlichkeit, or New Realism, in the 1920s in Germany.34 Moholy-Nagy becomes a touchstone for the New Realist photographic work of both August Sander and Albert Renger-Patzsch, two outstanding figures in this movement. Renger-Patzsch's late 1920s publication, **Die Welt ist Schön (The World is Beautiful)**, transforms the lessons of Moholy-Nagy into a full-fledged book production. Sequence is a major element of this book which stresses that "natural plant forms, animals, industrial products, and details of cathedrals and factories are related to each other through an inherent, god-given geometry and order."35 Here there is a clear distinction between the incidental collection of work into an album and the attentive structuring of photographs so that their sequencing becomes an aspect of their meaning. Renger-Patzsch succeeds in going beyond the portfolio or simple collection, using a technique which was later to be taken up in projects by Walker Evans (with James Agee, **Let Us Now Praise Famous Men**, 1941), WeeGee (Arthur Fellig) (**Naked City**,1945), and Robert Frank (**The Americans**, 1959).36 These are only some examples of well-known photographic books which articulate their meaning through an understanding of juxtaposition, movement, timing, and resonance within the bounded field of the book form.37 These were "crossover" books. That is, they were works which, no matter what the aesthetic motivation for their conception or production, were successfully published for wider distribution than either artists' books or **livres d'artistes**. Many of these would not have been easy for an artist to reproduce (the images in Moholy-Nagy's book were produced as relief prints from photographic plates, an expensive process which does not support the finest half-tone values) because of the expense and labor involved. They extend the possibility of artistic expression into a more commercial venue, sometimes with a mainstream audience, more often a limited one. In this regard they show that a form of artists' books can be industrially produced and widely distributed to a larger audience.38

The photographic book became a standard of artists' books activity, and its history belongs to the early 20th century in which the concept of the book as an artistic form was taking on a new, vital identity. All of the works discussed here were conceived as artistic works which permitted an artist to use the book directly as a form whose constraints and characteristics were an integral aspect of its aesthetic conception. They were made largely as inexpensive editions, freely circulated, and part of the common currency of artistic expression and exchange, and so they can be distinguished from the many elaborately produced editions of **livres d'artistes** with which they were contemporary. These were works which were considered avant-garde, experimental, and innovative when they were made; they broke with the formal conventions of earlier book production, establishing new parameters for visual, verbal, graphic, photographic, and synthetic conceptualization of the book as a work of art. That they were artists' books seems irrefutable, that they formed the background for much later work is somewhat questionable, since they were part of a history which was temporarily forgotten at the time artists' books

63

emerged in the 1960s. But that they have an important place in that history, and that they can serve as inspiration for both scholarly and creative work in the future should be abundantly clear.

1 The term "historical avant-garde" is used to refer to early 20th-century activities, thus distinguishing it from "avant-garde" as a generalized idea, though from this point on in the chapter, the shorter phrase will be used.

2 Again, without relying on technological determinism it seems clear that the availability of cheaper printing and mass produced paper made these possible.

3 The best known example of synaesthesia in French poetry is probably the poem "Les Voyelles" by Arthur Rimbaud (1854-1891) in which each of the vowels in the French language is given an identity as a color.

4 Symbolism, discussed earlier in relation to Stéphane Mallarmé, was a 19th-century movement in art and literature in which representations were believed to be merely material manifestations of metaphysical or spiritual Ideals. The result was intense, dense, ornate, even excessive imagery meant to invoke the power of these Ideals.

5 The Wiener Werkstatt was established by Josef Hoffman and Kolo Moser with the support of a wealthy young patron, Fritz Warndorfer, to continue work they were inspired by in the craft guild workshops of British designers — notably Charles Rennie Mackintosh and Charles Robert Ashbee. Peter Vergo, **Art in Vienna 1898-1918** (Cornell University Press, 1985).

6 Vladimir Markov's **Russian Futurism** (University of California Press, 1968) is still unparalleled as a source for the history of literary activities comprising the Futurist movement in Russia, though an interesting first-hand account is Benedict Livshits, **The One and a Half Eyed Archer** (first published in 1933; in English translation by John Bowlt, Oriental Research Partners, 1977). Markov explains the process by which the term "Futurism" was picked up by the Russian press and attached to any and all avant-garde art activity, without regard for the differences among Russian groups or their fundamental distinction from the Italian artists whom they knew only through publications until Marinetti's famous trip to Moscow in 1914.

7 See below for fuller discussion of **zaum**, an invented language meant to communicate without conventional words.

8 German artists, particularly the Expressionists, made similar synthetic forms by borrowing from folk traditions and making use of contemporary artistic developments at the same time. A key source for this section is Camilla Gray, **The Great Experiment: Russian Art from 1865 to 1930** (Thames and Hudson, 1962), still the best introduction to Russian art of the period, though the work of John Bowlt as both writer and editor are additional sources.

9 This is one of the major ways in which Russian artists' involvement with books was

different from that of German or French artists — the Russians actually **made** their books themselves to a far greater extent.

10 See Susan Compton, **The World Backwards: Russian Futurist Books** 1912-18 (British Museum Publications, 1978) and also her **Russian Avant-garde Books** 1917-1934 (MIT University Press, 1992), for detailed discussion.

11 The World of Art, and the periodical of the same name, had produced elaborate, well-financed productions, such as the Ballets Russes of Sergei Diaghielev, which had promoted Russian culture for export, as well as for Russian consumption. See Camilla Gray for more information.

12 Again, see both Compton and Markov for developed discussion.

13 In fact, as anyone who has made a book knows, there is much more work in even such a small pamphlet than may appear.

14 Christina Lodder, **Russian Constructivism** (Yale University Press, 1983) is a useful reference for both the debates and discussion of their effects in applied design.

15 The Transsiberian railroad had been completed in 1905 or 1906; the title translates roughly as **The Prose of the Transsiberian and of little Jeanne of France**. For an analytical discussion of this work see Marjorie Perloff, **The Futurist Moment**, (University of Chicago Press, 1986), including details on Cendrar's elaborate publicity for this "simultaneous" work and notes on its production.

16 See F.T. Marinetti, **Selected Writings** (Farrar Straus and Giroux, 1971) and work by Giovanni Lista **Mots en Liberté Futuristes** (L'Age d'Homme, 1987).

17 This and the next citation are from Marinetti's writings cited in Lista, **Mots en Liberté Futuristes.**

18 Apparently Sylvia Beach of Shakespeare and Co. in Paris didn't know what to make of **Dada** and kept it in a back room for several months — its graphic form was so alarming and unfamiliar to her.

19 See Michel Sanouillet, **Dada à Paris** (Jean-Jacques Pauvert, 1965) for a thorough listing of the dozens of Dada and early Surrealist periodicals produced between about 1916 and 1925.

20 Herbert Spencer, **The Liberated Page** (Bedford Press, 1987).

21 My book, **The Visible Word: Experimental Typography and Modern Art** (University of Chicago Press, 1994), Williard Bohn's **The Aesthetics of Visual Poetry** (Cambridge University Press, 1986), Herbert Spencer's indispensible **The Pioneers of Modern Typography** (Lund Humphries, 1969) and Gerald Janacek's **The Look of Russian Literature** (Princeton University Press, 1984) are references for further reading.

22 Since sources dealing with the Russian avant-garde list him as Ilia Zdanevich, I will do the same through this section. Later in the book, for works produced after 1940, I will refer to him as Iliazd. All references are cross-listed in the index however.

23 See Compton and Janacek, op.cit.

24 Shockingly little scholarship has been produced in this area in spite of how fascinating the work itself is.

25 Zdanevich is a fascinating figure; for writing about his work in print see several catalogues, both titled **Iliazd**, one from the Centre Georges Pompidou, 1978, and the other from the Université de Quebec at Montréal, from 1984. Both have excellent essays in them by Olga Djordjadze, Regis Gayraud, and François Legris-Bergmann. I have written a book-length biographical study of Iliazd, as yet to be published.

26 These should more properly be called Productivist, since Rodchenko moved beyond Constructivist principles, which he thought too aesthetic, to the more applied and politically active agenda of Productivism. See Lodder, **op.cit.**.

27 See Elena Barkhatova, **Soviet Constructivist Posters** (Flammarion, 1992) among other publications — there are many.

28 Established with his brother, Weiland Herzfelde; see both Douglas Kahn, **Heartfield and the Mass Media** (Tanam Press, 1985) and the splendid catalogue **John Heartfield** (Abrams, 1991).

29 See Ruari McClean, **Jan Tschichold: Typographer** (David R. Godine, 1975). Design as an institutionalized discipline is a post-World War I phenomenon. The Bauhaus and the several institutes for the systematic teaching of applied design established in the Soviet Union following the Revolution were the first sites in which design curricula were developed as a concept independent of either the Beaux Arts tradition or the trade and technical training which had emerged in the 19th century as an aspect of industrial manufacture of craft objects such as textiles and ceramics.

30 Renée Riese Hubert, **Surrealism and the Book** (University of California Press, 1988) is the comprehensive study in this area.

31 Francis Frith (1822-99) made regular trips to the Near East, especially in the 1850s.

32 The title in the original is **Malerei, Photographie, Film**. Another instance of wonderfully integrated design/content sensibility is **The Isms of Art** or **Die Kunstismen** published by El Lissitzky and Hans Arp in 1925 (Eugen Rentsch Verlag, reissued as a reprint in 1990), much of what Moholy-Nagy did as a designer was developed by Lissitzky and Rodchenko.

33 See Alex Sweetman, "The Photographic Book," in **Artists' Books: A Critical Anthology and Sourcebook**, op.cit., **On the Art of Fixing a Shadow**, the Exhibition Catalogue of the National Gallery and Art Institute of Chicago show (Bulfinch, 1989), and even Riva Castleman, **A Century of Artists Books** (Abrams and MOMA, 1994).

34 For the study of one of these precedents, see Molly Nesbit, **The Albums of Eugène Atget** (MIT University Press, 1993).

35 David Travis, "Ephemeral Truths," in **On the Art of Fixing a Shadow**, pp.235-237.

36 These works are getting short shrift here, but the point is to indicate their existence as precedents, rather than to detail their particulars. My convictions about the attention to sequencing in Frank's book are in part due to Ann Sass's (unpublished) disser-

tation on his work.

37 In his article on photographic books, Alex Sweetman (op.cit) cites an essay by Elizabeth McCausland, published in **The Complete Photographer** in 1942 (No.43, Vol.8) in which she discusses twenty-two photographic books published between 1925 and 1942. As I assume this does not include the many photographic journals, publicity works, and other design productions which were mainly photographic in nature, this gives some sense of the extent to which this form had developed between the Wars. I have not seen this article, but it would be interesting to see the range of ways in which the structure of the book is integrated into these pieces, especially given the tremendous output in this area in the post-World War II period.

38 Others might argue that these are not artists' books because their production is not under the artists' control, but with such criteria, most of what passes for artists' books would have to be discarded, since so many contemporary books are printed using offset, an industrial mode which requires skill, experience, and access.

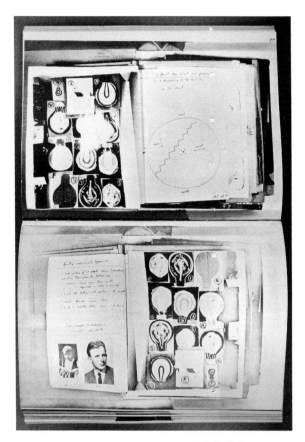

Dieter Roth, **Snow**, 1970

4

The Artist's Book
as a Democratic Multiple

The idea that an artist could create a book directly through means under his or her control was an important feature of the early 20th-century avant-garde. But the idea of the book as a democratic multiple, with all that the phrase implies, comes into its own in the post-1945 era of art and literary activity. Nonetheless, it seems that this concept is linked to even earlier history. Books, after all, were not always democratic — until industrial modes of printing appeared in the 19th century — mechanized typesetting and casting, high-speed presses, and industrial paper making — the book was still a rare commodity, expensive and labor intensive. The association of industrial production with the democratization of the book supports the 20th-century idea of mass-produced books as "democratic" multiples. There are some paradoxes in this term which have to be explored.

It would be a mistake to ascribe a deterministic role to technological changes — new technology always takes awhile to find its character and use. But it is still essential to take into account the greater availability of inexpensive modes of reproduction — particularly the combination of photographic and printing technologies — in the United States and Europe in the period following World War II. This greater availability combined with major changes in the mainstream artworld in the late 1950s and early 1960s to provide a crucial foundation for the artist's book as a democratic multiple. The post-war period saw the emergence of various avant-garde movements. Asger Jorn, a Danish artist, was one of the founders of CoBrA, an international movement of artists from Copenhagen, Brussels, and Amsterdam, and produced a number of handmade books, some in collaboration with the Belgian surrealist Christian Dotrement, in the late 1940s. Within Fluxus, the international movement, George Brecht staged mail art and events which became part of the publications in the late 1950s and early 1960s. Fluxus drew many participants in Germany, New York, and elsewhere and the ephemeral nature of their publications was character-

istic of both their sensibility and that of an artworld in which Happenings
and Events were replacing sculpture and painting as modes of expression.
The Romanian poet Isidore Isou, who arrived in Paris at the end of World
War II, and founded Lettrism, published with the well-respected literary
press Gallimard as well as publishing his own works. Isou galvanized an
entire group around him involved with Lettrist works. They produced
some books and experimented with letterforms and symbolic conventions. Much Lettrist activity was subsequently absorbed into Situationism
in France (in the 1950s), a movement which also fostered publications, but
not artists' books. And Concrete poetry in Brazil and Germany gave rise to
a host of publications, some of which were more literary than artistic, but
all of which were highly experimental. The beginnings of conceptual art,
pop, feminism, activist art, and minimalism also served to stimulate the
production of artists' books' — often in a hybrid synthesis of one or more
of these aesthetic points of view.

Distinct as these groups were they had in common with earlier avant-
garde movements a belief in the liberatory and transformative power of
art and a desire to communicate this conviction by non-traditional methods. They were increasingly caught up in the conceptualization of art as
an activity which was not bound to particular media or conventional
forms such as oil painting, and carved or cast sculpture. Instead, the idea
that art was primarily **about ideas** emphasized the conceptual practice of
art and beginning in the early 1960s conceptual art became the prevailing
mode. In such an atmosphere hybrid forms or, to use Dick Higgins' apt
term, "intermedia," became the norm rather than the exception.1 Books
were a form of intermedia par excellence since they could contain images,
texts, marks, and materials in a format which was flexible, mutable, and
variable in its potential to stretch from the sublime to the ridiculous, the
ordinary to the unusual, the inconspicuously neutral to the absolutely
outrageous — and to express personal, political, or abstract ideas.

One could argue that the basic premise of the artist's book as an alternative artform, one which was able to exist outside of gallery or museum
structures, had been established in the early 20th century. But it is overwhelmingly evident that artists' books become a self-sustaining, even self-
defining, realm of activity after mid-century. Works produced within an
art movement, such as those by Lettrist Isidore Isou directly expressed the
movement's aesthetic aims. Though his eccentric comic-book like **Les
Journaux des Dieux (Journal of the Gods)** produced in 1950 was not

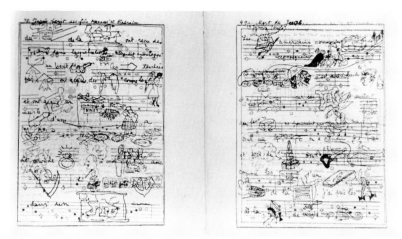

Isidore Isou, **Les Journaux des Dieux**, 1950

explicitly a manifesto of Lettrism, other of his publications and those of his close associates Gabriel Pommerand and Maurice Lemaitre demonstrated Lettrist precepts. Lettrism, like Dada or Surrealism, was involved with all kinds of activity. Lettrists did performances, made films, wrote poetry, staged events in order to garner publicity, made paintings, had exhibitions, openings, and so forth. For them, books were an aspect of their overall aesthetic campaign, and interesting though some of these works might be, they were not the sole or even main focus of Lettrist activity.

Following the mid-century, artists began to make books a primary or major aspect of their activity, without linking the content or form of the book to an already established agenda. This attitude makes the work of two pioneering post-war artists Dieter Roth (a.k.a. Diter Rot) and Edward Ruscha important and establishes their books as landmarks in the development of artists' books as a form. It would be a mistake to suggest that their work sprang from nowhere, separate from a network of influences and ideas in the arts. But they are unique in that they both systematically and innovatively explored the potential of the book form in sustained series of projects. Roth and Ruscha also serve conveniently to contrast two distinct attitudes toward artists' books as an inexpensive edition or democratic multiple.

The term "multiple" as it applies to artists' books is confusing, since it was originally linked, as Clive Phillpot has pointed out, to the production of three dimensional objects meant to be non-unique artworks.2 This suggested a "democratic impulse" as a part of the impetus to book production.3 Joan Lyons states this clearly in her introductory remarks to her 1984 anthology: "Artists' books began to proliferate in the sixties and seventies in the prevailing climate of social and political activism. Inexpensive, disposable editions were one manifestation of the dematerialization of the art object and the new emphasis on process.... It was at this time too that a number of artist-controlled alternatives began to develop to provide a forum and venue for many artists denied access to the traditional gallery and museum structure. Independent art publishing was one of these alternatives, and artists' books became part of the ferment of experimental forms."4

Undeniably true as both the historical facts and critical conceptions expressed in these lines may be, they have given rise (not necessarily through Lyons' work, but as a general sentiment encoded in the literature on artists' books) to certain misconceptions or myths about artists' books. The first of these is that it is **necessary** for artists' books to be inexpensive works in unnumbered or unlimited editions. The second is that they should be produced in small format, through commercial means. The third is that this produces a democratic artform — one whose democracy resides in its affordability rather than in the accessibility of its content. Finally, there is the terrific confusion which arises between the idea of what is affordable for the artist to make and for the consumer to buy. Offset editions are expensive to produce, require capital up front, and are printed on presses whose purchase price tends to be outside the range of independent artist's budgets, but offset books are considered the low-end of the book market in terms of pricing. That said, however, it is important to remember that in the affluent decades of the post-war period, printing services were relatively affordable. The first (1962) edition of Ed Ruscha's **Twenty-six Gasoline Stations**, for instance, which consisted of 400 copies of 24 sheets, sewn through the spine in pamphlet stitch, could easily have cost between $1 and $2 a copy to produce.5 In this first edition, the copies were also numbered, though in subsequent editions he abandoned this practice.

The importance of the democratic multiple as an idea in the proliferation of artists' books should not be understated — it became a definitive paradigm for artists' books. But to use it as a delimiting criterion for determining what is and is not an artist's book seems both unreasonably narrow and nostalgic, and also seems to ignore the realities of artists' lives and the economic conditions for the production of their work. Lyons' remarks point to another important historical fact which will be discussed below: the establishment of many institutions in this period which came into being primarily or solely for the purpose of producing and disseminating artists' books.

Dieter Roth, **Snow**, 1970

Dieter Roth

Dieter Roth's (b.1930) book production was the outgrowth of experimental work in graphic design combined with concrete poetry.6 His earliest publication was a journal produced collaboratively with Eugen Gomringer (one of the originators of German concrete poetry) and a graphic designer, Marcel Wyss. The journal **Spirale** appeared in nine issues, from 1953 to 1964 and was an elaborate production "oversize in format but finely printed on colored papers, which includes woodcuts and lino prints by established artists such as Hans Arp."7 Roth extended his graphic investigations to book forms in projects he began in 1954. Like his fellow designer, the Italian Bruno Munari, who had been working with alternative book structures since the 1940s, Dieter Roth brought an interest in formal problems to his work with books. Munari (whose work will not be discussed here in any further detail) made a series of works he titled "Libro Illegible;" these began as handmade works, but "in the fifties he rejected craft" and adapted his designs for mass production, anticipating this trend in artists' books.8 Like Munari, Dieter Roth made use of hand and die-cut patterns of overlapping pages whose structures in his early works served to sculpt the book's intricate interior space. Though he termed his first production a "Children's Book" (it occupied him from 1954 to 1957), the features of the piece became basic elements in his production vocabulary.

Roth focused on the book as a physical form, one whose codex conventions (binding, even-sized pages, and fixed sequence) became the basis of a structural investigation. Every turning in 2 **bilderbücher** (a cut book from 1957 and one of the first editioned works of his newly established imprint, Forlag Ed) produced new patterns. The layering of pages is an emphatic recognition of the standardized features of construction and a thorough deconstruction of the conventional flat surface of the sheet. The page's flatness is now actual and literal rather than merely serving as a visual support for illusion. No element of structure remains neutral in Roth's production since the whole functions only because its parts have been brought into sharp focus in relation to the way they perform. Conventions of bookness become subject matter — a turning page becomes a physical, sculptural element rather than an incidental activity. Linear sequence becomes spatialized. Surface pattern transforms into height and depth, channels of access and areas of blockage, which read simultaneously as a visual pattern and a shaped form. The fact that the work is bound goes beyond mere convenience of constraint and fastening and becomes a means to articulate these relations.

Finally, there is an interesting transition marked by these constructions from the craft of design to an industrial engagement with production processes. Even the hand-cut early editions of Roth's work seem to quote the methods of die-cutting, to mimic and imitate industrial modes in a manner which removes and represses the marks of authorship, artistry, at the level of markmaking or sculpting. In this sense, Roth's books anticipate the production processes associated with Minimalism, in particular with Donald Judd's use of industrial fabrication techniques for his sculptures. Industrial and graphic designers had been increasingly involved with these techniques in the early 20th-century (the organic forms of handdrawn ornament or design having become outmoded as the **mod-**

erne aesthetic took over), and a machine aesthetic had found its way into cubist and futurist painting as a motif. But the use of mechanical means as well as purely industrial forms as the basis of art production would become a conspicuous feature of the art of the 1960s.9

Dieter Roth published regularly under his imprint Forlag Ed and some of his productions were also republished by other editors in editions in the 50 to 200 range.10 Roth's work as a book artist rapidly received international recognition: in 1964 and 1966 he printed a collection of small books, **Snow**, as a project with students at the Philadelphia College of Art, and **Scheisse** at the Rhode Island School of Design, and was having editions produced by presses throughout Europe: Lund Humphries in England, Ives-Sillman in New Haven, Steedrukkerij de Jong in Hilversum, Holland, and literally dozens of others in Cologne, Berlin, Copenhagen, and elsewhere. But the most consistent and successful publishing collaboration has been between Roth and Stuttgart editor Hansjörg Mayer, who produces Roth's books in significantly larger editions.11 Roth's individual works will be discussed in subsequent chapters, but it is important to realize how he functions as a breakthrough figure for the book arts. Roth is the first artist to make books the major focus for his work and to engage with the book as an art work — not a publication or vehicle for literary or visual expression, but as a form in itself.12 Though early avant-garde artists had experimented with books, stretching their conventions, they did not take these conventions of format and structure as the subject matter for the making of books in the way which Dieter Roth does. There would be no way to translate a Dieter Roth book into another medium — the idea of the works is inseparable from their form as books and they realize themselves as works through their exploration of the conceptual and structural features of a book. In addition, by making these works in editions which function within the conventions of publishing, Roth made it clear that these were really meant to be books, not sculptures or multiple art pieces. This last aspect of his work is significant, since it allows structural work to integrate with the edition process in the hybrid form of the artist's book.

Ed Ruscha

By contrast, Ed Ruscha (b.1937) uses the book in an almost neutral manner, or at least, in a manner designed to neutralize the physical and structural features of his books by making them as conventional and inconspicuous in material terms as possible. Ruscha's 1962 publication of

Twenty-six Gasoline Stations is generally cited as the founding instance of artist's bookmaking. Clive Phillpot, for instance, stated unequivocally that "the principal credit for showing that the book could be a primary vehicle for art goes to Ed Ruscha."13 Phillpot's criteria privilege Ruscha's large-sized editions and the fact that he "produced books as a first-order activity," both criteria which would apply to Dieter Roth as well.14 More significantly, however, Ruscha made books visible within the art world in a way which would not have been possible for literary based endeavors or even cross-over trade published photo books.

Ed Ruscha, **Various Small Fires and Milk**, 1964

Ruscha's books combined the literalness of early California pop art with a flat-footed photographic aesthetic informed by minimalist notions of repetitive sequence and seriality. The title describes the contents of the book which is both absolutely banal and very precise: **Twenty-Six Gasoline Stations** is a book of exactly that — black and white photographs of twenty-six different gasoline stations. Thirty years later, with a quarter of a century of mainstream artworld activity between, the aspect of shock-effect and humor has diminished somewhat. But in 1962 this work read against the photographic landscape of highly aestheticized image-making, work which carried photography's claims to art status forward on the double engines of fine art imagery and/or humanistic critical visions (the Edward Weston, Ansel Adams tradition on the one hand and the Dorothea Lange, Walker Evans tradition on the other hand). Ruscha's sense of humor is more apparent in the titles and formats of several of his subsequent books. **Various Small Fires** (1964) and **Nine Swimming Pools** (1968) both of which disclaim their cover titles in their interior where the full

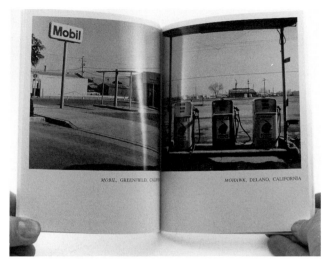

Jeffrey Brouws, **Twenty-six Abandoned Gasoline Stations**, 1992

phrases read **Various Small Fires and Milk** and **Nine Swimming Pools and Broken Glass**. The photo sequences parallel these full titles, with a glass of milk and a broken glass as the final image in each work, respectively.15

Ruscha's work was clearly established as an instance and icon of an identifiable artworld practice because he produced the series of these books in a consistent format. Each new work referenced the others, making its neutral flatness into something, rather than merely an incidental choice of words in square-serif type on plain white covers. There was nothing of the rare book or limited edition art book in these works — they could have been produced at most commercial offset shops. The paper and photo-reproduction methods are undistinguished. In fact, they are the stock-in-trade of commercial post-war printing. These aspects of Ruscha's books give them their distinct identity, though they were carefully designed. they were also calculated to have the look of a completely neutral, almost incidental publication. (The parody by Jeffrey Brouws demonstrates the cult status of Ruscha's books among artists' books.) Most of all, Ruscha's work was cheap —it was made to be inexpensive, to circulate widely, to be available to an audience which wouldn't or couldn't afford gallery art. The idea of circumventing gallery structures had already begun with Happenings and certain Fluxus events in the late 1950s and early 1960s which allowed art pieces to be staged anywhere, anytime, and by anyone. But it would be a mistake to see artists' books as absolutely disconnected from mainstream art institutions — often artists' publications were developed in coordination with museums or galleries who used the opportunity to create a publication which was a hybrid of artist's book and catalogue. Galleries saw these works as inexpensive sideline items or a good way to generate publicity rather than as a threat or subversion of their authority. Still, there is an idea of the book as a democratic, affordable, available multiple in which an artist is able to produce a vision and disseminate it widely which is indissolubly connected to the work of Ruscha. It was an idea which had many ideals in it, many hopes for a transformation of both artworld and wider worlds as arenas in which artists could operate without regard for commodification of their work. In the affluent era of the 1960s, still booming from the post-war economic rush, it was possible to have such a vision.

The Broader Field
While the works of Dieter Roth and Ed Ruscha establish fundamental new parameters for the basic concept of the artists' book, they did not spring from thin air or from the uninhibited genius of their creative instincts. In particular, their work extended the independent publication projects of artists and writers which had been in existence throughout the 20th century and had hardly suffered from diminishment in the post-war period. As Barbara Moore and Jon Hendricks made clear in their essay, "The Page as Alternative Space: 1950 to 1969" periodicals which flirted with the idea of the publication as a work of art in itself had sprung up in many different venues at this time.16 Aside from the periodical **Spirale** (1953-64) which served as a point of departure for Dieter Roth's book work, there are other examples which they cite: Swiss sculptor and artist Daniel Spoerri's involvement with the periodical **Material** (with Roth, 1957-59), German sculptor and conceptual artist Wolf Vostell's seven issues of **Dé-coll/age** (1962-69), publications by the Czech group Aktuel which were tabloid-sized sheets describing their happenings and political positions. Not all of these were artists' publications, many were produced from a more literary emphasis, such as Ed Sanders' **Fuck You: A Magazine of the Arts**, published in New York in the early 1960s or British writer Jeff Nutall's **My Own Mag** (1964-66). Formats varied considerably as did production methods — from ditto and mimeo to offset, with occasional linoleum-cut images or handcolored work and photographs. The French poet Paul-Armand Gette's **Eter** (begun in 1966 and also published in subsequent edi-

tions as **Ether, Eter Contestation,** or **New Eter**) was an assemblage work in which each artist contributed their own pages to be bound into the finished edition.

Nor were Roth and Ruscha alone in seeing the potential of the artist's book. The American poet and physicist Bern Porter began producing his found poems works in the 1950s, while in the 1960s, to quote Lucy Lippard, "if you were reading the signs, you noticed that the book was the coming thing."17 Other early instances of artists' books include Eduardo Paolozzi's 1962 production **Metafisikal Translations** (based on an animated film made in 1960) which brought into book form the eclectic pop culture sensibility which he had exhibited in lectures he gave in the very early years of British Pop, more than a decade earlier.18 In 1962 Daniel Spoerri made his first version of **Topographie Anecdotée du Hasard (The Anecdoted Topography of Chance)** to accompany an exhibition of his still-life sculptures in a Paris art gallery.19 And by 1962, George Brecht, George Maciunas, Ben Vautier and other artists associated with Fluxus were deeply engaged in the mail art and alternative art activities whose traces or documentation would become part of Fluxus publications like **Chance Imagery, Water Yam,** and others in the later 1960s. In addition, conceptual artists like Henry Flynt or the Art and Language group in England appropriated the book form to their own ends, as in Flynt's **Concept Art: version of the mathematical system 3/26/61 (6/19/61)**. By the end of the 1960s artists' books of the democratic multiple variety were an established form, though as Lippard pointed out in "The Artist's Book Goes Public," an essay in 1974, they had difficulty finding their place in the artworld.20 Typically self-published, artist's books were without any organized system of distribution until the 1970s, were rarely reviewed (even to this day) in art magazines or the arts columns of daily newspapers, and were not a fundable category in grants giving organizations.

Nonetheless, Lippard was optimistic in 1974 about the potential of the artist's book in its democratically conceived form. Her piece was written at the moment in which various institutions for the production, sale, or promotion of artists' books began to be estabished. Printed Matter (now Printed Matter Bookstore at DIA), a bookstore in New York City exclusively for artists' books had just been inaugurated leaving another, slightly older New York institution, Franklin Furnace, to serve as an archive and depository for this burgeoning production.21 Lippard envisioned the possibility of a large public for artists' books, ending her essay with this poignantly hopeful sentence: "One day I'd like to see artists' books ensconced in supermarkets, drugstores, and airports and, not incidentally, to see artists able to profit economically from broad communication rather than from the lack of it." Within this sentence are expressed the convictions and sentiments which saw the artist's book as a form capable of democratizing art by offering an experience of artistic vision through a wide circulation and affordable means. Lippard's optimism was rather qualified in another essay written about ten years later.22

In this later essay, Lippard expressed several points of concern — the first was that by imitating the forms of mass culture media the artist's book might loose its capacity to be distinguished from these forms and thus loose its critical edge. The other was that the artist's book had remained a novelty, a curiosity on the edge of the artworld, and that where these experimental works did find a wider audience, they left that audience baffled by the esoteric and complex conceptual terms of the work. This is one of the major paradoxes of the relation between artistic vision and the ideal of liberatory or transformative effects on consciousness within the body politic, that it was also an aspect of many artists' books is not really surprising given their point of origin within the artworld. But the democratic aspect of the artist's book could not, in Lippard's opinion, be recaptured and extended without attending to this basic problem. By her criteria the most striking and representative members of the truly democratic book category were works which politicized the lived experience of the audience through presentation of critical insights into real life, circumstances, or conditions in which people (members of the public as well as the artist) existed. She cited several dozen examples of this work in her article, some of which will be discussed in a later chapter, including Dona Ann McAdams, **The Nuclear Survival Kit** (1981), Paul Rutkovsky, **Commodity Character** (1982), and Masao Gozu, **In New York** (1981).

Nonetheless, the concept of the artist's book as a democratic multiple has both a highly developed history and its own well-established practitioners. Aside from the figures cited previously there are others whose names must be mentioned here for their longstanding contributions in this area. Some are artists, like Lawrence Weiner, John Baldessari, and Richard Long, who have made books an ongoing component of their work. Marcel Broodthaers, Daniel Buren, Maurizio Nannucci and Suzanne Lacy are other artists who could be included in this category. These are all established artists, well-known enough to guarantee some degree of visibility for their work.

Institutions

If the 1950s and 60s had witnessed the development of the artist's book as an inexpensive artform whose flexibility of format made it useful to artists' work and positions, the 1970s was the decade in which institutional sites dedicated to the production of artists' books as democratic multiples came into being, thus consolidating this aspect of their identity. There were many such institutions including: facilities for production, places for distribution or exhibition, and institutions for teaching skills associated with artist's book production, and private, independently run presses. Many of these are still in existence, their operations ongoing, sometimes in modified or expanded form.23

Printed Matter Bookstore and Franklin Furnace have already been mentioned, the former having performed the function of publisher as well as the major place for seeing, buying, and distributing artist's books. While other bookstores dealing with artists' books have come and gone in the last two decades, Printed Matter is distinguished by its continuity and longevity. Printed Matter's guidelines made clear from the outset that they were interested in the mass produced multiple, books in editions of over 100 copies, which were not expensive, precious, or over-produced. But the work published through their progam had to be farmed out for production. The facilities which provided production services as part of their fundamental function and identity included Visual Studies Workshop, established in Rochester, New York, by Joan and Nathan Lyons as a degree granting graduate program in media arts.24 Visual Studies Workshop Press came into being in 1972 and has been responsible for a steady stream of publications ever since. The works of VSW Press in many ways exemplify and define the elusive character of the artists' book as a democratic multiple. These are works made by artists as books, first and foremost, and are produced to sell in an affordable market, though often only because of the generous subsidies which the Lyons and individual artists are able to generate to support their production. In American artists' books, VSW Press has had a tremendous influence, with work by figures who made major contributions to the field having spun off from its graduate program or been directly produced under its auspices.25 Nexus Press in Altanta, which began in the late 1970s from the desire of a collective group of photographers to print their own books, has been directed and sustained through the efforts of Michael Goodman (who left the press in 1992) and Jo Anne Paschall (its current director).26 Nexus, like Visual Studies, has an unqualified commitment to publishing artists' books. Bookworks in London and Art Metropole in Toronto served similar functions, as did the short-lived publishing program of the Nova Scotia College of Art and Design, which produced a series of works under the editorial supervision of Benjamin Buchloh in the late 1970s. The Women's Studio Workshop in Rosendale, New York, has produced a steady list of productions. While other organizations — museums, galleries, or centers — have also sponsored artists' books publications, these are the major institutions for the publishing of artists' books. Private publishers dedicated to this field, such as the well-known and highly significant Hansjörg Mayer, have also existed since the 1960s, with a continually rising and falling tide of imprints coming and going in these decades. I will just mention them here, without attempting in any way to do justice to their identities as publishers, simply to enter this activity into the record: Beau Geste Press (at least in part the effort of Felipe Ehrenberg, established in London in the 1970s), Ulises Carrión's Other Books and So (also a bookstore of that name which he operated in Amsterdam from the early 1970s), Simon Cutt's Coracle Press (Norfolk, England), and Phil Zimmermann's Space Heater Multiples. Of these, one of the most successful at producing artists' books which used a more or less standardized format to "pass" as trade books was Dick Higgins' Something Else Press (1964-73).

Other facilities were established in the 1970s and early 1980s in the United States for teaching and exhibition purposes which focused on artists' books as multiples.27 These included Pyramid Atlantic founded by Helen Frederick, with contributing energy coming from Kevin Osborn, and the Press at the Woman's Building in Los Angeles, established by Sheila De Brettville in 1973.28 With a few exceptions, these are all organizations which have formally or informally sustained publishing programs from time to time, either through providing grants or training to artists for book projects. Many of these facilities have had regular exhibitions of the work of their members, students, or other artists. There have been a host of gallery exhibitions of artists' books over the last few decades, and exhibition catalogues from these shows provide a major bibliographic resource. Sites for these exhibitions include university galleries, art centers, and alternative galleries. More recently, mainstream galleries have evidenced some interest in this area, but a major museum show — not just a set of cases in a hallway, foyer, or restaurant waiting area — has yet to occur.29

The reasons for the slow acceptance of artists' books by the mainstream artworld are not that difficult to assess. Economics, politics, and logistics all play a part. The idea that these books have a democratic character resides in large part in their affordability and given the problems of distribution, this makes them less profitable as an artworld commodity than the **livres d'artistes** sold at substantially higher fees. This low price tag often diminishes the stature of the work in the eyes of some for whom expense is the hallmark of value, while it is the proof of authenticity for others to whom these appear to be the real artists' books. In fact, price, production means, and market stature don't define a neat aesthetic or conceptual category — the range of works which comprise books with the identity of a democratic multiple is quite varied. Many of the cloudy critical issues about identity, status, and affordability as myths or concepts of these and other artists' books will only be dispelled with critical and public debate. The recently established **Journal of Artists' Books–JAB** (Brad Freeman, founder and editor) is certainly one step forward in this direction complementing and extending the long-term efforts of Judith Hoffberg's newsletter **Umbrella** published since 1977.30

Exemplars of the Genre

The idea of the democratic multiple exercises no constraints on artistic conceptualization, and works which have been produced in this mode are wide ranging. To close out this chapter, I will focus on a few which are exemplars of the genre.

The first of these is a recent work, Philip Zimmermann's **High Tension** (1993), which was produced at Visual Studies Workshop as a project for Montage 93 a state-of-the-arts fair held in Rochester in 1993 to showcase electronic media.31 A highly complicated work, this could not have been produced without a considerable subsidy, and the high cost of its production shows up some of the paradoxes of so-called "democratic" multiples.32 Zimmermann is an artist who works creatively with every aspect of production. Photographic manipulations, stripping, and other pre-press activities transform the project in a way which differs significantly from simply sending finished designs (boards or disks or film) to a printer. This also means that the book doesn't exist in any other form until it is printed and bound — it is not a reproduction of a series of extant photographs

Philip Zimmermann, **High Tension**, 1993

which could just as well be viewed in a sequence on a wall. How would one even begin to separate out the images into discrete elements within a work where the facing sides of an opening complete each other or an overlapped page reads against the visible edge of pages below?33

High Tension has an unusual shape, when closed it makes a five-sided flat form bound on its longest side, with a jagged outside edge to its cover. On the cover is the image of the artist's face, printed in silvery-green and black, both runs in enlarged photographic dot screen which has been made into a relief plate so that the printing has a dimensional effect. The title, **High Tension**, is printed in purple metallic ink, its framed and bordered letters appearing to float above the image. Exploding tendrils of force reach outward from the outline of the man's head (which wraps, as a full frontal image, around the spine spanning front and back) like the lines of activity from the sun's corolla. Thus the spiked outer edge, cut in a sharp pattern, functions as an icon of the sun with regular, triangular, points. Within the book the pages match up with an edge of the book as a whole and with an edge of one of the triangular forms of the cut cover, so that this motif of the cover turns out, once one is inside, to have been generated by the internal relations of the pages. This isomorphism of page and cover is handled expertly, so that the structural arrangement is trans-

84

lated back into printed patterns on the page edges. Typical of Zimmermann's work, the piece is elaborately patterned throughout in both structural and graphic sense. The surface of the pages is a wealth of colored patterns produced through a combination of photographic, printerly, and computer manipulations.

The theme of **High Tension**, with its emphasis on pressure experienced at the intersection of many sources of stimulation and demand on an individual psyche (in this case, to be read against the autobiographical referent of the cover image), edges toward the paranoaic. The multiple, conflicting visual patterns on the pages with their continual reemphasis of the pointed spikes of the cover form, reinforce this sensation. Almost every page is divided along a diagonal axis which splits its visual field and aligns the mock horizon with the bottom of the next or previous page, thus making the design reference the structure visually even where the actual pages render that structure invisible. The book has a sharpness which feels slightly dangerous, as if the threats contained in the phrases "Your hair is falling out" or "You think people are gossiping about you" has intensified the anxious form of the book into another instrument of possible torment. This is, obviously, a work which could not exist in any form but that of a book: its internal complexities — the mirroring and quotation of page shapes, formal divisions of the whole, echoing of the outer edge's motif — are all elements of its total significance. The six four-sheet signatures of the book were sewn and glued, and the cover wraps on to the bound sections. The finished work is a fully realized piece of art, shiny, sensuous, engaging, seductive, which only comes into being as a book.

By contrast, the formal and graphic elements of Martha Rosler's **Service, a Trilogy on Colonization** (Printed Matter, 1978) are intentionally low-end and unglamorized. Similar in size, Rosler's is a book of about 64 single sheets, perfect bound, printed in black and white. There are only two images, the front cover photograph of a woman whose dress and posture bespeak her class position as a domestic, and the back cover of a postcard with Martha Rosler's address on it, stamped and postmarked. The text in the book was generated from a series of postcard accounts by three different women, each discussing her experience of domestic service. These three "food novels" revolve around accounts of exploitative working situations, and each has been transcribed by Rosler into a different typewritten narrative whose postcard unit structure is still suggested by the size of the book, its horizontal format, and the discrete chunks of

SERVICE

a trilogy on

colonization

martha rosler

Martha Rosler, **Service**, 1978

text printed on one side only of each page. Rosler's work communicates the contradictions and conflicts of working life as completely as Zimmermann's reflects those issues through the filter of an interior psyche whose external situation is left undisclosed. The women's individual voices come through their accounts, which are not entirely without hope as each comes to terms with her situation and its possible resolution. While Rosler's book sells (or sold, since prices are always subject to change....) for $5 a copy even in 1994 and Zimmermann's for $35, both are squarely within the category of the multiple in an unnumbered edition offset book. Both are self-conscious about the book form, Rosler's anti-aesthetic is no less calculated to suit her intentions than Zimmermann's complex design.

Finally, in contrast to the serious aesthetic and political tone of these works, with their highly thought out and professional production, the last work I will consider here is the genial **Your Co-Worker Could be a Space Alien**. Produced in xerox by Tatana Kellner and Ann Kalmbach, (KaKe productions, Rosendale, NY, 1985) the book's format is determined by folding four 8 1/2" x 14" pages in half into an eight page (16 sides) staple-bound volume. This is double-sided xerox and has all of the visual qualities of that medium — the broken letters, poor quality resolution, high-contrast images and occasional streaking of certain low-end xerox. The look of the work does not quote any other artform — it is not a quotation of an instruction manual, though there are hints of that, nor of a tabloid exposé,

Tatana Kellner and Ann Kalmbach, **Your Co-Worker Could Be A Space Alien**, 1985

though it borrows a few features from that form as well. In its brief but biting series of tips from "experts" (an unidentified, omniscient force of others who presumably exist somewhere as a network of power) the book uses its ruthlessly dark humor to point up the paranoiac stigmatization of homosexually oriented individuals. Played out as a guide to recognizing space aliens, a premise maintained throughout, the book nonetheless shows its double meaning through its imagery. The woman who serves as photographic model to demonstrate the "tips" is clearly not a glamourized female according to media standards. In the first image, for instance, showing off the alien's propensity to wear "odd or mismatched clothes" the model shows off her strong unshaved legs above baseball hightops and saddle shoes. By insisting that the assumed identity addressed in the book is that of an alien, the work escapes being a didactic treatise on discrimination in the work place and instead reads as a very funny series of one-liners about deviance and normalcy.

Your Co-Worker... is a book which could not be improved upon by changing its production values — it would only gain an unnecessary glossiness or finish. In its realized form, it is stark, unexpected, and startling, managing to throw one's norms and expectations into relief through the

87

use of a disorienting humor. As a book it is ephemeral, a mere pamphlet, a treasure culled from the massive oceans of constantly printed material. As an artist's book it is clearly democratic — produced with snapshot, xerox, a homemade pasteup, and typewriter text, something almost anyone could get access to if they wanted to make a book with low-end production input and high-end conceptual impact.

Each of these works is charged with a particular combination of aesthetic and political issues which make use of the book form to present a realized vision which can circulate freely in the world, with all the autonomy which a book possesses. The mobility of the book is one of its most unique characteristics, as well as its capacity to be preserved through that mobility (imagine a painting which had passed from hand to hand, been carried on the subway for two weeks, and then ended up in the pocket of an airline seat only to be rediscovered and enjoyed again). But these books also show a range of production approaches. Zimmermann, an artist who uses the medium of offset in all of its technical particulars achieves his effects through his understanding of film, color printing, and graphic form. Rosler deliberately uses a format marked as "unproduced" and undesigned — though her pages still require pre-production work, camerawork, and presswork. And Kellner and Kalmbach exploit the potential of cut-and-paste informal production whose aesthetic tolerances are much broader than those of either Zimmermann or Rosler. Offset and xerox are not the only methods for production of democratic multiples — letterpress, rubber stamps, stencil printing, silkscreen, linoleum cut — all of these can be and have been pressed into the service of books in this vein. The distinguishing characteristic is the artist's vision of a work which bypasses the restraints on precious objects. The vision becomes a book which is able to pass into the world with the fewest obstacles between conception and production, production and distribution. That is the nature of the democratic multiple — the ready availability of an independent artist's vision in book form.

---

1 Originally used in various lectures and writings, the term is recorded and defined in essays in Dick Higgins, foew&ombwhnw (Something Else Press, 1969). Higgins was an early participant in Fluxus as well as an artist and publisher, poet and scholar.

2 Clive Phillpot, "Some Contemporary Artists and their Books," Artists' Books: A Critical Anthology and Sourcebook, Lyons, ed. (hereafter referred to as ABs) p.101-102.

3 Phillpot, ibid, p.102.

4 Joan Lyons, "Introduction and Acknowledgements," ABs, p.7.

5 Coming up with $400 in 1962 could easily have been as difficult as it is today to come up with a sum three times that high; at that time $400 was 2 months rent on a decent one bedroom apartment in California, for instance, and minimum wage was still well under $2.00 an hour.

6 Barbara Moore and Jon Hendricks, "The Page as Alternative Space 1950 to 1969," ABs, pp.89-90. Moore and Hendricks's rich article points out the distinction between these works and the development of books within the literary tradition of alternative publishing.

7 Moore and Hendricks, p.90.

8 Moore and Hendricks, p.89.

9 One exception would be the sculptural works of Naum Gabo and Nicolas Pevsner from the 1930s which are in the quasi-industrial in character.

10 The bibliographic information in this section is from **Bücher** (1974), Kestner Gesellschaft, Hannover.

11 The first Hansjorg Mayer edition I can find a trace of is the 1967, **die blaue flut**, which is listed in Roth's catalogue **Bücher**.

12 A useful contrast could be made with Iliazd, whose work as an editor verges on artists' book production, but stops short of seeing the book in itself as a sufficient work of art. Iliazd innovates within the conventions, changing them, but Dieter Roth seizes on conventions as subject matter, substance, and makes their interrogation and transformation the basis of his books. These are grey areas at times — there are many artists' books which are conceived within traditions of book structure, don't challenge it, and are still very successful works.

13 Phillpot, **op.cit.**, p.97.

14 Phillpot puts great weight on the idea of the unnumbered edition as a criterion for artists' books and held to this principle as the basis of his collecting for the Museum of Modern Art Library during his tenure there. Obviously there are many contradictions in maintaining this or any other single criterion as the necessary one for defining an artist's book. Again, Ruscha numbered his first edition — does this disqualify it? That would be silly.

15 These details from Phillpot, **op.cit.**, pp.98-99.

16 All bibliographic details in this paragraph are from Moore and Henricks, op.cit., pp.87-95.

17 Lucy Lippard "The Artist's Book Goes Public," ABs, p.46.

18 Paolozzi's lectures at the Institute of Contemporary Art in London in the late 1940s in which he used props gathered from mass media and popular culture had been a watershed in the development of the British movement. See Simon Wilson, **Pop Art**

(Barron's, 1978) and Marco Livingstone, ed., **Pop an International Movement** (Rizzoli, 1991).

19 Emmett Williams' translation of this book was later reprinted by Something Else Press.

20 Lippard, **ABs, op. cit.**

21 This amazing collection, the Franklin Furnace archive, was sold to the Museum of Modern Art Library in 1994.

22 Lucy Lippard, "Conspicuous Consumption: New Artists' Books," in **ABs**, 1985.

23 My research here has been cursory. The details of their histories are often contained solely within the anecdotal experience of members of the institution and the trail of paper evidence they have produced. This is another area in which a thorough study is sorely needed.

24 The Workshop is linked to the State University of New York system.

25 Janet Zweig, Phil Zimmermann, Skuta Helgason, Kevin Osborn, and Scott McCarney were students at Visual Studies Workshop and Ulises Carrión, Francois Deschamps, Susan King, Erica Van Horn, Paul Zelevansky, and others produced books there. Don Russell and Helen Bruener, who ran the bookstore at VSW, later established Bookworks at Washington Project for the Arts in D.C..

26 Again, the list of people who have worked there on staff or for projects includes many significant book artists: Clifton Meador, Joni Mabe, Brad Freeman, Felipe Ehrenberg, Telfer Stokes and Helen Douglas, Bill Burke, and so on.

27 My focus on the United States here is merely a result of my restricted knowledge base.

28 There are other organizations formed during this period which were dedicated to book arts and/or printing, binding, and papermaking — such as the Pacific Center for Book Arts whose founding committee included Betty Lou Chaika, Betsy Davids, Tom Ingmire and Kathy Walkup, the Center for Book Arts in New York established by Richard Minsky, and the Minnesota Center for Book Arts, started by Jim Sitter in Minneapolis — but these institutions did not define their mission primarily in terms of the artist's book as a democratic multiple.

29 The MoMA show curated in 1994 by Riva Castleman was NOT a show of artists' books but of illustrated books, mainly **livres d'artistes**.

30 Very few other places have focused any critical attention on artist's books. For instance, Nancy Princenthal's regular column in **The Print Collector's Newsletter** has been both a steady and unusual contribution to critical writing in this area.

31 This is a book which involved a great deal of work in the trimming, binding, and production at every point in the printing process and could not have been an "affordable" edition without sizable subsidy.

32 The book cost about $19,000 to produce in an edition of 1000 finished copies. It sold

for $25 pre-publication price and $35 after publication. With distributor and bookstore discounts, this means there is a return to the publisher of only about $17.50 a copy — less than the price of production. When the artist's **unpaid** labor is counted in, this equation becomes increasingly skewed — especially as Zimmermann not only did the research, development, and design, but also the stripping and platemaking on the project. It simply isn't possible to make such work remunerative if one is the artist working on these terms.

33 I don't think these are requirements for an artist's book, but certainly a book which is so completely engaged with its production has a dialogue with book forms which is very different from even that of Ruscha.

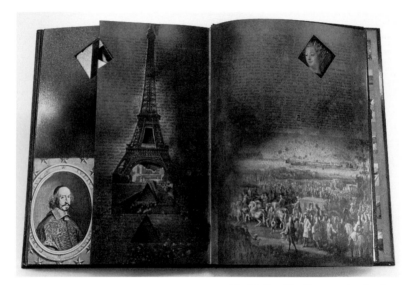

John Eric Broaddus, **France**, n.d. mid-1980s

5

The Artist's Book
as a Rare and/or Auratic Object

Artists' books are not all issued in editions. Not all artists' books are issued in photo-offset reproduction on neutral paper with standard, supposedly inexpensive, formats. An artist's book can be a unique work, a highly limited edition, or an inconsistent edition, and still be a work which is a direct expression of aesthetic ideas in a book form. And these works do not have to fall into the conventions of **livres d'artistes** or fine printing. In this section I will present works which demonstrate that fetishized, limited edition, transformed, or unique works can be considered artists' books.

Many of these books have an auratic quality an often inexplicable air of power, attraction, or uniqueness. Some are unique objects, one-of-a-kind works which emanate a precious or mystical or intriguing quality. Some are issued in limited editions (often because some aspect of production was too costly or complicated to repeat through a larger number of books). And some are fetish objects which make use of the book in an erotically charged way or to exhibit and/or demonstrate sexually charged behavior. Transformed books use an existing work as their base, and then make a palimpsest which is a combination of textual, visual, and material manipulations of the original. All of the books to be discussed here are undeniably artists' books — they are investigations of the book as a form through an examination of its material, thematic, and formal properties. These works extend the concept of the artist's book beyond that of the democratic multiple, demonstrating some of the range of 20th-century artists' explorations of the book.

Auratic Objects

Books which have an aura about them generate a mystique, a sense of charged presence. They seem to bear meaning just in their being, their appearance, and their form through their iconography and materials. It is

93

as though they have been imbued with a power which animates them beyond their material limits generating a metaphysically charged atmosphere which surrounds the work. In my own responses to such works, I am often aware that there are a complex of factors involved — from subject matter to production. Certain themes, as well as certain materials, contribute to this charge. While some books create this aura through elaborate labor and an intense investment of obsessive work which intrigues the viewer, there is no more a formula for the auratic book than for any other original artform. But the identifiable characteristics of these works — auratic or fetishistic — are qualities which produce a fascination which can't be easily explained. This is not the same as respect, interest, or other forms of engagement. It has to do with tapping into a certain level of the **fantasmatic** — a level of psychological engagement in which emotional energy attaches to an object for reasons which cannot be explained through reason or conscious analysis. There are many such books. The catalogue of the **Livres d'Artistes — Livres Objects** exhibition held in Paris in 1985, for instance, is replete with works bound in wire, with chicken feet, feathers, buttons, jewels, elaborate materials, ashes, wax, framed photographs all included.1 These range from votive objects to pieces loaded with personal meaning encoded in rich display of materials while still continuing to function as books with accessible (not always legible) pages of either text or image in some combination.

Timothy C. Ely, an artist who has made mainly (but not exclusively) unique books, has produced works which have a distinctly auratic character to them. Finely wrought, they are often in bindings whose production creates an effect of age — of magical and arcane references. They suggest a world in which the book is an artifact of wisdom, recondite and esoteric, secret and precious, available to the initiate rather than the casual or widespread reader. In the interior, Ely's signature style pages combine motifs of mapping with diagrammatic forms whose suggestions of cosmological information is borne out by tiny indications in glyphic writing. A subtle sense of color and timing is part of the success of these works, which occupy the ambiguous places of surface dimension and deep-space illusion while working in a web of intricate devices. This work intrigues the viewer because it seems to suggest the possibility of decipherment, a reading of a complex code according to a key whose power would release profundities from these pages. Whether this is true or not, the compelling sense of the work is this promise. **The Flight Into Egypt** (1985) sustains these stylistic inventions over the course of a full volume whose narrative implications are clear from its title. This work is a guide to reinvention through transgression and return, a spiritual journey for consciousness rather than for the body. But narrative is a minor function for Ely. His book **Elementals**, for instance, presents itself as its name suggests —as a catalogue of cosmic fundamentals — and has an equal impact. The spaces of Ely's work are spaces of possibly unknown realities, alien or mysterious, the products of civilizations past or in some hybrid future, conceivable within the combined visions of science fiction, the new age, and old alchemical belief systems.

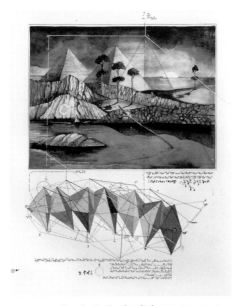

Timothy C. Ely, **The Flight Into Egypt**, 1985

Most of Ely's unique books are drawn in india ink, hand-colored with watercolor and iridescent paints and gold leaf for points of emphasis. The bindings are encrusted with textured materials (such as sand coated with acrylic) which are worked and distressed, as well as marked with signs and glyphs which are as inscrutably arcane as those on his thick interior pages. While this work might be successfully reproduced, the impact of Ely's work comes in part from the sense that one is holding an original manuscript in one's hands.2 His collaborative project with writer/philosopher Terence McKenna and typographer Philip Gallo, **Synesthesia** (Granary Books, 1992) carried some of the auratic quality of Ely's originals into a small edition. Ely handpainted the pages of each copy of this edition, so that each had some of the character of his unique books.

Other artists have successfully managed to produce a sense of aura in editioned books. Among them one particularly moving work is Tatana Kellner's **Fifty Years of Silence**. A work produced at the Women's Studio Workshop (of which Kellner is a founding member), **Fifty Years of Silence** produces a striking and disturbing impact. In formal terms, the book is comprised of printed pages which have been die cut to accomodate a sculptural element — a life-sized cast of an elderly woman's arm. Flesh colored and stencilled with a concentration camp number "71125" the arm represents Kellner's mother's own arm. Similarly, the title refers to her mother's fifty year silence on her imprisonment in a German concentra-tion camp during World War II. The arm sculpture lies on the inside back cover of the book so that it remains the center of the reading experience, because the pages are die cut throughout the arm never goes away, and as the pages diminish, its dimensionality is increasingly apparent.3 The theme of the Holocaust, with its taboos and its potential for diminishing the significance of historic events with aestheticization, is volatile mater-ial for art production. In Kellner's work a personal story is told against the weight of long repression and reluctance, a repression made all the more poignant as it has been maintained within the intimate bond of relations between mother and daughter. Kellner transcribes her mother's story in handwriting and in type, while images of her mother appear on the verso of the sheets. The arm, as a physical, tactile form in the midst of the text, and an echoing shadow form on the opposite page (the die-cut opening) has a macabre presence. Too realistic to serve only as an image, the arm has a presence whose status as a disconnected limb is horrific, grotesque, uncompromisingly insistent on its own materiality. As a result the book has the feeling of a reliquary in which a real fragment of a body has been preserved, though the papier-maché is not obsessively illusionistic, it is convincingly real, uncannily present. An unusual work, this book is com-pelling by virtue of its unusual tension between first-person narrative and physical objectification as well as by the intensity of its thematic con-cerns.4

The Book as Private Archive

Quite distinct from either of these works are document projects which by their genuine or simulacral production of an archive seem to present

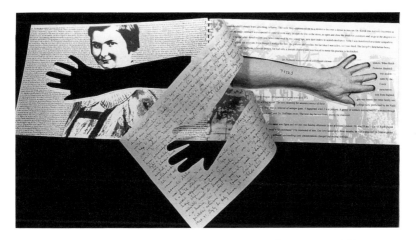

Tatana Kellner, **50 Years of Silence**, 1992

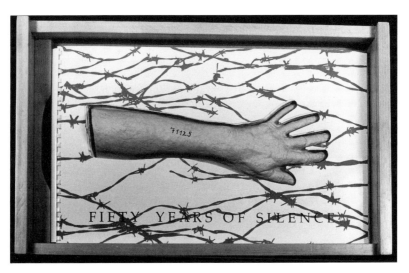

Tatana Kellner, **50 Years of Silence**, 1992

Marcel Duchamp, **La Mariée mise à nu par ses célibataires meme (The Green Box)**, 1934

the viewer with the raw materials of personal memory and experience. The precedent for these is a work by Marcel Duchamp (1887-1968), the **La Mariée mise à nu par ses célibataires, meme** known as the "The Green Box," which holds materials pertinent to his huge work by the same name **(The Large Glass or The Bride Stripped Bare by her Bachelors Even)**.5 Published under Duchamp's own imprint, (Editions Rrose Selavy) in 1934 this project contains loose leaves of notes for his "Large Glass" project reproduced in facsimile. Complex and conceptual, the "Large Glass" engages numerous calculations and manipulations of philosophical and representational material. Located at the Philadelphia Museum of Art, this work remains one of the most elusive and intriguing works of early 20th-century art. Begun in 1915 and left in a definitive "state of unfinishedness" (his phrase) in 1923 (after the glass itself cracked in transit, a fact Duchamp accepted with typical equilibrium considering the new pattern a part of the work), the "Large Glass" is highly enigmatic, and the notes for its production are barely sufficient even to introduce a viewer to its mysteries. As an auratic work in its own right, the "Large Glass" is a paradigmatic example of conceptual and process art from the early part of the century by an artist of unsurpassed inventive imagination. The "Green Box," contained almost a hundred facsimile notes produced in collotype, loose and unbound in a paper wrapper housed in the green suede-paper box which lends the work its familiar name and provides a dossier which passes as the artist's own jottings. For a viewer fascinated with Duchamp, this is just a step removed from having access to the artist's notebook.

The box and archive format provides a voyeuristic satisfaction. It allows one to replicate the act of going through someone's private and intimate papers or documents. It is an act which wavers between prying violation and necrophilic curiosity. These works often have a nostalgic quality — as of something preserved from a past whose only traces are these material bits and pieces. Two such works, both charged with this quality of preservation and distance, are Christian Boltanski's **Maison Manquante** (La Hune Librarie, 1990) and Yani Pecanins' **Un Viage en Zeppelin** (self-published, 1980s). Despite some similarities, the differences between these two are compounded at every level of production and thematics. Pecanins' work is personal, revealing fragments of her family history through bits of photographic, documentary, and other material evidence. Her work is self-produced, precious in its facture, as carefully constructed as a much-loved scrapbook album of reminiscences in which bits of wax or string or carefully glued pieces of bright foil or old tickets are placed. The work was an editioned work, however, not a unique work, and its fragments weave a loose but never explicit set of narrative connections concerning the arrival of members of her family from Europe to Mexico. The work is inviting because it is both beautiful and modest — housed in a cardboard box which does not announce the rich variety of its contents, it displays a charming and intriguing quality in the fragments which comprise its interior.

By contrast, Boltanski's work is without a direct link to his personal history. The book was motivated by an encounter with a bit of damaged geography, a block in Berlin in which an apartment house was destroyed in an otherwise nearly intact row of structures on February 3, 1945, near the end of World War II. Boltanski's archive is a documentary history of that hole, that gap, that absence. The void of the bombed out streetscape is the place of his book, the point of its departure. Boltanski researched the history of the building, finding the names and backgrounds of the former Jewish inhabitants and recovering any traces he could of them through neighbors and relatives. The result of this research is the compound archive housed in the box — a work done with the same materials archivists use. A standard box of grey, acid-free, cardboard in which are folders containing maps, photographs, transcripts of conversations and interviews, lists and city records — in short all the written and visual documentation he could assemble. The interior folders are mostly labelled to

Christian Boltanski, **La Maison Manquante**, 1990, Spencer Collection, NYPL

correspond to names of individuals, though a few are more general and
contain information about the building or the bombing which destroyed
it. Boltanski's archive, unlike Pecanins' highly personal document, is
almost clinical. It has the character of a dossier for a courtcase or a historical project. The emotional impact comes from identifying with the victims whose fate is a direct result of war, but a displaced experience of the

Holocaust, one removed from the experience of the camps. As in many of Boltanski's pieces which use the Second World War as a reference, the terror of the piece resides in its demonstration of the way such events insinuate themselves into the fabric of daily life. It is the documentation of normalcy, of small interiors of apartments in which unexceptional (and no doubt, some exceptional) individuals lived — human beings whose existence was subject to forces of history and politics over which they had little or no control — and in which they had no choice about whether or not to participate. Their existences are both incidental and individual, specific and generic, as represented by the archival evidence.6

Both of these works share an auratic quality which comes in large part from the faithfulness of the reproductions — each element in the archive feels real, seems authentic, appears original. While the Duchamp "Green Box" facsimiles are evidently facsimiles, in spite of their closeness to the original works, the pieces in Pecanins' and Boltanski's documentary archives are, in effect, indistinguishable from originals. When Boltanski includes a snapshot, it has the crimped edges and black and white quality of a photograph from the 1940s, and Pecanins is not so much replicating other originals as creating the sense of an actual scrapbook work. Authenticity in their work is thus mimetic in the case of Boltanski — the imitation at all levels of form and appearance of an original — and virtual in the case of Pecanins — a presentation with all the convincing earmarks and material qualities of an original. Only a unique work could assemble an authentic archive out of original materials and present it. Any editioned work, as in the case of Boltanksi and Pecanins, is a replication.

This archival format is used in a unique work by Betsy Davids' **Sites and Passages** (1992). The first part of a record of a three-month trip through several continents, climates, and zones of awareness and personal investigation, this work is constructed of the paper materials which track the movement and activities she pursued in that journey. Davids stresses the formal as well as substantive aspect of these pieces, giving them a relation as color, form, and texture which puts their informational content into material contrast, one to the next. Thus the feeling of a bus ticket and its details of destination is made to be both a physical object with weight and color of type and paper and also to show its inscribed linguistic information. The information on these pieces is inseparable from their facticity, and yet the formal structure of the unique work almost allows the physicality of information as material to exist in its own right.

Betsy Davids, **Sites and Passages**, 1992

Like many writers and artists, Davids responds to the notebooks she finds in foreign stationery or art stores, and this project was constructed on a binder structure of Greek manufacture. The narrative is taken from Davids' personal journal and notes, written in the space between private communication and possible readership, for oneself and for a possible other whose eye is our eye in reading the pages. Two dream accounts frame the piece, establishing Davids' psychic parameters for the project and the journey. As the work elaborated in the course of production, it became clear that a single book could not contain the full trajectory of the introductory dream texts, so this volume is now the first in what will be a series.

Journals and diaries are almost a cliché of artists's books — the manipulated notebook, the transformed sketchbook, the book of accounts or old ledger. And yet in their most successful manifestations they are almost always intriguing — for exactly the reasons that journals are — they offer a glimpse into the ongoing thought processes, jottings, projects in progress of an individual. The clichés occur because so many of these works contain predictable scrapbook accumulations and/or self-indulgent hand-written paragraphs surrounded by drawn or painted imagery in a sort of cottage industry of the cult of individualism. But when the journal form becomes an icon, an image which refers to these aspects of the cliché, and through referencing them, transcends its limitations to become an image of the conflictual structure of a journal form (its tensions of the interior life externalized, the exterior life internalized and so forth) then it can become highly charged. One such work was made in 1976 by Mira Schor, **The Book of Pages**.

Mira Schor, **The Book of Pages**, 1976

Schor's work has aspects of both an auratic object and a fetishistic one. It both gives off a strong field of energy and also embodies a cultish quality of ritual processes which inscribe private ceremonies of psychic activity. The rice paper pages are dark and discolored, as though weathered and ancient and hand-written in dark ink, a handwriting which allows only a percentage of the text to be read. But the pages are also translucent so that there is much visual bleed-through from one to the next. Legibility is further restricted by cross-outs and blots, and an occasional passage with white painted through it — the striking blank negation obliterating a record. Drawings, diagrams, notes and other graphic disruptions of the text give variety to the texture of the whole. The edges of the pages are frayed, brittle, cracking — as if the work has been through seasons of weathering and wear. The signatures are split along the spine, and some pages hang loose, attached only by a single corner still sewn to the binding. The work is fully fetishized; its marks, colors, materials all worked to a degree of obsession which asks to be recognized as substantive. One does not attempt merely to read this diary, but feels the experience of the material object as evidence of its distress, as a record of struggles and damage, survival and testimony. Such work constructs a metalanguage of the journal as a site of record, not only in a textual sense, but also as a physical, corporeal reality. Here the pages of a life are also the skin, surface, of a body which cannot help reveal its scars as the history of its experience. Ultimately these scars become significant not merely as incidental evidence — but also as the compensatory trophies of a life whose difficulties they record. The text of the work is an account of a love affair, blocked and unsuccessful. The male figure who is the object of Schor's attentions becomes a muse who refuses to speak, thus inverting the traditional relations of representation and artistic romance.

Susan kae Grant, **Giving Fear a Proper Name**, 1979-81

Fetishistic Books

Books which are more completely involved with fetishism tend to be more psychological than mystical in character. In psychoanalytic terms, the classic character of the fetish is its reference to the phallus. The fetish stands in for the absent phallus of a woman, whose supposed castration induces fear and impotence in the psyche of a male.7 Fetish objects have a formal relation to that supposedly lost phallus — thus the stiletto heels, knives, guns, whips, pointed brassieres, and so forth are the stock-in-trade of such imagery. The displacement of sexually based fears breaks out in other forms of neurosis such as phobias, and it is these which inspire Susan kae Grant's **Giving Fear a Proper Name** (Black Rose Press, 1979-81). The book was based on dream and nightmare journals, though little of the specifics of these is revealed. Instead, the book is a catalogue of names for various fears — "Topophobia, fear of place," "Eremiphobia, fear of solitude," "Scopophobia, fear of seeing and being seen" and so forth. The entire work is a fetish object — a pink diary in a plexiglass box, loaded with sexual imagery, an overdetermined vocabulary of femininity from which a small gun dangles loose, limp, free-floating. On every page a different fear is elaborated, first through the presence of these titles and phrases, and then through a torturously complex elaboration of small objects in a tiny collage. Each collage contains a photograph of some part of the female body, already fragmenting and dissecting the corpus in the manner of a fetishist — whose greatest fear is the recognition of the woman's body's wholeness (since it appears castrated, thus damaged and incomplete). In "Topophobia" a photograph of an eye is cut, peeled back, and pinned open; in "Eremiphobia" an image of an ear has a tiny plastic telephone attached to it and is pierced by actual straight pins. Throughout the book the pages speak a visual language of cutting, penetrating, and mutilating in controlled rituals of pain. The collages contain many small objects and are produced through complicated mixed-media assemblages, thus providing satisfying emblems of perverse imagery whose seductive quality is the fineness and care and even tinyness of their form. The paper on which these collages are mounted was handmade — and pink, again to underscore the femininity of the book — and contains hair, fibers, and other shreds of organic material which suggest bodily detritus. This is an editioned work of fifteen copies, but it gives the feeling of a unique book, and one of its subtexts seems to be a comment on the fetishization of the precious craft of the book — as if such processes (handmade paper, over-production, and obsessive work) often compensate for a lack of substance at the center of a work.8 In Grant's case, fetishism becomes the subject matter and method in a replete cycle of self-reflection.

Editioned Works with a Rare or Auratic Character
There are many other book works which have these fetishized or auratic qualities to them. But there are also editioned works which are neither fetishistic objects nor democratic multiples. These are not fine

print works or illustrated books or **livres d'artistes** — they are books made as direct expressions of an artist's point of view, with the artist involved in the conception, production, execution of the work. Often these are limited edition works which involve handwork or other features which prevent them from being produced in a more extensive edition. My three examples are all editioned books which involve elaborate production.

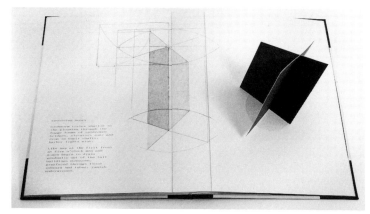

Sjoerd Hofstra, **They Pair Off Hurriedly...** , 1992

The first is Sjoerd Hofstra's **They Pair off Hurriedly**, a book which uses a passage of John Dos Passos's text from his novel **Metropolis**, and then weaves it through blueprint pages which support tightly engineered geometric constructions. In a crude sense, one could refer to this as a "pop-up" book, but it has much more sophistication and control than the run-of-the-mill book of that type. Hofstra's structures are perfect geometric solids whose construction is artfully concealed. As the pages turn, the solids materialize with a seamless skill which speaks of a merciless and mechanically flawless technology. This is not a world of cuteness and sentiment, but a world in which reason and order complete themselves in form. The quality of the blueprint reinforces the metaphors of technological functionality, and the tension between the sketchy, diagrammatic images in the blurred blue lines and the sharp, solid perfection of the crystalline geometric forms is striking. Evidently labor intensive, this is clearly an artist's book, a work of integral vision and structure, unrealizable through other means.

Keith Smith's **Book 91** often referred to as **The String Book** (Space Heater Multiples, 1982) is constructed of paper and string, without text or

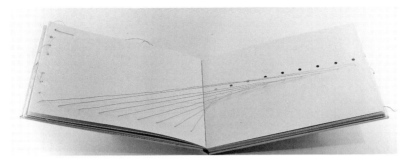

Keith Smith, **Book 91 (The String Book)**, 1982, NYPL

images. The structure is such that strings of a set length, knotted and threaded through the paper pages, expand and contract in response to the turning of the pages. The strings are cut to fit the openings and yet to move and breathe with the movement initiated by the reader, sliding with just enough resistance through their paper holes to make a gentle "shussing" sound as they do so. The work, like Hofstra's, is perfectly engineered.9 The simplicity of the materials, linen thread and thick, off-white paper, make the book a field for an ongoing experience of space and light. The cast shadows of the various patterns of the string, laid out in straight and crossing grids, with single and multiple threads interacting in a changing sequence of arrangements, are contained within the field of the page, which holds their image against the suspended taut line of the string forms. The whole is physical, sculptural, and textual — an interplay of material (string/paper/knots) and immaterial (shadow/light/sound) elements — which amount to a full experience of book as structure and significance, sense and experience. The edition size on this work was fifty copies, pushing the limits of such complicated handwork.

The final work is more traditional in form than these physically complex works, and stands as another instance of the handmade edition — a work which has combined elements of a printed edition as part of its production with elements of handwork. **Scrutiny in the Great Round**, by Tennessee Rice Dixon (Granary Books, 1992), makes use of photocopier reproduction of black and white collages on paper which Dixon then distresses by wetting, crushing, staining, and flattening. These sheets are the editioned aspect of the piece on which she mounts a montage of other elements — fragments of imagery, drawn areas, and watercoloring. The work is personal and arcane, not confessional, but intimate, with iconography of mating and fertility, impregnation and growth. The surface is highly

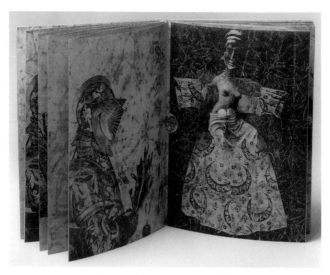

Tennessee Rice Dixon, **Scrutiny in the Great Round**, 1992

worked, and the paper takes on the quality of a tissue or web in which jewels of thought are caught — captured elements of a private alchemy of the myths and rituals of procreative energy. This work was produced in less than two dozen copies, each of which has the same elaborate finish executed by the artist. As in the case of Smith and Hofstra, there is no necessary reason to limit the edition, no structural prevention to extending it indefinitely — it simply becomes a matter of practicality and a sense of the limits of an interested audience as well — not to mention the limits on the artist's capacity to sustain interest in the project. Dixon's work, with its intensely personal interiority, its idiosyncratic and individual vision, is clearly an artist's book. Signed, numbered, and professionally bound, it would not meet the criteria of the democratic multiple, with its deliberately banal methods of production and non-precious forms. But to exclude such works from the realm of artists' books seems artificial and pointless since they obviously extend the paradigm of the book as a work of art.

The Book Transformed

A book may be transformed from an appropriated or found original through physical or conceptual means — or parts of a work can be cut out and used to make a new work. The book as a form is already a received idea, loaded with cultural and historical values and resonances. But it is a form which permits invention and innovation. The convention of the book is both its constrained meanings (as literacy, the law, text, and so forth) and the space of new work (the blank page, the void, the empty place). But working on an existing book is not quite the same as either of these — it is not a replication of a conventional form and it is not a completely new statement within the existing vocabulary of forms. The transformed book is an intervention. It generally includes acts of insertion or defacement, obliteration or erasure on the surface of a page which is already articulated or spoken for. There is an aggressiveness to this violation of an existing text which is related to the gentler act of making a layered palimpsest. In a palimpsest, the original bleeds through, interweaves its presence with the new materials to a greater or lesser degree. In a transformed work the presence of the original can be reduced to almost nil, or be so fragmented and restructured as to be a Frankenstein monster of the original. All of these practices of working onto or into an existing work are interventions into the social order, and the text of the world as it is already written. These transgressions are marked with an apparent physicality of means. Transformation also recuperates works whose status is canonical or its opposite — obscure and unremembered, part of the dross of continual production.

There are many instances of such transformations, and one which has become a canonical work is Tom Phillips' **A Humument**. This is the recuperation of a work which would have otherwise probably been left in increasing obscurity. The project was begun in 1966, when Phillips, inspired by reading William Burroughs' descriptions of his "cut-up" technique, decided that he wanted to make a work with similar techniques.[10] He set rules for his purchase and selection in advance (it had to be cheap — threepence in English currency — and it had to be a book) and then proceeded to find the book in a local shop's book bin. It was a victorian novel by William H. Mallock, **A Human Document** (1892). At first, Phillips states, "I merely scored out unwanted words with pen and ink. It was not long though before the possibility became apparent of making a better unity of word and image, intertwined as in a mediaeval miniature."[11] Phillips elaborated on his procedure to the point where every page became dense with pictorial and verbal imagery. From the existing romantic narrative of Mallock's work, which is almost entirely effaced by the paint applied to the surface, Phillips allowed another story to emerge whose hero is named "Toge." This word can only occur on pages where the words "together" or "altogether" appeared in the original text (the only words in which these letter combinations occur), thus the story of "Toge" is always delimited in advance by the possibilities latent in Mallock's text. It is this relationship of overlay and latency, of invention and constraint, which gives the transformed book its tension.

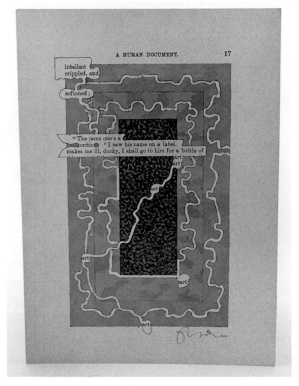

Tom Phillips, **A Humument**, begun in 1966

Part of Phillips' skill is his sensitivity to the existing structures of the page, as well as the complexities of the book form in its entirety. As he notes in his remarks on the work's construction, the only way to link bits of text excised from a whole page is by preserving the link of the "gutter" — the empty white spaces between type — between them. Without this link all of the pages would have presented text in a "staccato" fashion.12 But Philips also makes use of the basic block of type on the sheet as a framing structure, allowing an image to fill out to the margins. In fact, his respect for the margin is so strong throughout the work that in the few sites where it is broken through or bled into these read very clearly as gestures by contrast. The linear form of the type, when allowed to show, sometimes functions as an element of a pictorial composition — a break between paragraphs becoming a point of demarcation for a horizon line in a sketched landscape. But the type can also function simply as the grid on which an abstract design is enmeshed or from which a pattern is elicited. The work is infinitely varied, the range of opacity and translucency permitting the Mallock work differing degrees of preservation. In terms of strategies of representation, each page and each opening makes visual interventions at different levels of literalness and illusion — either using the page as the support for a visual image, a pattern, or taking its typographic layout as the basis of a design. The work is impossible to pigeonhole — its visual and textual interventions are not strictly pop, conceptual, or pointed by a particular agenda. It is rather a full-scale work of invention and variation — an obsessive doodle onto a framework which repaid this labor with a rich harvest of discoveries. Let free of the responsibility of making a new invention the book artist is able to allow associative processes free reign, to let the work happen — which is not to discount either labor or intention in the process, merely to point out their framework. Phillips worked on the book as a whole, rather than in a linear manner. He picked pages and developed them, then went back, picked another, and so forth while leaving the structure of the original volume intact. The result is that the work does not have an overdetermined linearity to it — it has a more sculptural, dimensional feel as a text than a story or narrative would have in a regular format. The internal page motifs — books within books, scripts which are invented, designs which mass or mask the underlying work, painted frames and occasional views into or out of rooms drawn into the text — these all work at the level of each page, one at a time, while the work as a whole unites in a kaleidoscopic vision of transformative energy. Though Phillips emphasizes that the title has an "earthy sound to it suitable to a book exhumed from, rather than born out of, another," the work is light and spacious, for all its dense intensity.13

Phillips' transformative gestures nearly exhaust the possibilities for taking the structure of a page of print and remaking it — but there are other artists who have performed their own interventions on existing pages. The work of John Eric Broaddus derives from attention to the visual structures of a printed work. Broaddus's unique works would be almost impossible to reproduce in editioned form: they contain elaborately cut

John Eric Broaddus, **France**, n.d. mid-1980s

out pages which would have to be die-cut, sheet by sheet, in any reproduction. Conceptually, Broaddus' work makes an interesting pendant to
that of Phillips, since Broaddus is attentive to the potential of the visual
elements in page structures and uses these, rather than the text, as the
basis of his investigations. France, (finished in the 1980s) one of Broaddus's last pieces, is a major work by any standards — complexity, exhaustive artistry, and conceptual interest. The book is a transformed encyclo-
pedia volume which focuses on French culture and history. Broaddus cuts,
paints, draws on and into the elements of the pictorial iconography. The
changes he makes, however, are such that only echoes and phantoms
remain: the outline of a famous architectural monument, a glimpse of a
well-known work of art, the cast shadow or profile of a famous political
figure. Broaddus has an uncanny capacity to zero in on the precise bit of
visual form which carries the maximum amount of resonant associations.
Because the pages are cut, not merely reworked on their surfaces, the
book becomes a layered space. The process of revelation in each turning
offers new, unpredictable, vistas through the pages. Broaddus is particu-
lary expert at manipulating figure/ground relations. What appears as an
icon in one cut surface turns out to be part of a field of amorphous or patterned elements as the page turns — thus the transformations occur as
part of the dynamic action of the book, not merely as an intervention into

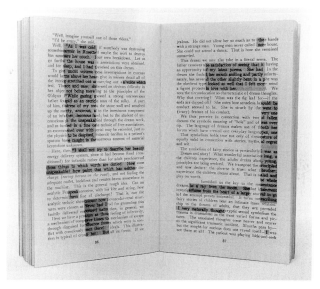

Mary Lum, **The Final Results of Psychoanalytic Treatment**, 1991

its received form. In part this is possible because the changes Broaddus makes in the pages are physical and spatial as well as visual: the work has become a sculptural codex, richly polyvalent with suggested and emphasized meaning.

Broaddus and Phillips do not deplete the range of possible transformations of existing books. Many book artists are less ambitious in visual terms, though no less thorough in their treatment of a preexisting text — such as Ian Murray's **Image and Appearance** (Halifax, 1974) a philosophico-critical treatise extracted from a work whose full title (before deletions) was **The Image and Appearance of the Human Body by Schilder.** Murray's systematic crossing-out is straightforward — all the lined-through words are still present and still readable, and the new text reads against its original — a liberated soul against the dross of a cast-off body. Mary Lum, in her reworked version of Sigmund Freud's **The Final Results of Psychoanalytic Treatment** (Pyramid Arts Center, NY, 1991), relies on subtlety, rather than drama, for effect. Barely noticeable interventions (a slice through the page, an area of highlight several words long, a patch of alternate text whose halftone screen is clearly visible pasted in over a column three letters wide and six lines long, and so forth) disrupt the regularity of text like neurotic symptoms which never achieve their own coherence either as or within the work. The variations on this theme are many — Claude Lothier's **Les chemins de la vie**, a unique book made in 1980, is painted with thick bands of color which run throughout the found book, obliterating a part of the text on every page as they streak through from front to back "to temporarily override meaning, which feigns to disappear only to resurface a little later, unsynchronized."14 Merapi Obermayer took pages from a love story, folded them into tiny squares, and placed them into a gridded box with only phrases offering themselves to be read, making a reworked book called **Dream for Every Page** (1981), while the Japanese artist Matsutani picks up books in the flea market which are "lonely" and gives them whole new "chapters" made of vinyl and graphite which bulge out from the ancient bindings in a physical bid for renewed attention. I mention these examples to concretize the idea of the wide range of possibilities for such projects, but there are also artists for whom this work is the central focus of their practice.

Helmut Löhr is one such artist. His sculptural projects involve the transformation of existing books through physical means — tearing, shredding, reworking fragments and pieces into highly aesthetic new objects whose relations to their original is through a field fraught with reference and resonance. The concept of "reference" becomes embedded in materials — the repressed content of the original work having been put at the service of a physical form in which it is still, nonetheless, visually apparent. He shredded the contents of a telephone book into a thick, soft, bulk with frond-like fingers of tissue-thin paper thwarting the condensed index of the familiar resource. Or he might warp an entire paperback, curling its spine and pages into an emotionally charged spasm of response to the world, or fold its interior pages into a solid, geometrical form composed of the delicate ribs of individual pages, each looped back on itself and tucked into the spine to form an open fan. Löhr's works in this vein began in the late 1970s, anticipating many of the manipulations which have become commonplace.

Physical and material transformations often produce a resonance through the changes wrought on the substance of paper itself — Denise Aubertin's "baked" books made in the early 1980s darken the pages of found works invoking the image of book burnings or of some post-apocalyptic condition of earthly existence turned to ash. Books made in other materials imbue their own intensity through the associations of such materials. Anselm Keifer's large-scale books made of heavy dull grey lead, laid open on stands designed to hold their outsized form and ponderous weight absorb the viewer into their profound depths, rather than offering themselves for communication. Such works become affective pieces rather than textual vehicles or message bearing forms, their physical, tactile presence takes the iconic and cultural resonance of book forms and plays it out through an extenuated spectrum of propositions — "what if" this were a book and a book were this, what then? Books of bread, marble, granite, soap and dried leaves pressed with flowers delicate and impossible to manipulate without destroying them. Books of lost objects, found texts, destroyed titles, remade photographs — all gaining some value by using the book form, insisting on its familiar structure as a frame to the otherwise elusive meaning of these constructions.

At their most banal, these works simply rely upon the codex as a convenience — the books of appropriated images taken directly out of mass culture sources which Richard Prince composes are deliberately affectless. He makes the least possible intervention into his sources or their relation to each other, composing a giant found-image poem from the materials at hand — advertisements and media photos rephotographed, reprinted, into an incidental sequence of non-events. This is almost an anti-book, an attempt to negate the structuring principles of sequence, relation, flow and event within the bound conventions of the codex.

Finally, there exist works which make a conceptual transformation of an earlier piece, skillfully citing and restating its premises in a manner which dialogues across historical time and cultural assumptions. One such piece is Marcel Broodthaers' version of Stéphane Mallarmé's Un Coup de Dès (1969).15 Broodthaers took the structure and layout of Mallarmé's proposals for the poem (which went unpublished in his lifetime) and re-presented them as a schematic work. Where each line of the poem should lie on the page a dark black line, simple, geometric, stark is placed in its stead. This is a physical equivalent, a moral inequivalent, a recapitulation and an obliteration. Where is meaning in this work? It is flattened into form. And yet, Broodthaers', in a gesture which is appreciative and humorously insightful, attends to the structure of Mallarmé's work with far greater concentration than any typographer's reworking could do. Broodthaers reduces Un Coup de Dès to its structure — or to put it another way he elevates the structure of the work to a concept worthy of study in its own right, thus acknowledging Mallarmé's own fetishistic attention to this aspect of his work. Rendering the structure concrete, visible, almost tactile, Broodthaers offers a conceptual analysis of Mal-

Marcel Broodthaers, **Un Coup de Dès**, 1969

larmé's poem across the distance of a nearly a century. Broodthaers used a translucent paper for the project, thus permitting the spatial suspension of the phrases on the page to read against each other in dimensional rela- tion — the whole is the constellation Mallarmé envisioned, hanging in a space of its own creation in which its linguistic structure makes the coor- dinates and also maps the form. It would be hard to imagine a more subtle treatment of Mallarmé's work, or one more capable of demonstrating its essential properties, than this reworked book by Broodthaers.

Poetics of the Book

The work of German artist Barbara Fahrner extends philosophical and poetic investigations of the book as a metaphor for the world. Fahrner is an artist for whom making books is a fundamental way of processing her experience into symbolic form — to give it meaning and to give it a per- manence which counteracts the transient inconsequentiality of the pas- sage of time. She poses her projects through highly structured organiza- tion, but there is a dialogue in them between obsessive ordering and eclectic receptivity which participate in the "collecting" sensibility which motivates her.

Fahrner's Das **Kunstkammerprojekt** was produced in the course of a year — from November 1987 to November 1988 and it was inspired by the concept of the kunstkammer as it existed in the Renaissance: the idea of a

116

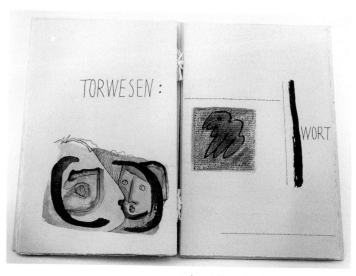

Barbara Fahrner, **Japetus Steenstrup**, 1987

chamber devoted to an individual's collections.16 These collections were not merely comprised of artworks — they might contain anything from biological specimens to antiquities to that all encompassing category known as "curiosities." Fahrner combined this idea with that of the Heimatmuseum — a form of local, provincial museum dedicated to preserving the artifacts of lived local culture (everything from farm implements to items used in daily life). The conceptual parameters of these two museums intersect in an image of eccentricity and the quotidian. The unsystematic order of her kunstkammer becomes the depository of the lived, the vernacular, and the immediate as well as of the extraordinary and rare. Fahrner used the kunstkammer concept as an image to structure a work comprised of many books, all of which were related to each other within an outline of the whole. The final form was eighty-four books which were arranged according to several thematic divisions taken from the **Idea del theatro** of Guilio Camillo published in 1550 in Florence. These themes were sufficiently open in themselves — the seven planets, simple elements, complex elements, creations of man, unity of body and soul, activities of humans in nature, and the arts — to allow Fahrner considerable freedom in their interpretation.

The **Kunstkammer** is literally an expanded book, one comprised of many smaller works — some containing long abstracted texts from various sources, others containing Fahrner's drawings, diagrammatic charts, and notes. The whole weaves together in a form she compares to a net "a structure without a recognizable order, but nevertheless a system that branches out in all directions. These ramifications are accompanied by countless holes, and these holes represent the holes in our own under- standing and knowledge." If Fahrner's project has any resonance with that of Mallarmé and his desire for a book which would be the equivalent of the world, it stops short of the cosmological totality to which Mallarmé aspired. For Fahrner the completeness of the form demonstrates its inabil- ity to accurately represent the fullness of the world and also shows the limits of human knowledge as well as individual understanding. The book is an ordering — singular and indefinite, not the order — definitive and transcendent. It is a collection which is able to expand to include the reach of the artist's inquiry and imagination rather than bound or contain it. And yet as a finished work it is finite and offers its own typology as a particular, individual collection of ideas. Thus its incompleteness serves metaphorically to indicate the limits and lapses of Fahrner's own processes, while its repleteness serves as symbol of her existence as what she calls "a nomadic collector."

The theme of containment also informs A Passage (Granary Books, 1994) a work by Buzz Spector. Spector's investigation of the book as image, icon, and symbol engages with the metaphoric role of the book through many facets of its cultural identity. The themes of the library, authorship, and language have all found their way into his sculptural and installation works. But here discussion will be limited to a single work which con- denses many of Spector's concerns into a single book object. The work is bound like a conventional book, sewn and glued into a case binding. The full measure of pages fill out the spine to a thickness of slightly more than an inch. Standing on a shelf or seen from the spine side the work appears to be a regular book, stamped with its title, author's name, and publisher. But inside the book the pages turn out to be torn, each page slightly longer than the next, so that the entire body of the book slants at an oblique angle. The same text has been printed on each page and the tearing allows the text to be read through the wavering, flickering disruptions caused by the physical transformation. The word "A Passage" appears at the top of the page, suggesting a running head — as if this were the title of the work — and since the text begins in mid-sentence there is good reason to believe that the page is supposed to exist within a larger book. The frag- ments of text recount an anecdote about a visit from an old friend from

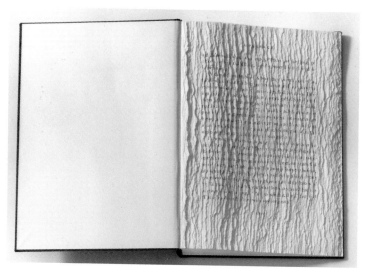

Buzz Spector, **A Passage**, 1994

Hebrew school days to whom Spector shows a collection of his altered books. The friend responds to the torn pages of these various volumes (the torn sequence has been a form in Spector's work for some time) with a story of Talmudic erudition. A learned scholar knew the Talmud so well that when shown a single line from anywhere in its text "he could tell you what letter occupied that site on every following page." Spector's response to this account of a feat of memory is to reply that he is clearly not a scholar since "These books only show what I've forgotten."

Spector's book is about the absence, rather than the presence, of record. Here life is what is missing from the book, experience is always elsewhere, and the text, form, and material of the work are a thing in themselves rather than a symbol or substitute for the world. The metaphor is one of loss, of continual escape and slippage of life from its containment within representation. Spector's work suggests a fundamental impossibility for the book to contain anything except the sign of absence; it is the empty field showing all that it cannot enclose.

1 Livres d'Artistes — Livres Objects , Editions C.E.R.P.M, Paris, 1985.

2 Chronicle Books in San Francisco is publishing a trade edition of Ely's **The Flight Into Egypt**.

3 The historical antecedent to this piece is an anthology, **Le Surréalisme en 1947**, for

THE CENTURY OF ARTISTS' BOOKS

which Marcel Duchamp designed the cover: a cast mold of a female breast, painted realistically, (Pierre Le Feu, Maeght Editeur, Paris, 1947).

4 There are two interesting parenthetical points here. One is that Kellner has managed to integrate the book-object aspects of sculptural work into an actual book, rather than reduce the work to a non-book in order to have it function as an object — thus making it an unusual hybrid. The other point has to do with the resonance between this work and Joan Lyons' **My Mother's Book** which is conceived and executed within the codes of book structure and yet both thematically and in its emotional impact, has certain similiarities. In spite of its non-precious, offset production, Lyons' work has some of this aura about it as well — perhaps because the transcribed first-person voice combines with the photographs to create a sense that the dead are present, still with us.

5 Rudolf Kuenzli mentions another box work by Duchamp, **Box of 1914**, but does not describe it, "Introduction," **Duchamp Artist of the Century**, R.Kuenzli and F.Naumann, eds., (MIT University Press, 1989).

6 Some of Boltanski's other catalogue/archive pieces will be discussed in Chapter 12.

7 Sigmund Freud, **Introductory Lectures on Psychoanalysis** (Penguin, 1973) and his most orthodox interpreter, Jacques Lacan, **Ecrits** (Norton, 1977), among other writings are the primary sources for this concept.

8 This is purely my speculation, and many of Grant's works have this seductive fetishistic quality, not all of which can be subsumed under this theme of the preciousness of book production.

9 This becomes clear in the presence of a similar work which is not worked out — such as the Museum of Modern Art's version of one of Munari's **Libro Illegible**, a disaster, which doesn't open properly and feels like it will rip at every turn.

10 The technique of cutting up found materials and reassembling them according to random techniques was first used by the Dada poets. Tristan Tzara has a famous piece from the late 1910s describing this way of making poems.

11 Tom Phillips, **A Humument**, (Thames and Hudson, 1980), endnotes.

12 **Ibid.**, n.p.

13 **Ibid.**, n.p.

14 **Livres d'Artistes / Livres Objets** , op.cit., is the source for this and a number of other works in this section. Virtually every one of the more than a hundred objects in this catalogue could be described as an auratic, fetishistic, or transformed book.

15 A joint publication project of Galerie Wide White Space in Antwerp and Galerie Michael Werner in Cologne.

16 Barbara Fahrner, **Das Kunstkammerprojekt**, Herzog August Bibliothek, Wolfenbüttel 1992; this catalogue, particularly the interview with Harriet Watts, serves as the source for this paragraph.

6

The Codex
and its Variations

A book is a highly complex organization of material and conceptual elements. While there are other forms which books take, the most common, versatile, and frequently manipulated is the codex form. Made from a set of bound leaves or pages, the codex is a very restrained form — conventionally made with standard-size pages fixed in a rigid sequence by being clasped or held on one side. The codex was a later invention than other material supports for writing such as clay tablets or bark because it depended on a thin, pliable sheet of something like paper in order to function. Papyrus and skins used for making parchment were often pasted end to end to make scrolls, but the limitations of scroll forms are obvious — access to the textual material is limited to the unrolled area and skimming, scanning, and searching the document are extremely difficult. In Jewish religious practice the gradual unrolling of the Torah scroll follows a set pattern throughout the year, with elaborate ceremonies attached to its handling, opening, and closing. Scrolls are liable to damage, since the tightly rolled material must be kept from drying out and cracking with the movement.

Parchment and vellum (parchment made of calfskin) served as the basis of book production throughout the early Christian era and into the early years of the invention of printing. Douglas McMurtrie, the book and printing historian, notes the last official use of a papyrus support for an official document was a papal bull issued in 1022, "long after parchment had become the common material for writing and just before paper came into common use in Europe."1 Paper had been invented in China in the first or early second century A.D. and gradually made its way west into Europe, coming into use and then manufacture in the Near East and Egypt by the 8th century and into Spain and Italy in the 12th and 13th centuries respectively.2 (Paper was also produced in the New World in copious amounts as part of Mayan culture in the 7th and 8th centuries.)3 Paper can be made of a variety of fibers and other materials can be used to make books — in artists' books every material imaginable has been used from cloth and metal to wooden planks and glass sheets in the assembly of a codex form. Likewise, writing materials — which have traditionally included inks from various pigments and binders, paints, and graphite, among others — have expanded to include everything from thread to spray paint, glitter to milk, blood and body fluids, to pigments made from organic matter in the site in which the work is undertaken, and so forth. In short, there are neither rules nor limits in the use of materials in artists' books — though the permanance or longevity of these may be extremely variable.

In examining the way artists have interrogated the structure of the book, it is important to begin with the obvious but also profound realization that a book should be thought of as a whole. A book is an entity, to be reckoned with in its entirety — the most successful books are those which account for the interrelations of conceptual and formal elements, thematic and material concerns. As in any mode of artmaking, there are no formulae for coordinating the parts of book. There are artists for whom structural issues take priority — Keith Smith's philosophy of making a book, for instance, relies on resolving structural considerations first so that the physical organization of the book becomes, for him, a substantive and critical area of activity. This is not to say that he then turns content into an incidental element, simply filling up the pages' blank space, but that for him form can only serve content if it is well-resolved. Other artists, like Dieter Roth, realize the book through a process whose production of form and content are often one and the same idea. Many of these are works which depend upon sequence and the permutations of a formal gesture through serial repetition. Other artists work up a book from an interplay between thematic elements, or texts, photographs or other images interacting with propositions for form until the relation works out. There are also over-designed books — as well as overproduced ones — works which have such a neat "fit" of elements that it suffocates them. They are locked into a single frame of reference as design which renders them superficial and decorative, rather than communicative, or their production values are inflated in relation to their concerns.

Though the codex is the dominant book form — and with good reason, given its efficiency and functionality — there are various shaped books which have found their way into the world of artists' books with faithful regularity — polygons and fold-up works, boxes and accordion folds, scrolls, pop-up structures, and tunnel books.4 To remain artists' books, rather than book-like objects or sculptural works with a book reference to them, these works have to maintain a connection to the idea of the book — to its basic form and function as the presentation of material in relation to a fixed sequence which provides access to its contents (or ideas) through some stable arrangement. Such a definition stretches elastically to reach around books which are card stacks, books which are solid pieces of bound material, and other books whose nature defies easy characterization.

The codex will be the focus here. But aspects of this discussion — such as conventions or determinants of form — have resonance for some of the book-like objects whose identity rests in their reference to such conventions and also for the as yet to be worked out character of whatever books will be in the electronic universe.

The Codex Form: Order to Chaos

The parameters of the codex form can be defined by stretching its basic elements to two extreme poles. At one extreme, the codex is a set of uniformly sized pages bound in a fixed and intentional sequence. At the other extreme it is an accumulation of non-uniform pages in an unintentional and unfixed sequence which is barely recognizable as a book. I suggest that both of these are book forms — that work equally with the idea of the codex as their point of reference — conceptually speaking. Michael Snow's **Cover to Cover** (Nova Scotia College of Art and Design and New York University Press, 1975) is a work which uses the structure of the codex as an aspect of its conception as well as calling attention to it throughout the execution.5 Isidore Isou's **Le Grand Désordre (Chaos)**(1960) is about as remote from Snow's work as a book could be — it practically inverts and nullifies every aspect of order, structure, and sequence. It could be argued that Isou's work is not even a codex except that its identity depends so clearly upon subversion of the paradigm.

Snow's book is entirely visual. Black and white photographs of what appear to be the front and back of a door comprise the front and back cover images.6 These cover images, examined closely, turn out to be the front of an actual door and the photograph of a back door held in Snow's own hands, his fingers showing in the margin. Thus the illusionistic character of photographic truth is already pointed out in the contrast of the covers, which comment on each other. The book is rigidly sequential, following Snow himself through the space of the door/book which he opens as the pages turn. The recto and verso of the sheet are literalized: the recto shows the front view of Snow coming through the door, the verso the back view of him passing through. Each page in the sequence is thus granted a dimensionality, as if the full space of the event of Snow's movement were contained within its flatness.7 The play of literalizing the photographic illusions in the sequence becomes a means of analyzing the conventions of the book form.

From the first, Snow aligns the door he walks through with the edges of the book. Door frame and page edge are one and the same. Once through the door his body — so far the only object in the frame/door/page — moves aside to show the photographers who are positioned to shoot him from each side. Obviously what we are seeing is the photographers shooting each other — now that the object (Snow) has been removed from the line of sight. The intersection of their photographic fields — Snow's now absent body — thus reveals them as objects (though it was from their points of view that we "saw" Snow). As if shy of being recognized, the photographer on the left sheet raises a blank white page over his face which then, immediately, comes to fill the full page opposite. A device within the structure of the narrative returns again to the structure of the book — the white sheet is precisely equivalent in dimensions to the page size. That sheet of paper then begins its own sequence, being handled by fingers which enter from the margin, thus turning the blank sheet into a physical fact, referring constantly to the edges and limits of the book, until it is fed into a typewriter. At that point it functions again as both illusion and actual sheet on which something typed enters the book as a text. What is typed is the bibliographic information of the book, thus keeping the self-referential aspect of the work in a closed circuit of reference and meaning.

This kind of play continues (I have described only the opening sequence) throughout the work, which moves according to a cinematic logic through the space of Snow's residence and out into his driveway to his car. In the exact center of the book two halves of the front end of the car join in a mutant automobile body with the door to his house on the left and a speed zone sign with the word "begins" on its bottom providing the punctuating text. From photograph to page and from page to book the work is continually structuring its illusions within the formal constraints

Michael Snow, **Cover to Cover**, 1975

of book form. In the process the book's structural features are emphatically called to attention. Spine and margin are delimiting factors. The codex is sequence raised to the power of a conceptual device. Edges are the finite limits of the universe — anything beyond them falls away into a void of unrepresentable space. They are literally the edge of the image as well as in alignment with some element depicted in the image. The central gutter is a point of mirroring, of reversals and inversions (later in the book Snow's car turns upside down through the turning of the photographic page after which the entire work moves upside down and backwards to the end of the book, which thus functions as its own beginning). Every aspect of a codex has been made use of to form the conceptual underpinning of this work. It enters into the production of meaning page by page and is integrated into a two-headed, two-sided work which functions from either direction. The linearity of the codex has thus been subverted by making it bi-directional.

Isou's **Le Grande Désordre** is easier to describe than Snow's work — its disorderly structure doesn't require or even support the same kind of analysis. A manila envelope is its housing. Printed on its cover the name "Isou," the title **Le Grand Désordre** under which the word **Roman** appears, identifying the work as a novel, and then the editor's imprint. Inside the envelope are the elements of the book. First, a cover, also printed with title, author, subtitle, and the description "a hypergraphic, polyautomatic novel." Hypergraphy was the term used by the Lettrists to describe their invented writings — glyphs whose meaning was supposed, like that of Russian **zaum** sounds, to communicate without regard for convention. The Lettrists attempted to pulverize language into fundamentals and recreate writing from scratch, imbuing this activity with political and poetic revolutionary significance. There is little actual hypergraphic writing in this work.8 Here the Lettrist agenda has mounted to another level, replacing signs with things. The envelope contains more than the cover for the book — it also contains its content. These are elements which spill forth as so much trash and debris: matches, cigarette butts, theater tickets, cancelled stamps, torn postcard invitations to exhibition openings, announcements, a bit of writing paper, wallpaper, paper clips, a twisted coat hanger, and so forth. This is all detritus of a life lived and cast off. The evidence, factual, real, and irrefutable in its literalness is all that is offered to the "reader" for whom the text of the "novel" is to be constructed from this mass of disorganized material. There is no set sequence. There is no

Isidore Isou, **Le Grand Désordre**, 1960

structure, order, or framework. And yet the empty cover of the codex form serves as the major object according to which the rest of the elements gain their identity. They are meant to be "in" this book and part of it. The cover does more than name the project as a book, it physically permits the contents to be in or out of the work. The codex is the destroyed but still functioning reference of the piece — this gives the fragmented, narrative elements some coherence. Otherwise the disorder would be meaningless, unbounded, insignificant. All the missing features of the codex, are invoked by the mess of miscellany whose imaginary text is the actual life of the inscrutable author.

With the highly conscious structure of Snow's **Cover to Cover** at one end and the disordered debris of Isou's **Le Grand Désordre** at the other we have the extremes of the codex paradigm: self-referential or only functioning as a referent, an idea, an abstraction which by its existence binds elements together because they are read and experienced in relation to the idea of a book. Between these two extremes, almost all codex forms find their place and identity — from Dieter Roth's works of found and cut press sheets to the highly articulated pages of Telfer Stokes and Helen Douglas's WeProductions. From the uniform and intentional at one extreme to the non-uniform, unintentional, and anti-intentional, at the other, the codex gives definition to the structure of these works. Whether the limits are literalized or transgressed they function to define these works. While the codex can also be taken for granted and simply used, in all its conventional convenience and efficiency, there are many ways in which artists have expanded its vocabulary through manipulating its features. There are many structures which are a variation of the codex form, making use of the conventions of uniformity and intentional sequencing. A few of these will be discussed here to demonstrate the suggestive possibilities of integrating structure with concept, theme, and materials.

Structural Investigations

Structures and binding are not the same. Binding methods and their conventions — expanded and normal — involve choices of material, assembly, and coordination of the elements of the codex into a workable, functional whole. Binding aesthetics range from the functional to the decorative, minimal to excessive, and everywhere in-between. The structure of a book and its binding are intimately related, however, my discussion will center on form, not mechanics, with an emphasis on structure as an organizational apparatus rather than a craft of production. Keith Smith's writings have done the most to conceptually integrate structure and production. His works, **The Structure of the Visual Book, Text in the Book Format**, and **Non-Adhesive Bindings** are sourcebooks which provide a wealth of information and insight into investigations of concept through form in the making of books.9

Variations on the codex can be created by changing the way the binding structures the sequence or access to the pages as in fan or blind books. Joan Lyons' 1975 **Untitled** fan book uses a single screw and post, like those used on paint sample books, to hold the pages of the work together. The shapes of the pages, as well as the material on them, changes as one moves from top to bottom or front to back. The first sheet has a marked, organic curve to its top edge which gradually flattens out on each successive sheet as the book progresses. When the book is closed, part of every page is visible because of the gradual slope engineered by the cutting. The image of seascape, water, rocks, and clouds spreads into a dynamic spiral when the book is open, though the image itself is the same on each sheet. Because of the cutting, a different part of the image serves as the top edge thus stretching the image through the continuity formed by the cuts. Con-

Conrad Gleber, **Chicago Skyline**, 1977

rad Gleber's **Chicago Skyline** (Chicago Books, 1977) is a fan book which reveals the cityscape through a series of linked photographs, and here again the single point of fixed binding allows the viewer to reveal or conceal a wide or narrow band of that skyline according to individual whim. A fan book could be used for a textual work as well as a visual work, but the inherent elasticity of the image and the effects on its internal relations of scale have a particularly attractive effect in the adaptation of this format to visual books.10

Slat books are bound into a venetian blind structure using threads which run up both sides and pull the book shut. Slat books are a traditional book form in Asian and Indonesian cultures — Douglas McMurtrie describes Hindu slat books made from palm leaves in which the writing is incised with a sharp instrument then filled with dark pigment to increase legibility.11 Slat books can structure revelation and disclosure within the book through visual and physical means. In Scott McCarney's **Memory Loss**, (Visual Studies Workshop, 1988) this aspect of the structure embodies thematic elements of the work.

Using an accordion-folded sheet, rather than traditional slats, **Memory Loss** stretches out in a line of ridges printed on both sides. Several colors of ink (black, red, and light blue on one side and black, yellow, and

Scott McCarney, **Memory Loss**, 1988

light blue on the other) are manipulated to maximize the effects of fragmentation being described. The book deals with physical therapy treatments undertaken by a victim of an accident who has suffered from memory loss. The book may be viewed from various angles — across the slats from right or left or else faced straight on. In each case, different parts of the whole are made available but never all at once — as the fragments of a damaged memory refuse full access to the complete past or integrated self. McCarney's design sensibility serves this content well — with the play of repetitions and variations on images and themes worked out across the structure of the book. A man's profile from a lithograph in 19th-century style (appropriated from an anatomy text) announces a sequence in which cutaway interiors of muscle, bone, blood, and brain are revealed across the faces of successive slats. Likewise, a text, oriented to rise along the horizon of each folded ridge, places the emotional experience of the victim into headline statements: "Dependency," "Euphoria," "Impatience." Fragments of the young man, various weaving snakes (benign and deadly varieties), snippets of correspondence, postmarks, cancelled stamps, are all pastiched on a large graphic halftone screen of the man's face — only readable as an image from a distance which turns the rest of the visual and verbal material into mere pattern. This is an intensely personal book, though it does not announce itself as such — the materials were all drawn from McCarney's experiences with his brother, but the emotional quality comes through even if one doesn't know this.

Thus the processes of viewing the work recapitulate some of the activities and difficulties of a rehabilitative therapy. Because the book is an accordion fold, the "slats" are artificially made into discrete elements by the folds which allow the book to be collapsed into its binding, sliding along its strings like a camera bellows.

Both fan books and slat books take the discrete unit of the codex page and put it into a new syntagmatic arrangement. Rather than remaining separate spatially, the pages are able to connect in relations of continuity, their surfaces functioning as part of a whole image or field. The effect is the re-ordering of the determined sequence of normal linear reading. While in the codex there is a jump from opening to opening and the break functions as a moment of transformation (or is overridden by elements of continuity) the fan and slat books have the possibility of subsuming the individual pages into a larger pattern. In these books the page functions as a segment — as in the structure of layered tile or lapped shingles. There is a physical relation of contiguity, not only the possibility of a thematic relation, while the codex form is described as a continuity with continual interruptions. This is similar to the scenes of a film, where the viewing experience is in relation to those breaks whether they are emphasized or repressed beneath the illusion of a continuous image.

The codex can be varied by changing access to the information in the sequence of pages by either cutting, drilling, or perforating the page, or through the use of materials of varying opacities. Possibly the most renown cut book is a literary one, Raymond Queneau's **Cent mille milliards de poemes (A hundred million poems**, Gallimard, 1961 — designed by Robert Massin). Here the normative literary page has been sliced between every line so that each can be peeled back independently through the full depth of the book, making a different poem with each combination. In Keith Smith's **Out of Sight**, (Keith, 1985) a series of pages which bear only text have been cut at intervals so that each succeeding page is exactly one letter wider than the next. As a result the first page which the viewer sees on opening the book is a complete text reading left to right, top to bottom, except that every line reads across the cut series of pages. As each page is turned, the page below reveals another text which also reads across the full set of letters, but with a different meaning in each turning. So "Dearly I draw him near" becomes "Tenderly I draw him near" and then "Erase today I saw him appear" in the first three turnings

Raymond Queneau, **Cent mille milliards de poèmes**, 1961

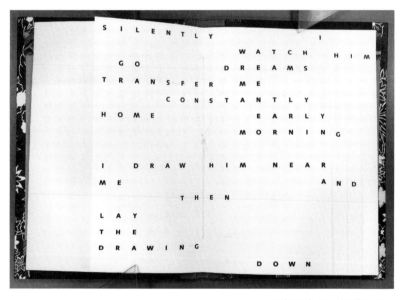

Keith Smith, **Out of Sight**, 1985

of the top three lines. The cover of the book is printed with a title just barely distinguishable in tone from the color of the black ground on which it lies, thus expressing the theme of visual concealment and revelation. In this work the cutting changes the alignment of the edges, allowing the pages to read against each other rather than in isolated sequence.12

Turn next page for instructions.

Sally Alatalo, **Past Due**, 1980s

Sally Alatalo's **Past Due** (du da, vol.2, no.4, 1980s) uses the same structure to a different effect. Alatalo's color-xerox piece has a single image on it, repeated through the whole of a cut stack of about fifty sheets. The overall effect is an elongated gentle curve which dimensionalizes the image. The variations in the xerox give a slight flicker to the surface as the whole image — a wrapped or draped sculpted bust of what appears to be a woman's head — is comprised of these slim strips of almost matching color. The book doesn't perform the way Smith's does, transforming itself as one turns its pages. Instead, it seems to breathe and stretch in the hand with a peculiar animate quality. However, this work functions within the codex convention, using its object-character to a physical and conceptual end — embodying the codex and rendering it a corpus in its very structure and being.

Clifton Meador, **Up Cog Bridge Hope**, 1988

Clifton Meador's **Up Cog Bridge Hope** (Center for Editions, 1988) uses cutting to reveal interior spaces within a sequence of folded pages. A single long sheet is folded to make an accordion book of three openings with the long end of the sheet wrapping around the outside to form a cover. The inside folds of the openings are cut, the interior fold inverted, and thus a smaller reverse-fold page protrudes into the opening. This sets background and foreground apart within the opening, which Meador exaggerates showing a large bridge in grainy halftone in the background and in the foreground photographs of renowned celebrities intoning. Typical of Meador, there is both a critical message and an irreverence: Marlon Brando as Marc Antony, Richard Burton as Sir Thomas Beckett make up one pair whose thought-bubble captions read: "His accusations in vain" and "His prayers ineffectual." Behind the cut opening is an image of a large mechanical cog, a geared wheel, the motif of fate, human systems, knowledge, life, the inevitability of grinding forward without remorse. By cutting through the page the entire text can be read against that central motif printed across the inside of the spine, an Orwellian meta-image and inescapable referent to the work. Thus the spatial manipulation generates a changing set of meaning relations since the physical relations of text/image/motif all intersect simultaneously. Rather than reading the flat space of a page, one reads the dimensional space of a field of significant elements.

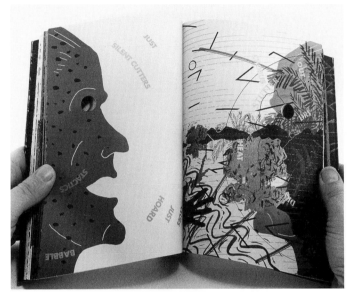

Kevin Osborn, **Tropos**, 1988

Other forms of cutting or interfering with the intact surface of the codex pages include drilling or die-cutting. Dieter Roth's **Gesammelte Werke Band 7** (Hansjörg Mayer, 1977) made use of holes cut through the pages as a way of literally "opening up" the reading experience. The pages were cut out from the color section of newspaper and other comics, bound, and trimmed to uniform size. Conventional expectations about the nature of the text were mooted by the radical intervention in surface, thus allowing the eye to penetrate from one page to another, affording unexpected juxtapositions and irruptions in the field of the page. Kevin Osborn, in exactly the inverse gesture, used a hole drilled through the entire of his book **Tropos** (Osbornbook, 1988) as a means of unifying the complex interior visual field. **Tropos** is multi-layered, its verbal elements making an active interplay with its visual icons, patterns, and graphic motifs. It is also a complex book, one which does not immediately reveal all its aspects on first viewing. The transformations of patterns, for instance, in page to page sequences, allows them to function as background and then in the foreground as recognizable imagery. As the profile of a Janus face comes and goes from the outside edge of the (folded) pages — facing each other across the spine — the drilled hole functions as eye and then opening, then as arbitrary point of constant reference in a field as the pages change. In a few sequences a faint echo of the drilled hole gains intensity until it becomes a round, dark, spot capable of passing for a double of the actual hole only to disappear again — thus emphasizing the real hole's representational nature and its dimensionality.

Joan Wolbier, **Arachne/Amaranth**, 1983

Opacity and Translucence

Varying the degree of opacity in the paper or materials used for the pages of a codex work can create an internal space within the codex form without transformation of the physical form. In **Arachne/Amaranth** (True Grid Editions, 1983) Joan Wolbier used translucent paper (#17 weight,U.V. Ultra II) to its fullest potential. The square format book is comprised of a single signature of ten sheets, each printed with images drawn on mylar and burned directly onto positive plates. This process eliminates a photographic negative in the offset process, preserving a drawing, line, and shading unmediated by the dot of the halftone screen. Each translucent sheet is printed either on one or both sides with a discrete visual element — not so much an image as a part of a whole which is composed through the layered sequence. The work is like a single mandala or meditative diagram, with grids, a triangular frame, a central floral motif, a ring of glow-

136

ing circular forms themselves layered on the next page by shadows marking them as a waxing and waning celestial body — each sheet reads over and against the next. The book is bi-directional, reading right to left and back. There are two title pages, one at each end, each following the cover in the conventional way so that neither end can be identified as the "true" front. Wolbier successfully integrates surface and dimensionality — the work is not merely layered, but becomes a spatial composition, with the elements rising and receding from the field of the page. Wolbier's work transcends the major clichés of the translucent page — her formal investigation is so thorough, and her awareness of the design of these pages and facing pages is so carefully articulated, that subtleties of arrangement become substance. This is both a web and a floral form expanding, a metaphor and an enactment of growth as structure, form as dimensional movement, the connection of elements across the punctual units of time all layering into a spatial illusion. The result is not an image of wholeness — rather the codex sequence resonates relations through the field of the book, evolving a structure over and through the pattern of pages.

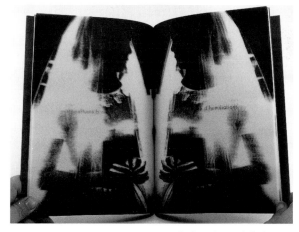

Francine Zubeil, **Panique Général**, 1993

A far simpler work structurally, Francine Zubeil's **Panique Général** (Editions de l'Observatoire, 1993) uses a single image — a high contrast image of a bride — to create an uncanny work. A feeling of obsession is generated by the relentless repetition of the image of the bride whose face is entirely dark, her veiled form with hands just touching, elbows out, her figure delicate as only a very young body can be. Because of the translucency of the paper, there is an effect of ghostliness and also of a blurred,

137

eerie dimensionality. The images are not quite perfectly aligned and the slight displacement from left to right expands the form of the woman beyond the boundaries of the single image — as if she were moving slightly within the confines of the frame of the page. Occasionally there are phrases in red ink overprinted on the black and white image — "forgetfulness," "a sensation of being crushed," "a sensation of suffocation." These phrases anchor the floating image of the bride in an emotional experience of claustrophobic panic. In the last phrase, "one no longer knows if one is lying" the image flips direction, turning the other — the same — dark cheek, a ghostly presence. In this work translucency becomes darkness, a space of enclosure and fear, private, interior, inescapable.

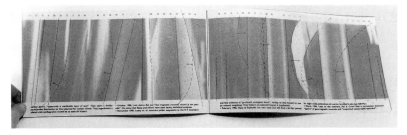

Lyle Rosbotham, **Extinction Event**, 1988

Lyle Rosbotham, in **Extinction Event** (Press 451, 1988), uses U.V. Ultra as a way of transforming or overdetermining meaning. This is a work about natural disasters as a statistically certain event — and on a scale likely to effect planet-wide devastation, if not outright destruction of the earth itself. Hence the name. This is an elegant work, with an elongated format, and sensuous black and white images printed on thick coated stock — images of movement, indistinct patterns of activity at an often indeterminate scale (ion chambers? red shift spectrograms? photo traces of microscopic refractions of light through organic matter?). The translucent pages layer onto these photographic images, in the first sheets simply marking out a cross-hair grid onto their field then moving in to diagram aspects of the photograph itself. A blurred out, stretched image of a freeway seen from below, its concrete swath cutting across the full length of the book, has blue marks charted against the grid, as if to analyze stress or fault lines through the structure of the photographed element below. Rosbothom terms this a "workbook." The accompanying text, printed to be read against a clear white margin below the photograph, is extracted from the work of astrophysicists who study "extinction event" phenomena

— the "Alvarez and Alvarez theory now prompts a search for the extraterrestrial mechanism that can bring debris into the solar system on a regular basis." A railroad track, a spot of light, the base of a streetlamp, a window open in a concrete structure — these are the photographic materials provided to "work" through the probabilities of the extinction event. Interspersed among these pages are frosted sheets of mylar printed with images of dinosaur and animal excavations — the grim reminder of what extinction means.

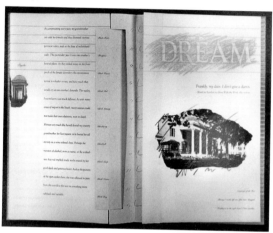

Susan King, **Lessonsfrom the South**, 1986

Translucency works as a textual manipulation as well. Susan King's **Lessonsfrom the South** (Nexus Press, 1986) used printed inks on a heavy vellum sheet. These sheets hold a hard fold, the crease of their edges functioning as a rigid element of the book structure. To open these folded sheets requires fighting their resistant impulse — consequently their interior spaces don't invite the reader in. The printing on the reverse side contains the title of each section — a fragment taken in sequence from the phrase "A Mid/Summer/Night's/Dream" — which appears muted, faint, and remote by contrast to the surface elements. The binding is a concertina variation — a structure in which a paper folded back and forth in small strips serves as the spine. The sheets of the pages are glued onto the concertina strips, giving the book an openness and breathing quality which bound books don't have.13 Folded into three parts, the panels of the pages layer onto each other making an interlined text in pale green and bright red typefaces she identifies as Goudy Oldstyle and Roundhand. King's work contains several levels of linguistic material — keywords in

the margin, notes in the spine, quotes on the section title pages and ongoing citations from "The Language of the Fan." The work is both conceptually and physically layered throughout, counterposing translucent and
opaque papers and inks and interweaving the themes of memory and
experience, expectations and actualities, filtering received knowledge
into consciousness.

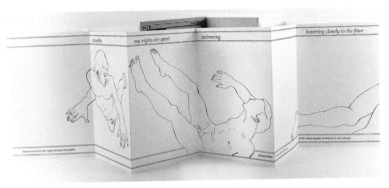

Keith Smith, Swimmer, 1986

Complex Structures

Further variations on the codex involve changing the structure of signatures into folds such as: accordion, concertina, french door, dos-a-dos,
and other folded or opening forms. Accordion books have the advantage
of creating a seamless continuous surface which is also broken up into discrete, page-like units. This allows the work to have the uninterrupted flow
of a scroll while also functioning as a book whose pages and openings can
be accessed at any point in the sequence. Keith Smith's **Swimmer** (1986)
takes full advantage of this aspect of the accordion-fold work. A continuous text runs along the work as a footer — linguistic and linear — while
the image of a naked male swimmer (dreamer?) floats through the blank
fluid space. The movement of the body renders the space liquid, unfet-
tered, unbound by limiting coordinates though it is literally the same surface which holds and supports the text. The duality of representation —
the tension between surface and illusion — is thus manifest as is the other
tension — that of flow and break which is the basic internal dialogue of a
book form.14 Part of Smith's skill is maximizing this tension even with the
large open drawing of a figure which crosses the boundaries between
what he calls the "frames" which are the panels of the accordion-fold
work.

140

The accordion is a popular form, and its adaptations are as varied as its producers. At the other extreme from Smith's activity of linking and repetition is the emphatic use of abrupt transition from space to space marked out in the accordion structure of the Brazilian Hugo Denizart's **Regiao dos desejas** (undated, presumably late 1980s).15 In this photographic work each turning reveals a new set of images linked by theme and underscored in their connection by an overall tone or color. Arranged in a long top-to-bottom accordion structure, the openings are radically distinct one to the next, with the complexities of photographic meaning multiplying within and across the breaks. The hard edge of the fold becomes a knife edge to vision, cutting through the continuity of thought as the field shifts from children to mothers from rich to poor from city to jungle in a multi-faceted visual experience. Editing, rather than verbal material, provides the "text" — the montage of juxtapositions demonstrating with vivid clarity the discrepancies of condition and situation among the photographed subjects.

Susan Bee and Charles Bernstein, **Fool's Gold**, 1991

In **Fool's Gold** (Chax Press, 1991) a collaborative project by Susan Bee and Charles Bernstein, printed by Charles Alexander, the accordion can be read back and forth, without particular linearity. Graphic elements override the folds, moving the eye through the work as a painterly field, letting the verbal elements interact without the constraints of page structures which generally determine their reading. The undeniable linear direction of fragments of language, as in the unpunctuated sentence, "Efficiency without reason is desperation" is given a counterpoint by the hooking, sweeping, or diagonal thrust of visual forms or by the placement of blocks of type at 90-degree angles, thus dislodging the dominant orientation from its insistent axis. Breaking and overtaking the folds, running off edges, floating in indeterminate space, objects and elements take the certainties of language and book conventions and throw them up for question. **Fool's Gold** integrates the fundamental feature of the accordion-fold book — the fact that its continuous surface can be used in imitation of the codex's discrete pages or to overcome those boundaries — into its thematic interrogation of the conventions of artifice and the artificial value of conventions. "Of course I take an interest in English as the host language," one of its resonant interior lines, points equally to the necessity for self-conscious attention to what is assumed to be normal, natural, and what is taken up for investigation — rather than for granted.

Another finely tuned use of the accordion-fold structure is Karen Chance's **Parallax** (Nexus Press, 1987). The title's reference to two irreconcilable points of view condenses the theme of the book — misperception. A gay man and straight man intersect in the course of their daily lives, their movements mapped across the vividly patterned real and fantasy spaces they inhabit. From bedroom to suburban streetscape to commuter train, office, and back home again, the two men's activities are connected in the narrative (they are in the same train car) through small windows cut in the pages. The book is printed in many colors on both sides of the paper, exploiting the printing medium by layering colors, patterns, and varied speckle tones to produce a work whose finish is densely saturated. As a result the rich images in the small peek-through sections function as framed vignettes of another life and consciousness. These cut-outs work two ways — the viewer looks first through one perspective and later, returning on the other side of the accordion sequence, from the other. The graphic manipulation is such that these two spaces work independently, emphasizing the difficulty of seeing from another's point of view. The duo-sided aspect of the accordion articulates a social division which cannot be crossed, and whose perforated spaces of intersection are only small irruptions in an otherwise habitual pattern of thought.

The concertina form permits the elements of a fixed codex sequence to have more physical space in it than a sewn or glued binding. The pages are separated from each other by the folded concertina spine onto which they adhere, or are sewn, so that their autonomy as pages is given more attention. Variations on the concertina abound, and it is a structure which also supports cut pages or other interior subdivisions or orderings. Though poets and literary publishers have tended not to make extensive use of book structures, Charles Alexander of Chax Press (originally Tucson now Minneapolis), used a concertina binding for a book which was a collaborative work of two poets, Kit Robinson and Lyn Hejinian, writing in responsive dialogue to each other. In **Individuals** (1988) each "page" is in essence two pages, a top and bottom strip, on which the text of one poet is printed letterpress. The articulation of the dialogue becomes an exchange of spaces, as well as linguistic remarks, through the sequence of the book.

Lyn Hejinian and Kit Robinson, **Individuals**, 1988

A "flag" structure which Susan King attributes to binder Hedi Kyle was the basis of **Women and Cars** (Paradise Press at Women's Studio Workshop, 1983) an offset printed book. The center of each "page" is a cut strip which can be moved independently of the top and bottom of the page. The images are photographic, printed in pale greyish pink, and the cut in the work disrupts the unitary sequence. The central strips can be aligned with or serve as a counterpoint to the top and bottom pieces of the page. Thus, the work presents the idea of the relation between women and cars and also, by its interruption of that representation, serves as a rethinking of the cultural category "women and automobiles." This counterpoint, embodied in the structure, reinforces the thematic reading of King's work just as it does in another such piece produced by Julie Chen, **Are You Listening?** (Flying Fish, 1992), in which the difficulties of conversational communication are marked out in the directionally opposed strips of alternating voices. To read or "hear" or see one side the viewer has to miss the other — thus making the physically irreconcilable duality of the page into a metaphor of social exchange. The two sets of opposing strips form the spiky, spatially aggressive character of the piece which reinforces the charged tension between defensiveness and hostility in verbal exchange.

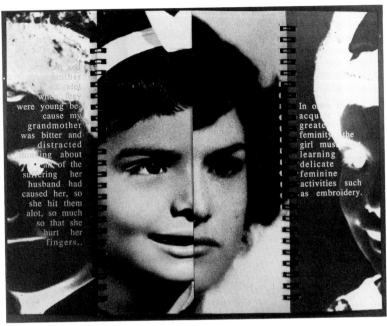

Ann Chamberlain, **Family Album / Album Familiar**, 1991

But codex bindings need not be singular or simple, either. "Dos-a-dos" and "french-door" formats allow an internal dialogue to develop within the structure of a work. Both of these are double codices — in one case bound back together so that two volumes share a back cover, each opening in the normal way from the front, in the second case, opening side by side, one half in a reverse of the conventional page turning pattern. Ann Chamberlain's **Lourdes: A Love Story** (1989), and **Family Album / Album Familiar** (1991) use a "french-door" format which is well-suited to address the theme of identity and family. **Lourdes** uses a spiral binding on each edge to hold the two sides of cut sheets in juxtapostion. These are images of Lourdes Menendez from her childhood to adulthood which have been blown up to match each other in scale. Turning the first flap one combines the image of a five-year-old with the image of a ten-year-old in a nearly synthetic whole, turning the second flap reveals the second half. On the inside or back of these flaps are texts — one from an interview with Menendez, the other from a book cited as **The Psychology of the Mexi-**

can by R. Diaz-Guerrero. Unlike the images, which form an uneasy but recognizable unity, the two texts are irreconcilable. The psychologist prescribes submission, marriage, and maternity as the fulfillment of the Mexican woman while the interview recounts specifics from Menendez's life — unprogrammatic and unformulaic. The split structure is the split identity of an individual (feminine) consciousness and social expectations for patterns of behavior. **Family Album** is slightly more complicated, using the successive pages of lapped french-door format to perform an exchange, interpenetration, of two aspects of family identity — maternal and paternal — but as in **Lourdes** the bifurcated structure establishes lines and limits whose broaching become significant through formal as well as thematic means.

Nance O'Banion and Julie Chen, **Domestic Science**, 1990

Hybrid and Spatial Forms

Many works make hybrid structures out of codex conventions to achieve their ends. **Domestic Science: Icons and Idioms**, by Nance O'Banion and Julie Chen (Flying Fish, 1990) uses an accordion form to hold a series of codices which in turn fold or open out. The book has a number of pop-up structures in it, and the openings become small interior spaces — as in the domestic interior suggested by the title. Brightly graphic, the work uses linoleum cuts with much surface area to produce a striking black page with white line work and hot fluorescent colors highlighting the whole. "Idioms" — like "to be floored" — which come out of or have some relation to the domestic environment proceed along one side of the base sheet's folds. On the other side the "Icons" open in their own extended accordion folds to detail metaphors which collapse mundane terms and psychosocial meanings. While much of the strength of this work derives from its graphic intensity, the unfolding structure gives it both physical and conceptual dimensions. One enters into the book, trapped and engaged in a way which would not occur if the same sheets simply followed in sequence.

Bookscape (1986-88) is a piece I made to address the inadequacy of any literary form I knew of to record or describe the experience of living in Dallas, Texas. The work is about literary form (not just in relation to the oddly alienating unfamiliarity of life in the "metroplex") as a set of conventions and traditions. The theme phrase of the work, "the book pretends to its own completeness" comments on the distinction between representation's apparent unity and the fragmentary, partial capacity of a work to represent a life. The tropes of narrative form, the conventions of bookmaking, and the absence of any clear legacy in which a feminist writer could find a history and place were all themes explored in this work — which took the form of a large, double-layered box of boxes. Tightly fitted to make a solid whole, the bookscape boxes each contained a book — around twenty in all — made with found materials, varied papers, and different methods of producing text (stencils, typewriter, handwriting, and so forth). The whole work can be set up as objects — each of the small books has enough substance to stand as a built form in the full landscape of the work — or to be looked at and read independently. Here, Mallarmé's whole book is a fragmented field unable to achieve even the final pretense of unity since each fragment both is and isn't a self-sufficient element while it functions as a part of the larger whole.

Other works which open out beyond the limits of the codex are folded works. These can be designed to function both as a codex, paged through sequentially according to the hinged edges of the piece, and as opened works, taking up floor or wall space with imposing graphic presence. Here again I discuss examples by Keith Smith because of their familiarity and because they are graphic and clear in their articulation of structure as a thematic element, not merely a material support. Smith has used the opening forms in several pieces, some in a format refined by Scott McCarney which they have named boustrephedon, for the Greek term describing the ancient practice of writing right to left and left to right (the word means "the way the ox plows"). Smith's Book 141 (1989) for instance, is comprised of a photograph printed onto twenty-five separate panels, all hinged together. The photograph is the stripped torso of a young man. Encountered piecemeal when the work is folded down the whole image is made available when the work is opened up in a play with the erotics of physical exploration and discovery. **Prepositional Space, Book 124** (1988) is a work Smith printed on panels from digitized images. Less overtly erotic than **Book 141**, the work has far more references to book structures within its imagery since it is an electronically produced image of an illusionistic drawing of a codex book with its pages being turned. While its iconography denies the immateriality of the electronic medium its form is a product of that technology — large in format and editioned on an Apple Imagewriter. The "preposition" may or may not be explicitly sexual — it is certainly an intellectual **proposition** about the illusory nature of the codex form — and its anticipated existence as a mere simulacrum of its former self.

Scott McCarney, **In Case of Emergency**, 1985

Both Scott McCarney and Clifton Meador have worked with the potential of the folding book. McCarney's **In Case of Emergency**, (Nexus Press, 1985) is designed with a bright "emergency" red cover closed with three yellow and black striped tabs in a standard "civil defense" pattern. The title is printed in stencil type, quoting the codes of emergency design. The text is appropriated from a cold-war era manual on emergency preparedness and steps to take in case of a nuclear attack. "It is a little difficult to open and extremely so to close," as Keith Smith has noted.16 He goes on

Clifton Meador, **The Book of Doom**, 1984

to add, "This is not accidental, as it suggests Pandora's box." The work is made of "two intersecting fold books" and the graphic patterns which link the pages allow connections to be made through motifs of bombs, extracted texts, jet trails, and mushroom clouds. The folded structure makes a matrix, rather than a sequence — not so much structuring it as unstructuring it. Meador's **Book of Doom** (Space Heater Multiples, 1984) by contrast, uses a regular pattern of unfolding pages to layer its apocalyptic elements into a full image.17 Inspired by 13th-century Spanish beatus texts with their focus on the apocalypse, **The Book of Doom** lives up to its title.18 Within the codex sequence the pages are folded so that their edges neatly lap, each extended just the same amount of margin beyond the previous, in a deceptively ordered universe. As each page unfolds, it turns out to have an open center, to serve as a frame around the hollow core. Each successive page narrows that core, lying on the previous page to make an image of intensifying implosion. The stencilled pages are edged with a savagely dark humored text beginning with "Men become aware of a strange dark star in the sky," and continuing with an image of late-model used cars falling into a deep dark pit of hell. The colors, the crudeness of the written marks, the rough but relentless patterns (influenced by African textiles) create a vision in which reason collapses, unsustainable under the sheer force of the hypocrisy and superficiality of modern consumerism. The regular sequence of the codex becomes a part of that machinery, equally relentless in its systematic evolution, while the painterly intensity of the surfaces — their images of cars, tires, rocket-

148

ships, and humans — has an air of the carnivalesque macabre, a dance of techno-destruction and doom.

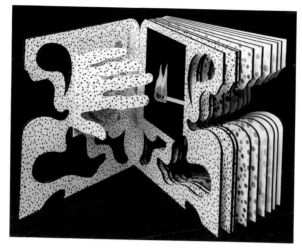

Lucas Samaras, **Book**, 1968

Interior Spaces

Books within books are another variation on the codex form. Two works which do this to very different ends are the landmark work by Lucas Samaras, **Book** (Pace Editions, 1968) and Susan Baker's **How to Humiliate your Peeping Tom** (Visual Studies Workshop, 1989). Both use books within the book as a means of expanding upon the graphically dense pages and the main themes of the text. Samaras' work refers to book making and book conventions many of which have been taken up by other artists (not all aware of this work). Samaras' "pages" are made of board cut in an organic pattern, full of large curved holes which echo the shape of the whole. Page is thus a violated surface, as much shape and sculpture as support for images or text. It is a play of patterned presences and equally deliberate absence — the dark tone of the plexiglass shows in the gaps as a black hole. The book recounts — in truly obsessive fashion — the exploits and adventures of first "Dickman," then "Shitman," and "Killman," and others. True to his name the first character is intent on outdoing Henry Miller in an endless cycle of sexually explicit encounters, many of which are merely masturbatory fantasies, and each of the characters plays out the suggestions of their name in similar fashion. The nonstop compulsive tone of the text is underscored by its typographic treatment — there are no breaks, indents, or openings anywhere in the solid blocks of text

149

set in six point (or smaller) copperplate type. Tiny little booklets of these texts are inserted into various openings — pockets, envelopes, folded enclosures — within the pages. These are highly patterned (a printed paper laminated onto the thick plexiglass sheets) — with multiple marks reminiscent of confetti, candy sprinkles, magic marker ticking, or some combination of these. The book has a slick, pop character — the image of hands — part cartoon, part real outline — dominates the first opening, covering the cut-out shape of a face. The book plays with itself — letting the elements be theatrical and mimetic, inscribing a drama of disclosure and revelation. In one opening a fork and knife face each other, in another the hand images move toward the gutter — always in a self-conscious recognition of the book's structure as a book. This is a pop comic of book-ness: the text is damned by its banality and by the absence of any really serious content beyond the raving sexual fantasies — which try to make themselves into as much of a pattern as possible.

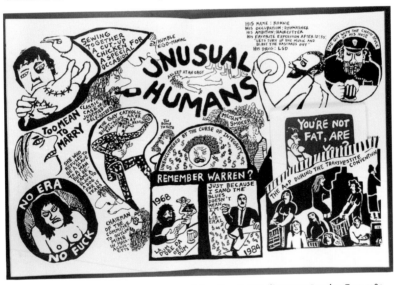

Susan Baker, **How to Humiliate Your Peeping Tom**, 1989

Susan Baker's work is far less monumental in materials or status. **How to Humiliate Your Peeping Tom** is a how-to book which uses biting humor to address self-image, identity, and insecurity issues which women live with. The book is at least as sexually charged as **Book** by Samaras, but its anecdotal, grounded-in-real life experiences quality belies pure aestheticism or the use of text as pattern. Baker's pages swarm with images and writing in a now classic 1980s "bad drawing" style. "Unusual humans," "My centerfold," and "All the guys I slept with in the 60s" are both parodic and sincere indictments of cultural norms. Baker's books within the book are developed inserts, real stories or asides which expand the nonexistent lacunae in the pages. In an already too dense field of graphic activity these extra entries push the sensory stimulation to a multidimensional pitch. One of these entries "You're not fat" tells the story of a single blind date while another "Car Log" shows in painfully drawn detail the many features of a trip or "six days of pain in the car." The book within a book format in Baker and Samaras's work amplifies the fixed structure by opening spaces within it. This inserts a spatial axis into the work which opens a window into the flat plane of the page and articulates a full text within it. Baker printed these inserts in blue ink to contrast them with the black and white field in which their pockets hold them. In Samaras's case the works are dense extensions of the patterning which makes the bits into a whole. The dimensions which they open are extensions rather than contrasts to the elements on the page. Books within a book expand the codex exponentially, embedding the exploded narratives or explications in the frame of the original, deceptively contained work. These mini-works are like tunnels out of the work or into its interior following rich veins of investigation or projection.

The counterpoint to the books which open out into other dimensions are books which contain discrete interior spaces. Maurizio Nannucci's **Some Texts** (Peter Weiermair, 1982) is bound so that most of its pages cannot be opened. They are printed, folded, but not trimmed, and thus the book reveals the production process as it conceals part of the text. Not simply to be read through the surface of another page (which would be impossible — the paper is opaque) these are spaces of enclosure and self-reference in a physical sense. Nannucci's work is about the relation between representation and factuality — to what extent can representation surpass its limitations by being about its own properties? "When red is red, blue is blue, and yellow is yellow" reads the first page — each statement printed in the ink it names. Type runs along the outside edges, tops, and inside places of the enclosed pages — pages bound uncut. "The missing poem is the poem" reads one line of blue type edging a closed sheet. Missing or blocked. Missing because blocked? Or merely blocked? The enclosed empty space becomes the lost space of an articulation unrecuperated in the book — but there as a space, present and unoccupied, indi-

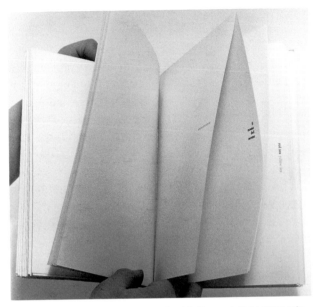

Maurizio Nannucci, **Some Texts**, 1982

cated but unfulfilled. This work literalizes the conceptual features of the book in its dis-functions and non-functions just as Smith's **String Book** literalizes the book in its sequential and material dimensions.19

Most of the works I have discussesd fit within a relatively small, familiar range of what passes for a book — from palm-sized to tablet-sized with the occasional wall pieces. But books have also been explored as spatial works of very large dimensions — big enough to wear, walk-through, and perform in. In 1967 Alison Knowles did a work called **The Big Book**. This was a huge work, with arms as long as the outstretched reach of an adult, all hinged onto a central pivot point. Collaged with photographic, painted, hung materials, shelves, objects, lamps, even a typewriter were all included in the piece. The form of this work was, overwhelmingly, that of a codex. Page followed page in this exaggerated version of the book. Knowles went on to even more ambitious projects, making a book-form maze or labyrinth which was an environment as much as a book, a room-sized work which took concepts of page, sequence, and turning into three-dimensional modes of expanded, exploded proportions. At a certain point these works, like those of other sculptural or installation artists, rely on a highly tenuous connection to the idea of the book. But Knowles' work made the concept of the book into an environmental experience in ways which broke new and now familiar ground.

Non-Codex Books

Non-codex forms include scrolls, which are few and far between. The form is so rigid as a means of access and sequencing that it has rarely appealed to artists. The renowned Sonia Delaunay and Blaise Cendrars collaboration, referred to earlier, is one notable exception. Rebis Press produced a scroll book in the late 1970s, **Jacob's Ladder** by Vicki Nelson, from a text which used that image as a major structural metaphor for the writing. In both cases, the work lent itself to a hanging or wall display more readily than to reading in the scroll form. Given its potent value as a symbol, it is surprising how few scrolls have shown up in the current book as object mania. In **Livres d'Artistes — Livres Objets**, a book-art-object exhibition from 1985, there are only three scroll works in the entire catalogue of 200 or so items.20 Of these, one **Sefer Thora** by Sylvia El Harar-Lemberg makes specific reference to "Judeo-Christian and Islamic liturgical objects which are the basis of my culture...." The other two emphasize the slow, restricted process of reading which the scroll structures into the work. Andre Lambotte, describing **Sans hiatus**, states that "the scroll cannot be apprehended all at once as a limited entity, but must be read... without beginning or ending." And Liliane Camier terms her **Untitled** handpainted scroll an "adventure in reading, a slow journey between the lines, plunging between pages as the pattern is unrolled." Though the reference to pages seems contradictory, these works emphasize aspects of the scroll which are not replicated in the conventional codex.

Other works which go beyond the codex or scroll form include box books or archives of documents, such as those discussed earlier, and works which have a geometric form which pushes them toward object status. One of the most famous of these is the tetrahedron form which Buckminster Fuller perfected for **Tetrascroll**. Fuller's work was produced in an edition with the assistance of Tatyana Grossman in 1977 (ULAE Inc, St. Martin's Press). It is a twenty-six page construction which folds into a thirty-six inch solid tetrahedron with four triangle faces. Each page has a text and a drawing with an analysis and projection of sane solutions to real problems — reasoned, realistic, and holistic. The work proclaims its vision of a balanced and functional universe. **Tetrascroll** could be unfurled to a full scroll length of forty-feet, but was engineered to fold and link into a sequence of solids. Neither codex nor, really, scroll-like in

form, this work, like all of Fuller's pieces, was both proposition and resolution of an idea in form.21 More significantly within the history and vision
of the book, Fuller's work takes the idea of book as a series of surfaces in
sequence into a rethought set of relations.

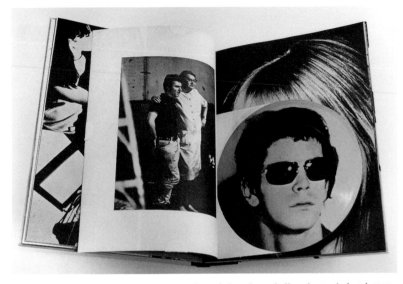

Andy Warhol, **Andy Warhol's Index Book**, (1967), NYPL

There are other structures which extend the book into a spatial
domain — such as tunnel books and pop-up works. There is a tendency for
such works to be more structure than content, cute and gimmicky rather
than actually for reading or interaction in an open-ended way. However,
both tunnel and pop-up forms find a wide and ready popular audience.
Andy Warhol's Index Book (Random House, 1967) "helped open up possibilities for artists who were interested in the form of the book."22 This
early work, like Knowles' large-scale books, codified techniques which
have been used by many artists who are unaware of its existence as a
precedent — as well as many who were. Very much a trade publication,
Warhol's work was both commodity and investigation of commodity — not
so much critique as reification. Warhol's pages of highly fashionable
underground and mainstream photographs of glamorous people in
extreme poses, lighting, and costume, are punctuated by the pop-up
appearance of such merchandise as a bottle of ketchup or a can of tomato
paste with all its proper labelling and illusionistic attributes. While the
transformation of the book as a structure had been ongoing in the course

of the 20th century, there had been less self-conscious attention to the artist's book as a place in which to examine books in relation to production and commerce. Though it would be specious to make Warhol's **Index** into a self-conscious analysis of the book as a commodity, it makes sense to put it within the framework of his other works — with all of their complex ambiguities about identity of object/art/commodity. If no other book of the 1960s embodied the book as commodity, Warhol's pop-up does — intruding this unwanted status into the realm of the book just as abruptly as the cans of vegetables intrude into the seamless glamour images of its pages. It is the one pop-up work which seems to sense the irony and specific peculiarity of trying to make the conceptual space of the book into a physical space — the transformation of idea and illusion into physical, literal, object — with all the reductive force which such transformations effect upon the open ended form of the codex.

The Book in the Electronic Field: Immaterial Structures
Finally, while considering book structures, it seems worth at least musing on the question of the electronic spaces of the book. There are several major ways that electronic media reorganize access to the conventional features of books as information. One of these is the book as archive. The archive concept suits electronic media because digital storage can contain vast amounts of information and even offer simulacral documents on the screen. The notion of the archive is at once hierarchical and diagrammatic and also, because it is so structured, is also openly accessible. Like a good filing system, the archive has an apparent order to it, and if one imagines an elaborate tree diagram in which a logic of categories and subcategories is followed through with precision and care, then the archive offers a means of structuring knowledge through organization — as well as through the information it contains.23 But an archive need not be merely an encyclopedic or dry treatise on knowledge — it can also be as rich as a personal inventory of information or the interlocking data bases of spy thrillers, voyeuristic lurkers, or other obsessive record keeping.

Another form of electronic manipulation is the book as a hypertext. In hypertext formats elements of the ongoing linear text are points of access to another area of the text base. Though each individual section may unfold in a linear manner, the strings of text loop into and out of each other in a mutable sequence. Thus a story may be told from multiple points of view, a reader may access one or more of these either in turn or through cross-cutting. Certain hypertext programs allow the reader to write into the text, thus transforming it, its content, theme, structure, or outcome. In a strict sense, a hypertext is not narrative, since it is a linked set of possible text strings, rather than a single text. Hypertext can be accessed passively, letting the story follow a course set by the writer as it scrolls on the screen, or actively, by the reader's expression of preferences at points where the story forks. Crude though it may be, this can be compared to reading a newspaper or magazine in which multiple stories proceed through the pages with "continued on" instructions moving the reader through the maze of fragments. Inevitably one reads across the columns of print, rather than simply following a single story, thus making a primitive hypertext montage of the elements. In hypertext these montages and connections are deliberately worked up to make the whole text into a web of relations linked through the tissue of that network — there are spots one can't leap across — you have to move through the connecting strings, forks, or stories.

The last electronic book is the book as a field, a floating matrix of information not linked by hierarchical diagrams or by story strings. The paths through such fields have to be imagined in a spatial/dimensional model, though that is merely a visual abstraction. But if one imagined a three-dimensional matrix along three coordinate axes — height, depth, width, in which elements were organized either randomly or by affinity, then the "reader" would browse by moving through the field in a manner I have always envisoned as that of the "diving mouse" — a mouse with a three-dimensional playing field, not a two-dimensional screen. Such a process would have little to do with conventional narrative or reading patterns, and instead, function through free montage. If each of the encountered modules also had the potential to expand through a time-quotient (imagine individual filmic units) then an internal set of time-based factors would also function within the structuring of the "text."

It is clear that certain conventions of the codex form — hierachical organizations of information, some indexing and access devices — will find their simulacral equivalent in the electronic "book." It is also evident that there will be new paradigms and parameters to the ordering, structuring, and experiencing of books as technologies facilitate new patterns of thought and creativity. Whether these forms will be so different from present-day books that it becomes impossible to envision them as new versions of an old idea or whether they become radically new, it's clear

that electronic and conventional media are forging new forms and definitions of the book as we know it.

1 Douglas Mcmurtrie, **The Book: The Story of Printing and Bookmaking** (Dorset, 1943) p.16.

2 See McMurtrie, "Paper and Its Origins," **The Book**, pp.61-75.

3 Mary Miller, in a lecture at the Yale University Art Gallery, February 10, 1995, on Mayan Painting. Miller made the point that paper existed in such quantities that it was wasted — burnt, thrown out, used carelessly in the 8th century A.D..

4 I find many of these become gimmicky of form, except in the most whimsical or sophisticated works, but they are frequently big crowd pleasers and I will leave their detailed exaltation to someone more sympathetic to their virtues.

5 Snow is best known as an independent filmmaker, and the book shows the influence of structuralist film in its rigor.

6 Anne Moeglin-Delcroix, "Qu'est-ce qu'un livre d'artiste?" in **Les Allieés Substantiels ou le Livre d'artiste au Present**, Actes du Colloque de la 2ieme Biennale du Livre d'Artiste, 28 & 29 Sept. 1991, Uzerche, Pays-Paysage, France (1993) has an excellent analysis of this book, and my remarks here have been influenced by that reading.

7 There is a complex issue to be developed here I have to at least sketch out. Ferdi-nand de Saussure, in constructing his model of the semiotic sign in the famous **Cours de Linguistique Générale** (**The Course in General Linguistics**, the basis of modern structuralist thought published from notes taken at Saussure's lectures given in 1907-11) described the two aspects of the sign (the acoustic image and the mental image, or the signifier and the signified as they are known in semiotic parlance) as discrete but inseparable — just like two sides of a sheet of paper. The manipulation which Snow makes of the paper sheet here as an illusion of real space which is impossible except as representation would make an interesting point of departure for semiotic analysis.

8 Maurice Lemaitre's **Roman Hypergraphique** will be treated in a later chapter, how-ever.

9 Standard books on binding are also useful for production and Dover Books has issued several of these in inexpensive formats, such as Pauline Johnson's **Creative Bookbinding** and A.W. Lewis's **Basic Bookbinding**.

10 Here, and throughout, see Keith Smith's notes on these forms in **The Structure of the Visual Book** (Keith, 1984, revised and expanded 1992, with even newer editions of this and **Non Adhesive Binding** forthcoming in 1995). He also has many more exam-ples of each and a more technical description of their construction.

11 McMurtrie, **op.cit.**, p.18.

12 I used this same device in a book I did in 1980, **'S Crap 'S Ample**, which I made as a

portrait — with the evident aspects of the person's character visible on the top page flaps and the unconscious elements of interior life on increasingly remote areas of the flap in smaller sizes of type.

13 In this case, unfortunately, the concertina strips were cut to form the flaps for attachment — the result is that the spine has a bowed quality along the cuts which doesn't quite hold up to wear. Though I like this book very much, there are aspects of its design that are not perfectly worked out.

14 See Smith's discussion of the complexities of this work in **The Structure of the Visual Book**, p.133-37.

15 Hugo Denizart is an artist I know only through this one work, found browsing the online catalogue of the New York Public Library.

16 Smith, **Structure of the Visual Book** (1992 edition) p.205.

17 This book was produced as "process color spray paint" — red, yellow, blue, and black sprayed through stencils. A Space Heater Multiple, the labor on the book was done by Meador (with Zimmermann buying materials) at a time when he didn't have access to other printing equipment.

18 This detail from Meador.

19 An interesting book to mention here is **Five Kwaidan in Sleeve Pages** by Karl Young (Chax Press, 1986) — again, a literary work rather than a bookwork it nonetheless demonstrates the printer Charles Alexander's sensitivity to the intersection of the two modes. The pages of Young's book are not merely uncut, they are reglued at their bottom, thus making the "sleeve" pages referred to in the title. The hidden text becomes a dimension of the book which can only be looked at obliquely, keeping itself from the sharp forthright gaze of the world, only revealing itself in a private reading. This is an agoraphobic gesture of publishing and writing in secret which is presented, yet, still marked with the signs of its hiddenness.

20 **Livres d'Artistes — Livres-Objets**, (Shakespeare International, Editions C.E.R.P.M., 1985) all citations are taken from the artists' notes on their own work, but the pages are unnumbered in the catalogue.

21 There are other examples of polyhedron extensions of the book as page/sequence/surface such as Barbara Fahrner and Daniel Kelm's **The Philosopher's Stone**.

22 Clive Phillpot, **op.cit.**, p.109.

23 This idea goes back to 17th century attempts to organize human knowledge in obvious and self-evident schematic outlines. The most complete outline ever achieved in this process was that of Bishop John Wilkins, who hierarchized every feature of the spiritual and physical universe so that he could make a universal language scheme to which it corresponded. The idea of a language system which is isomorphic with knowledge was the impetus behind Wilkins' work, and he invented such a scheme as well as a notation system in which to write it out. Wilkins' **An Essay Towards a Real Char-**

acter was published in 1666. See John Knowlson, **Universal Language Schemes in England and France 1600-1800** (University of Toronto Press, 1975).

Jan Voss, **Detour**, 1989

7

Self-Reflexivity in Book Form

Artists' books are often self-conscious about the elements of book structure. This can involve self-reflexive humor or serious philosophical interrogations of a book's identity. Disturbing conventions of reading by calling attention to these structures is often a feature of artists' books through an emphasis on the features of the page and pointing to the book as a whole. But a book can also be a self-conscious record of its own production — it can simply examine itself as a proposition — one laden with specific ideas about the ways a book can embody an idea through its material forms. There are really two subtexts here. One is the "idea of the book as idea" — the self-reflexive creation of books which are about being books, or what a book can be as an idea in form. The other is the "idea of the book as art idea" — which takes these investigations of the book into a dialogue with the concept of art, and shows that books are an art idea.

Self-Conscious Attention to Book Structure

Self-consciousness and self-reflexivity in any art form require a critical language which describes structures and methods. Such a language is termed "metacritical" — it is able to articulate critical issues rather than engage with formal or thematic concerns. There is always an aspect of metacritical thought to any work which calls attention to itself and its production. The familiarity of the basic conventions of books tends to banalize them: the structures by which books present information, ideas, or diversions, become habitual so that they erase, rather than foreground, their identity. One can, in other words, forget about a book even in the course of reading it. A book can simply work in a fine and functional way. But when a book calls attention to the conceits and conventions by which it normally effaces its identity, then it performs a theoretical operation. In critical parlance, one could say that such work calls attention to its own processes of **enunciation** (the acts of speaking, representing making a

161

work) rather than allowing a work to be enunciated (spoken as if it were naturally there). Self-conscious attention to the means of enunciation often lay bare the devices of literary or visual strategies of illusionism — as when a character in a novel addresses the reader about the fact that he or she is a character in a novel. The classic in this genre is the 18th-century novel, **Tristram Shandy** (1786), by Lawrence Sterne, which was one of the first novels in the English language and was also clearly aware of the novel's conceits and conventions.

Artists who focus on the elements of book structure are frequently making similarly self-conscious gestures from within the conventions of bookmaking. They show a margin, gutter, page, or frame to be both **the thing that it is** and also, show an awareness of the features that form the identity of that element. These self-conscious acts need not be tautological — a book need not be composed, for instance, of a text which uses only the word "text" in the main block, "running head" above, or "footnote" below in order to announce its self-consciousness. This reductive attention sometimes has its place in a preliminary study or examination, but the critical investigation of the "bookness" of the book can be far more resonant in its particular attention to an individual "text," "running head" or "image." Here again one could invoke Tom Phillips' **A Humument** for its analyses of almost every feature of a page through a deconstructive demonstration of its form without ever straying from a creative activity. In Phillips' work the idea of what a margin is becomes materialized, excavated, turned inside out so that the reader/viewer can see just what it is.

Self-conscious attention to the book form occurs at many levels. The book can be examined according to the conventions of the page — and the page in turn examined according to literary and/or visual traditions of form, layout, and illusion. Secondly, the book can be examined as a whole, as an entity, and an object. A book can call attention to the external factors which determine its structure or the book can become an object whose structural features are its subject matter. Finally, a book can be about the process of its own making — either its conception or production, or both. All of these elements can interact, playing with each other across the full field of the book, for instance, Helen Douglas and Telfer Stokes' **Real Fiction** is a work which incorporates a wide range of such processes in its finished form.

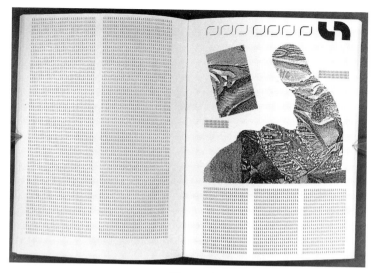

Ulises Carrión, **For Fans and Scholars Alike**, 1987

Conventions of the Page

The features of the page can be approached through the literary conventions of the text in all of its many linear, non-linear, and spatial forms. A page can also be analyzed in terms of its use of visual conventions such as the page as a flat field, a window, or a printed sheet taken literally, treated abstractly, or conceptually. Many pages combine elements of both visual and literary conventions.

Literary Conventions

Over the centuries, text and book formats have evolved a specialized internal organization to facilitate their communicative potential. Footnotes, endnotes, marginalia, head, gutter, flyleaf, running heads and footers, the table of contents, indices, and title pages are all codified book elements which are shared by other printed forms such as magazines or newspapers. These elements are so codified that they can be quoted without any verbal content, as shapes and forms on the page and function as a self-conscious investigation.

In **For Fans and Scholars Alike** (Visual Studies Workshop Press, 1987), Ulises Carrión composed pages which are organized in graphic terms but do not contain any specific verbal or visual messages. The text blocks on these pages are tightly laid out, shaped around the opening of image elements so that they make frames, windows, and spaces for those images in the exact manner of magazine or book layouts. But these blocks are composed entirely of the letter "i," with "headlines" made of brackets in bold and semibold weights. The image blocks have more information — they are patterns of graphic marks at various levels of legibility. At one extreme they are merely marks — gridlike lines or tonal values extracted from a larger image, blown up, and taking up space as if they comprised a readable image. At the other end of Carrión's spectrum, these images are snippets of leaves, or of wrinkled cloth, architectural fragments, or washes suggesting sky, water, or ground. The cover is a simple grey paper wrapper, with the same pattern of "i"s as in the interior. The format of the pages changes from double to single to triple columns and back again. Heads and subheads stretch all or part of the way across these units, the image blocks have nice gutters of space around them and are "captioned" in slightly smaller, denser "text" blocks. The book displays a self-conscious level of organization as a structural feature of a work, not necessarily tied to the production of meaning in the pedestrian sense. But the book is neither nonsense (silly gibberish) nor without sense (meaningless) — instead it presents structure as meaning, as the sum total of means for producing meaning, and thus offers structure to our view for analysis.

What distinguishes Carrión's book from the work of many concrete poets is that he attends to the book form as a whole, not only to the forms and structures of work on a page.1 It is the right hand page of each opening which bears headlines and images, while the left page (the verso of each sheet) has only "text" blocks. The sequential reinforcement of this through forty-eight sheets or ninety-six pages gives the visual analogue a reinforcement it wouldn't have as a single page exercise. There are other visual artists who have drawn the pages of newspapers, tabloids, and magazines in schematic form in ways which complement Carrión's work. Mertha Dermisache's **Diario no.**1 (Guy Schraenen, ed., 1975), like Carrión's piece, "interprets" a newspaper layout with an invented sign language of glyphs. But a book work which serves as an inversion of **For Fans and Scholars Alike** was **The Shooting of Pope John Paul II.**2 This work is composed of newspaper front pages which give accounts of the assassination attempt on the Pope. The event serves as a common point of reference, thus, the difference in the relation between format and the communication of meaning is foregrounded. The ways in which the layout and graphics emphasize certain aspects of the event rather than others becomes strikingly clear and though this is not a book about book-ness, it is a work in which format issues are accentuated.

Book elements have standard sites on the page and thus these locations come to carry a certain value. Alastair Johnston's **Heath's German Dictionary** (Poltroon Press, 1975) contains only beginning and ending words for dictionary pages. These words, standing at the top of the page, above a line of rule, straddling the page numbers, enclose a field of nonexistent entries. So "bunk" and "burst" on page "62" are next to "bursting" and "butt" on page 63. Though each opening preserves its even/odd paired numbers, and the page numbers progress as the book moves from front to back, there are as many leaps in numbering as there are leaps in concept. A leap-frog ride through associations in language, the work functions as a text but also suggests the absent text of the dictionary whose accidents of extraction in those headers are experienced as a found poem.

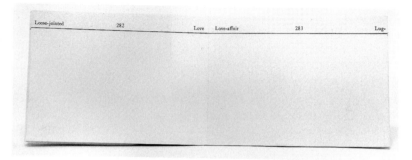

Alastair Johnston, **Heath's German Dictionary**, 1975

Attention to conventions can extend to the form of a book as a literary type — the use of index tabs, referred to earlier in the discussion of El Lissitzky's design for Mayakovsky's **For the Voice** (1923) is a case in point. Dick Higgins' **foew&ombwhnw** (Something Else Press, 1969) is designed to look like a bible. Bound in black leatherette, the book has a black woven page marker and the edges of its pages are stained deep red and its corners trimmed to a decorous curve. The interior pages of the work, which is subtitled "a grammar of the mind and a phenomenology of love and a science of the arts as seen by a stalker of the wild mushroom," are divided into two columns with a thin line of rule between them. Thus each opening spread is four columns across, each column topped by its own running head in delicate italic type. Subheadings in bold break up the pages, the paragraphs are neatly justified, except where they contain verse. There are occasional diagrams, drawings, or photographs, but not so many that

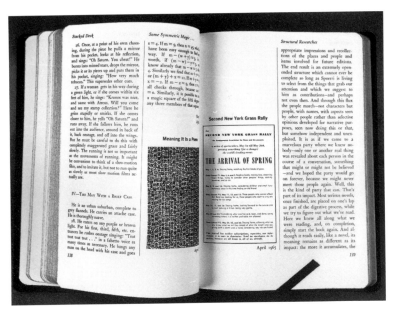

Dick Higgins, **foew&ombwhnw**, 1969

the constrained and religious look of the pages is disturbed. The biblical quality of the object (the thin paper, small serious black type, stained edges) gives its contents a particular cast — is this meant to be interpreted as a guide to new spirituality, a blasphemous slur on biblical texts, or a playful creative vision? The reading proceeds through each column independently. Each of the four spaces are on a specific theme — essays on asthetics and "intermedia," poems which detail personal life and observations, texts for performance pieces, and so forth. The character of a column can change, for instance, the contents of the column at the far right of the page, at first highly theoretical, ends up containing sections "from Thunderbaby's Book." Thunderbaby is a monster (a tantrum-throwing visionary infantile ego) whose fragmented ravings are part genius, part child, part idiot. Because of the careful order with which the book's format codes these elements they gain a certain respectability though the non-integrative aspect of the contents overrides the unifying biblical look of the work.

From A to Z (Druckwerk, 1977) was my most sustained exercise in using conventions of the literary page to structure a creative work. This letterpress book, an elaborate **roman a clé**, parodying the work and attitudes of poets encountered in the Bay Area in the mid-1970s, has every possible

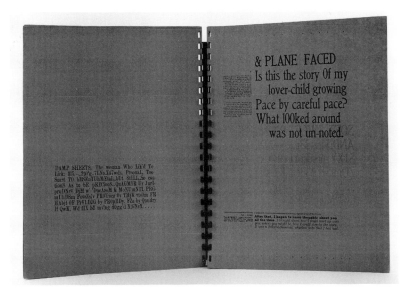

Johanna Drucker, **From A to Z**, 1977

form of appendix. The title page, table of contents, introductory notes, and so forth contain elaborate amounts of information about the characters in the book — who are each designated by both a letter of the alphabet and the number which corresponds to the place of that letter in alphabetic sequence (e.g., B=2). The interior pages, one for each character, are divided into running heads and footers, marginal notes, main text, and footnotes which are further subdivided into marginalia, headings, and subheadings. The placement of each element on the page establishes its relation to the text as a whole and to the same element on each succeeding page. For example, a narrative of an infatuation which character A has with character Z is worked out across the headlines and subtexts of the footnotes, while subliminal emotional reactions, sexual innuendo, and fantasmatic thoughts of each of the two characters find their own specific place around those notes as marginalia. Each page also bears a full poem on the recto, as well as bibliographic information about the source of the work, its critical reception, and so forth on the verso. Marginal notes in the upper half of the page recount conversations, letters, and other exchanges among the book's characters. All references are made by letter name "P" did such and such to "A" at a poetry reading by "X" so that the work is entirely self-referential. The sources for these marginalia are explained in the endnotes. The work was generated from the type in forty-eight drawers of lead letters (each to be used once and only once). Thus the legibility of the texts in the sections vary as letters in each size and typeface were gradually exhausted. By the time the endnotes were set, for instance, many substitutions of punctuation, dollar signs, uppercase letters, and other inventions were necessary to produce meaningful (but highly cryptic) statements.3

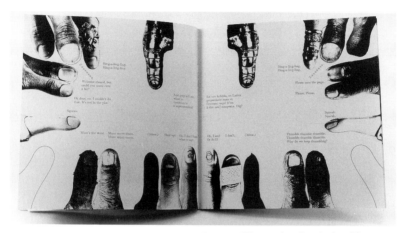

Emmett Williams and Keith Godard, **Holdup**, 1980

Visual Conventions in the Page

The self-conscious use of literary conventions increases the readers' awareness that there are such conventions and that they help structure meaning. The visual elements of the page structure are more elusive in their meaning — while a running head, for instance, reminds a reader of their place in the text, neither a gutter nor a margin is assigned a particular symbolic role. Both serve a visual function — to contain the text block, keep the spine from appearing to swallow the type, and generally improve legibility. Both gutter and spine are created in the making of the book — the gutter in the binding and the margin through decisions about the trimming. They may seem to perform passive functions which facilitate rather than contribute to the meaning of a page. But in an artist's book, these elements often become points of focus for the investment of meaning. In a collaborative project by Emmett Williams and Keith Godard, **Holdup** (Works, 1980), the margin of the page becomes a dramatic space. Godard and Williams use the edge of the sheets as the edge of a stage. They take advantage of the fact that it is the literal edge on which a reader's fingers normally rest in reading, and that it is a point of demarcation between what is presented and what is absented from the page. One after another, fingers of different shapes, sizes, colors, and degrees of grooming make their appearance. The book is humorous, each finger is the **pars pro toto** representative of a full personality. The fingers are printed photographically, in black and white, while an accent color of green is used for the spoken dialogue the fingers exchange as well as for overprinted areas representing fingernail polish, jewelry, tattoos, and other distinguishing features. The margin is the only active space of the book, the fingers being too small to penetrate to the center of the page, and an empty outline of a thumb is printed at the lower edge of both left and right pages so that the reader's own digit can participate in the action by occupying that space. By literalizing the margin, making it the site of a representation which could pass for an illusion of reality, the book uses as its only active area a stretch of space usually left completely blank. The frame is the work, rather than its boundary, and the permeability of that boundary promotes the action which is the content of the book.

Not all investigations of the visual elements of the codex form are apparent as this work by Godard and Williams. Margins are an obvious spot for intrusion and penetration, the play of the boundary between book and world, illusion and reality. But gutters are the spaces where the page opening goes into the binding. They are the unconscious of the book — a dark area of repressed activity which seeps into the book's open spaces subverting its autonomy. In **Rising Converging** (1988), Clifton Meador uses the gutter in a threatening and insidious manner, indicating a seepage from one area of global activity to another. The book consists of two signatures of four sheets each, reinforcing its binariness. The cover of the offset printed work (its title printed letterpress in silver ink), which looks like a pamphlet, has the close-up image of an exploding volcano with dark, thick rolls of billowing smoke rising from the naked cone. Iconographically the image resembles a mushroom cloud, the sign of apocalyptic disaster in our time, but is actually an image of a "natural" disaster. The tension between these two categories is the topic of the work, and the back cover shows the same image overprinted with a swirling mass of marbling. A vortex of pink and green and bright yellow ink churns over the image of explosion turning it into pure chaos. But it is in the interior structure that this book uses gutters to insinuate its message into the work. The first opening is of an old volcanic cone rising from a desert landscape. Yellow ink suffuses the black and white image, flushing the

Clifton Meador, **Rising Converging**, 1988

scene with unnatural intensity. The first images in this signature are "natural" scenes — landscapes with plants and animals in desert, mountain, plain — into which, two thirds of the way through, human figures enter on horseback. As the openings proceed, the margins turn into a strip toned with colored ink, but the image area stops — almost as if there is a mistake in the printing or trimming of the book. After several pages this "error" shows up in the center of the book, in the gutter. A bright streak or orange-toned image area (with fragments of zebra stripes, a carryover from an earlier image) suddenly erupts in the midst of a red scene of wooly mammoth-like creatures. On the next page a bright yellow strip of cacti (from the earlier desert scene) rises through the converging space of two pages of blue-toned imagery. On one level this merging of worlds is the meaning of the title, **Rising Converging**. However, as the book moves into the second signature, across an opening which seamlessly matches two sides of a green-toned view of a mountain valley with a winding road on which a truck descends a circuitous path of hairpin turns, the nature of the convergence is transformed. The interrupting imagery in the gutter turns violent in color — harsh, clashing red, green, and yellow stripes break into images which depict men with weapons. The imagery proceeds from arrows to airplanes and on the full pages bright hard triangular patches of tone add a disjunctive harshness. The interrupting strips fade out of the picture as the book goes on, but the message is clear: the relation of humans to their environment has the same destructive force as this "convergence" of images. The gutter, a place of non-action, a normally passive site erupts into violence, asserting its latent potential for power in the structure of the book.

Jan Voss, **Detour**, 1989

In **Detour** (Boekie Woekie, 1989) Jan Voss activates the fore-edge of the book.4 This is the outside part of the pages which turn into a surface when the book is closed and which is sometimes decorated with marbling, paint, or gilding, but which rarely plays a role in relation to the book's interior structure. In **Detour** a wandering line makes the images which sustain a continuous frieze throughout its two hundred pages. Other line work completes each page, but the basic movement of the work is achieved by the drawn images which work around the pages, wrapping over their edge, and moving onto each succeeding page. The front and back covers depict two small figures, each holding onto one end of what looks like a thin rope — the "line" of the book — which they pull on as if in a tug of war. It is this line which, in the course of wrapping page to page, shows up on the front edge of the book. Since the pages are printed on one side only of their surface and folded at their fore-edge (the open ends of the sheets are bound into the spine) there is enough area to sustain a tiny, pixilated contribution to a whole image. The bulk of the two hundred edges, aligned and shut, carries the image of a figure in the midst of a landscape, clouds above, water below. The book is simple and yet overwhelming in its epic scale and the sheer volume of drawing sustained in its pages, and this final touch integrates the interior and exterior faces of the work. A hint of the interior is glimpsed on its edge, though that edge disappears as soon as the book is opened — nor does the fore-edge image repeat the interior images, rather, it supplements them with its own integrity, activating another latent site for meaning in the book form.

The Literal Page

The literalness of a page — either as a blank surface or as a field of color — is another visual convention which can be imbued with meaning through self-conscious reflection. In Giovanni Anselmo and Gian Enzo Sperone's **116 Particolari** (1975) a binarism of black ink on white paper is set up to articulate a system of difference so that the relation of these two elements becomes meaningful. Almost all of the pages are entirely black, and the dark scene of the book becomes a space defined by this unified color field. Into this dark unity come occasional areas of white space, geometrically defined from the edge, a triangular cut of white light across one corner of a page. There are also a few pure white pages. Because the book contains no other variation in its sequence of darkness, these interruptions serve as a signifying break. In the finite pagination of the work the alternation of black, white, and parti-colored sheets differentiate from each other. In this instance the book is only structure, and meaning, such as it is, exists only at the level of form. Though quite different in concept and execution, this is not dissimilar to the formal manipulations of Keith Smith's **Book 91 (The String Book)**, (discussed in Chapter 6) and the punched, folded, and torn paper in George Maciunas's, **Flux Paper Events** (Hundertmark, 1976). Though the notion of meaning becomes collapsed through the manipulations of the pages and other elements of these works, they continue to function as books through their finitude and the boundary which such a limit imposes. The book is the framework within which these forms can be related in a significant way.

Color also plays a part in structuring a book, though its conventions are far less rigorously coded. The red and black opposition so familiar

Helen Douglas and Telfer Stokes, **Desire**, 1989

from the history of printing, for instance (and whose history goes back to Egyptian papyri in which the opening phrases of each paragraph were distinguished by red ink — a format picked up by the Romans and thus passed into printing conventions in Western Europe), is also a standard feature of 20th-century artists' books. The red and black on the bright white page is a standard element of Russian Constructivist design. This combination has become detached from its manuscript and fine printing background to serve as the visual code of "modern avant-garde." But outside of this convention, the use of color becomes a matter of context, effect, and deployment. Though color is often used in images, or even for differentiating registers of language, there are few instances of the use of color to structure a work rather than merely filling out an existing structure. I am differentiating here between a work in which color enriches a page and a work in which color makes relations on pages or among pages which would not exist in its absence. In **Desire** (Nexus Press and Weproductions, 1989), Telfer Stokes and Helen Douglas's book, a bright blue line which appears in some form on every right-hand page becomes a unifying "thread" — both referentially and literally — through the work. This book, which abounds in color — bright, neon, intense fields of color which fill the backs of the sheets and support the fragmentary text and images of their fronts — uses this device to provide continuity. The work has no single narrative, no evident sequence in the pages, and its sheer density fights the reader's own desire to unify the complex field of activity into a single work. But these bright lines — which twist and contort through the other elements on the page — referring to fence wires in their knotted ends and interlinking patterns — provide this. The lines are both surface and illusion — literally appearing as bright blue lines and also staging the page as a field glimpsed through wire fencing. The blueness of the lines is conspicuous, and thus, effective.

There are many other ways in which color functions within artists' books — and some of these will be discussed in the next chapter — "The Book as a Visual Form." However, the book's self-consciousness about visual conventions of the page brings in references to pictorial traditions. I distinguish these from literary traditions in so far as pictorial traditions invoke the possibility of a representational illusion in which the page functions as picture plane. An image may use the page as visual support without focusing on the way in which edges, orientation, and the possibility of illusion function within the book. An early practitioner of experimental typography, Filippo Marinetti, used the field of the page as a structure for the distribution of verbal elements in accord with pictorial conventions in his 1919 publication **Mots en Liberté (Words in Liberty)**. He structured his "Battle at nine levels" as a "pictorial" image — using a schematic diagram of a mountain rendered with typographic elements. By taking advantage of both the visual structure and linguistic value he doubled the potential of the page. It is both a picture and a poem.

In **Voy Age**, (Hansjörg Mayer, 1975) Emmett Williams carries this idea through an entire book work, and makes the book into a kind of filmic work. In punning short-phrase sequences, he describes a sea voyage in succinct and humorous language: "cam / era / poe / try / act / ion." The words are laid out on the page like the images of sky and sea with a horizon line between (invisible, but implied) and the ship of language moves through this page. As the work progresses, the ship begins to move away, into the distant horizon and to indicate this, Williams shrinks the typeface, letting this diminishment indicate increasing distance as it would in a perspectival rendering. The visual field thus become spatialized, acquiring a dimension which it did not have in the first sequences — those which merely used the page as a pictorial structure. Williams' work uses visual conventions without relying on pictorial means — the pages and their sequence are an image though no pictures are present. The back cover of the book shows a full schematic outline of the movement of text as it proceeds through the pages.

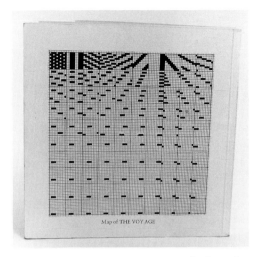

Emmett Williams, **Voy Age**, 1975 (back cover)

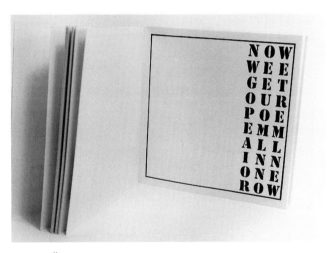

Emmett Williams, **Voy Age**, 1975,
courtesy of Arts of the Book Collection, Sterling Memorial Library, Yale University

There are other visual conventions, for instance — the act of turning
or opening of a page is inherently visual as well as temporal and spatial.
Ellen Lanyon's **Transformations** (Chicago Books, 1982) combines the
metamorphosis of each succeeding image in a book-length sequence with
a clear demarcation of the edge of the page and its turning.5 This use of
the edge of the page to manipulate the tension between continuity and
discontinuity is so fundamental to the book form that it shows up in many

Ron King, **Turn Over Darling**, 1990, courtesy NYPL

works. In every book a decision has to be made about how to either emphasize, ignore, or overcome the fact that the openings are discrete units, separate spaces, each from the next and yet part of a continuous whole. Ron King's **Turn Over Darling** (Circle Press, 1990) makes this separation into a unity by calling attention to the physicality of the sheet of paper. Here, the images are impressed into the thick paper so that they form a relief. The image is of a woman's body — top or bottom half on each side of the page, uniting across the middle of the opening. But as the page turns, the negative space of the impression is turned into positive space, giving the sculptural form a completely different reading. As the "tops" then match up with another "bottom" of a body across the new opening, there is a transformation of movement, form, and action as the body seems to roll around on the page. But the literalizing of the turning insists on the fact that the two sides of the sheet belong to the same entity —

while when they serve as a surface, they can pass for discrete elements. Motifs and elements which give regularity to the structure of a page — such as a page number placed consistently (or, moved around to disorient the viewer) also establish continuity or discontinuity. The works just discussed provide conspicuous examples of the self-conscious attention to the structure and function of various aspects of the visual forms of books.

David Stairs, **Boundless**, 1983, courtesy NYPL

Maurizio Nannucci, **Universum**, 1969

The Book as a Whole

It is possible to call attention to the book as a whole as well as to the discrete elements of its internal structure. Two works which insist on the book as an entirety, in which the recognition of unity transcends all internal structure effacing its significance are David Stairs' **Boundless** (1983) and Maurizio Nannucci's **Universum** (Biancoenero, 1969). Both are "unreadable" books — bound shut, into themselves, so that they only sig-

177

nify bookness by their form. **Boundless** is a tiny circular book, the size of a cookie, with white pages and brown covers which is spiral bound on its full circumference. If there is a content to its interior there is no way to know, and the round form of the work adds additional consternation to the viewer — which would be the open edge, if the work were to function. There is only one edge, the outside circumference, and it is the spiral binding and dense stack of paper which reads as "bookness" rather than the shape of the work. Nannucci's earlier piece, **Universum**, has a very different character. The book is a classic book form, with leather binding, beautifully curved spine(s), hard boards, an absolutely iconic book — except that it is, also, bound shut. (Both of these make an interesting contrast to the work of Buzz Spector, which is essentially "bound open.") What would, in a conventional book, serve as the fore-edge for opening the pages is here turned into a hard spine, enclosed in the same highly conventional binding as the first edge. The book has two spines. It is a mutant form as aberrant as some unfortunate genetic mishap and yet for all its apparent monstrosity it has an enigmatic beauty. The spines are decorated with the title stamped in gold, an array of gold-stamped stars, and the volume number — either "I" or "II" — depending on which side one has in hand. The paradox of this — that the book is itself and its sequel — cannot be resolved. The book is a Janus-faced, two-headed creature — but one which always looks inward on itself, its contents sealed against intrusion. Both Stairs and Nannucci reinforce the idea of the book as an enclosure, here taken to the extreme of a final closed space. These are books whose potential cannot be released from their object status in spite of the glimpse of the pages held captive in their bindings.

External Determinants of Whole Structure

In conceiving of a book as an entirety, there are artists who structure their work through an external determinant. That is, they use a structure which is already in existence either as an idea or a form as the basis on which the book is built. An example of this is Ed Ruscha's **Every Building on the Sunset Strip** (National Excelsior Press, 1962) in which the real referent of the totality of buildings on that infamous Hollywood boulevard provides the delimiting parameters of the book. This kind of minimalist gesture is often the basis of works determined by external structures. Such gestures often rely on other systems — alphabets, numbers, mathematical progressions, or propositions.

Ed Ruscha, **Every Building on the Sunset Strip**, 1962

Barbara Schmidt-Heins, **1949-1979**, 1979

Barbara Schmidt-Heins's **1949-1979** (1979) uses chronology as an external structure. The premise was simply to show one photograph of the artist for each year of her life. The vicissitudes of photographs, the changing features of her face as she goes from infancy to young adulthood, the inscription of styles and fashions of doing her hair, makeup, accessories are all recorded, foregrounded as information by the rigid structure of the work. In another such instance, Sol Lewitt's **Brick Wall** (Tanglewood, 1977) a wall is photographed repeatedly through various times of day, changes of light which at first rake the surface, then blanch it, then return it to higher contrasts of tone. This gives an emphatic focus to the visual image as information. The set structure of chronology, its division into years, is a far more rigid structural device than that which determines the moments at which a wall might be photographed in a different light. But they are both external structures, without any relation to narrative, pagination, or sequence, which then become perfectly aligned with these internal structures of the book. The placement of Schmidt-Heins's images is always exactly the same and the images have been scaled to the same size so that they have a strong formal relation, one to the next, as variants of a single image. Lewitt fills the page with his "image" so that it functions as a pattern as much as a pictorial illusion.

Maurizio Nannucci, **M40/1967**, 1976, courtesy NYPL

Both Keith Smith and Maurizio Nannucci have used the alphabet as a structuring device. In **Book 106** (1985), Smith allows the alphabet to disappear, letter by letter, from the book. As it does so, the text changes in response, trying to save its coherence from the vanishing references. The book communicates the sense that it is the act of turning the page which removes the letters, almost like a sieve straining out one element after another from a substance. The letter removed from the text shows up on the backside of the page — so that all of the "b's," "a's," or other letters are on the reverse of the sheet from which they have disappeared. The book is a gallery for the alphabet — each letter getting its moment of attention — while the work is driven by the decision to follow through until there are no letters left on the front side of the page. Though quite different in content and character, Nannucci's **M40/1967** (Multi Art Points, 1976) is also partially grounded in the structure of an extended alphabet. This book was made from a work produced on a typewriter. In the original, a page was produced from each key repeated to form a full field of grey tone on the page. Typed out in a regular pattern, left to right, the grid formed by each character has a different "color" of greyness. Nannucci systematically went through the keyboard from left to right and top to bottom in order to produce the full set of the pages, two to each key (shift and unshift positions). The result is a tonal poem (reproduced in an offset edition) whose sequence and length have both been determined by the keyboard. Thus the book is conceived and executed according to terms which are exterior to it, yet produce its substance and content. This is not work which grows from an image or text and then takes form, its form is prescribed by an external determinant and then produced in accord with those limitations. The work is the concrete realization of an idea in a form which is inseparable from that realization. The book does not exist in any other form — it only comes into existence as a book by following through a proposition ("start with a typewriter, take every key in turn... etc.").

There are many other such propositions. Almost all of these rely on some numerical feature to determine the number of pages in the finished book. In Christian Boltanski's **Classe terminale du Lycée Chases**, (Kunstverein fur die Rheinlande und Westfallen, 1987) he used a group photograph of a high-school class and then enlarged each face in turn to make a gallery of pages, one for each visage. It is this concept of the "each" or "every" in the first image or structure which gives rise to the second structure in a numerical analogue. Other works by Sol Lewitt use graphic propositions such as **Four Basic Kinds of Straight Lines** (Studio International, 1969) or **Geometric Figures and Color** (Abrams, 1979) as their basis, working through the combinations offered by the elements until they are exhausted, thus forming the book's structure. In **The Word Made Flesh** (Druckwerk, 1988), I used the single phrase of the title to establish the number of pages in the work, one for each letter, another frequently used external determinant.6

Finally, a book can function as a dynamic whole through linked or sequential movement or action. The classic form this takes is the "flip book" — in which each page functions like a frame in a film — only partially significant in its own right and dependent upon an entire sequence to produce its full meaning. There are dozens of flip books — Printed Matter bookstore in New York City keeps a small basket of them by its cash register, worn copies which patrons may flip through waiting for their pur-

Conrad Gleber, **Raising a Family**, 1976

chases to be rung up. One of my favorite in this genre (and I think it does qualify as a genre, a sub-field of work with its own distinct identity) is Conrad Gleber's **Raising a Family** (Chicago Books, 1976). This is a gem of a book, small in scale (like most flipbooks, which need to make use of the resistance of the paper in order for the pages to move quickly), and easy to hold. It is printed in black and white and the image is printed from the outside of the fore-edge up toward the spine. It is an image of a family, and at first only the very tops of their heads are visible. As the book flips, more of their faces, hair, and then shoulders and upper body appear. Because the pages are printed on from the edge backward, one can also hold the book so that the fore-edge slants back at an oblique angle, revealing the "risen" family (in a manner similar to a slat book or fan book — aligning its edges to link the fragments on a various pages into a single image). The pun makes the work funny, but the book also succeeds because all of its elements are in the right scale and handle beautifully to articulate the visual image which makes the pun of title clear. This book is a successful, apt, and pointed one-liner, which pulls the whole of its small structure into the meaning of the book as a single form.

The Book as a Conceptual Whole

There are books which attend to their own conceptual wholeness as an idea and which make use of that idea as part of their subject matter and structure. Two books which do this in interesting but contrasting ways are

Marcel Broodthaers's **Mademoise** (1986) and Davi Det Hompson's **Hook** (Tom Ockerse Editions, 1977). Both include internally self-referential texts and images which can only be decoded by reading through the whole book and finding the extra information necessary for understanding a reference. But they both enclose those references, folding them into the text and images as content.

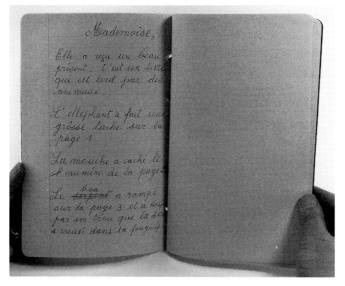

Marcel Broodthaers, **Mademoise**, 1986

For example, **Mademoise** looks like a small copy book, a notebook for a child — an image which the title, the partial word "mademoiselle," also implies. The book (based on a manuscript written in 1972) reads from back to front, also like the work of a child who has gotten part, but not all, of the idea of what a book is. Mischief has been performed on all of the pages. On the first, an elephant has left a stain, on the second the page number has been hidden or stolen by another insect or animal, and the third page is empty (except for the explanatory text) because the boa which was there has escaped through a hole in the paper made by the mouse which was on page four. A crocodile has eaten page six and on page seven a bee takes off and does not land again until page fourteen. This is about all that happens here, but the cleverness of its structure is that it continually refers back to itself. All the explanations for the problems (missing pages, blank pages, etc.) depend upon taking the book literally as a spatialized object, one which serves to support these animal activities.

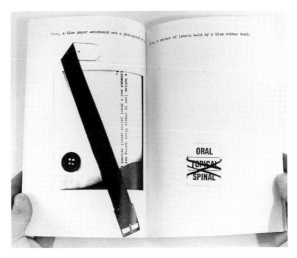

Davi Det Hompson, **Hook**, 1977, courtesy NYPL

Hompson's **Hook** is similarly self-referential, but does not show its hand quite so quickly as Broodthaers's piece. The work was produced from photographs Hompson made with a pinhole camera. They are images of objects on a page, reprinted to be images of objects on a page, each accompanied by a bit of text. The texts require that one know the whole (short) book in order for them to make sense. On first encounter, for instance, the text of page two "A button lost by Jeanie Black during her visit to Richmond and a short yellow pencil removed from eight" leaves the last part of the sentence hanging. Arriving at page eight one is confronted with the statement "Eight, one sentence and a short yellow pencil" and then the phrase "I remember now." Suddenly the book becomes a unified field of reference, one in which what follows is the affirmation of anticipations already turned into actions in the earlier part of the work. There is no way to "know" what becomes "remembered" in the first encounter — so memory, which should be grounded in the consciousness of an action, turns out to be a way to become aware of that earlier reference. The missing pencil which one finds first was "removed" from something one could not have knowledge of at the moment of encounter. Thus the temporality of the book, its conventional sequence, is obliterated by references which have to cross backwards through the book to its first pages. Since the book has to be held in mind as a totality to be understood, the normal linear sequence is replaced by the idea of a single, simultaneous space, of the conceptual whole.

The Self-Referential Object of Production

Books can reflect on their identity and form through a self-consciousness of the act of their production in a physical as well as a conceptual sense. The work can derive its parameters production processes as well as from the parameters discussed above. One of the clearest examples of this kind of work is George Gessert's **Dust and Light** (Green Light, 1987). Gessert's book, a series of standard-sized, 8 1/2 x 11 inch sheets, is a record of the xerox process. Its title refers to the fact that Gessert started by xeroxing a blank sheet of paper and then proceeded to xerox each succeeding sheet in turn, thus intensifying the areas where dust in the machine or on the surface of the glass produced a spot. With each successive generation, the dust spots swell and the area of dark shadow around them increases (the fattening effect of xerox). As the pages proceed the barely visible spots of dust resemble constellations, then ink splatters, then raindrops, and so forth until, on the last page, the book has a mottled surface which is more than fifty percent black. As a book about its own making, this is quite straightforward and about as fundamental as such a self-referential physical process can be.

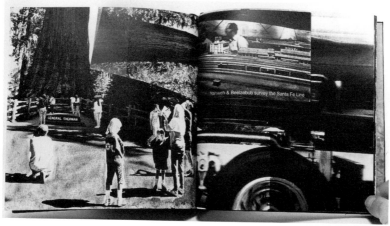

Brad Freeman, **Overrun**, 1990

At another extreme is Brad Freeman's **Overrun** (Varicose, 1990). The term "overrun" contains both a reference to printing as a process in which colors are layered on top of each other in successive passses through the press and to the cultural condition in which humans gradually overrun the planet, a dark vision of humanity. The two conflate and the images which Freeman produces for and in his book are about the process of overcrowding and embody the process of overprinting. Freeman manipulates the form of the photographic documents in the various phases of the printing process including changes made on the press. Using photographs he took himself, he then transforms them with areas of color which wash these pages with swaths of ink whose paths were determined in the dark-oom, through stripping, or painting directly onto the film. The effect is a disturbed color image, one which has the look of a television out of synch — photographically askew in every respect. In the hardbound part of the edition, Freeman laminated printing plates used for the images to the sur-face of the book board, and used the much overprinted set-up sheets as endpapers, thus binding the work in the materials which had facilitated its production. The process of overprinting which Freeman uses requires manipulation of the process at the press, where he changes the color of ink, plays with the placement of the image, and develops other features of the final print in the course of printing, rather than using the offset appa-ratus to reproduce a preplanned or pre-existing image. Freeman is not alone in this, but the artists who are most successful at this kind of manip-ulation are those who are actually printers, not merely designers.

Joe Ruther, for example, was very much involved in these manipula-tions, also with offset as his medium. **Down and Dirty** (1986) is Ruther's "collection of quick printed trash" which takes its title from a printing term meaning printing which has as its basic requirement that the ink land on the page — but not much else. **Down and Dirty** is a running rant from Ruther, who recounts the foibles and peculiarities of the printing process in his run-on prose while interweaving the dense verbal pages with vari-colored photographs of genitals (mainly but not exclusively female), nudes (likewise), and sexual acts. Many of these images have been manip-ulated with a mirror or other effects so that they are fragmented, bifur-cated, or doubled on themselves. The book is an excuse to print these fan-tasmatic images — the embodiment of raunchy male wet dreams — while Ruther recounts the story of the book's making. This double onanism rein-forces the sense of the title, **Down and Dirty**, and the prose reflects its own self-consciousness about the masturbatory character of art making and the accursed difficulties of running a press. The foreward is about the foreward, the text is about the time and space of its own writing with ref-erences to the making of the images and the printing of the book. "Truth is, I didn't intend to write any sort of introduction," the foreword states,"but after I got through printing the text it looked such a barebones

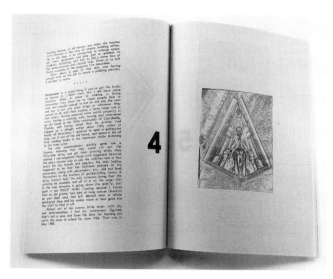

Joe Ruther, **Down and Dirty**, 1986

thing, and it also needed a bit of lip service to cover three or four boo-boos that I decided to flesh it out a little." Later on, Ruther explains his way of working, first disparaging printers who get the press to work through applied diligence and then "trudge through hours of checking out the press all the time seeing the one image. I cringe when anticipating that sort of thing. Therefore, being not desirous of entering a state of stultification in the process...." he manipulates and plays and varies the process all along. The farthest thing from Ruther's mind was the consistent edition or the static image — each book contains variations reflecting his continual intervention in the printing process — as well as his accounts of this activity in his inimitable redneck prose.7 Ruther represents the outsider artist in the book arts field, one who, in his own words, "drops out of the commercial rat race in order to indulge his whims, experimenting with materials and sloughed off equipment. Enjoying life. Playing."8

Other works which foreground the artist's fascination or engagement with the printing process include such pieces as Ann Noel's **CYMBOLS** (Rainer Verlag, 1985), Philip Zimmermann's **Interference** (Nexus Press, 1982), and Mark Pawson's **Life Has Meaning** (1992). Noel's title is comprised of the letters C/Y/M and B — for cyan, yellow, magenta, and black, the colors of process printing. In her work the sequence of printings and overprintings, elegantly designed and manipulated, results in pages layered with visual information but no specific message or content.9 By con-

Philip Zimmermann, **Interference**, 1982

trast, both Zimmermann and Pawson turn their process-driven work into a metaphor for social issues. Zimmermann's **Interference** is thematically concerned with microwaves and their effect on the bodily functions of living organisms, but visually he creates a gallery of dense pages, each framing an iconic image in a mass of patterns made by overlaying halftone screens onto each other in both platemaking and printing processes. The "interference" is the result — the scrambling of one pattern by another in a manner which reflects that of the microwaves he is describing in the running footer of the text. Pawson's work is stencil printed on duplicating machines using exceedingly bright inks. The slightly blurry, off-focus, and out-of-register images are overwhelmed by the graphic intensity of the pages, on which patterns of ants, planes, miniature dolls, suns with spermatoid rays, paisleys, swiss-army knives, skeletons, and cartoon eyes are among the many tiny icons which layer into meaning. Unlike Noel's marks, which are always about markmaking, Pawson uses a vocabulary of images to build the patterns on his pages, while Zimmermann's work sits right between iconicity and pattern, at that point where meaning emerges in their intersection. In all of these works there is a highly self-conscious process of production which contributes to the meaning of the books and is apparent in their pages as a part or most of their substance, not merely their means.

Dieter Roth frequently makes works based on production process.

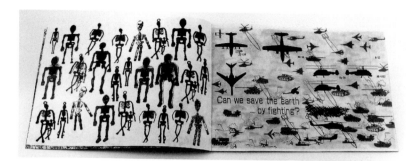

Mark Pawson, **Life Has Meaning**, 1992

Gesammelte Werke Band 3 (1960/61, Hansjörg Mayer) is composed of a block of lines on a single negative which is printed repeatedly at right angles to increase density on the page.10 This is a book which becomes the record of its own production as it proceeds since each page is produced through overprinting the negative on one area of the page. A grid builds up from the intersection of the lines as the pages pass through the press. By shifting the register slightly, the overprinting moves just enough to put ink onto a bare area of the sheet. Each page has one run more than the page preceding, and the increasing density tightens the grid until almost all white space disappears from it. It is important to distinguish this kind of print-process driven work from that of Sol Lewitt, whose work this book resembles superficially. Where Lewitt's patterns of grids, lines, or forms are made in a pre-press manipulation of elements which are then used as the basis of a photographic reproduction which recapitulates this process in printed form, Roth's work is made in the printing process. There is no other form in which this work exists. In this regard, Roth's attitude toward the making of a book provides a conceptual basis much like that used later by Freeman, Voss, and Zimmermann. In all of these cases, there is no book until there is printing, and the printing process determines much of the final form of the work.

The same process can develop within letterpress activity as well. The work of Ken Campbell, particularly such printerly works as **Skute Awabo** (1992), **Father's Garden** (1989) and **Ten Years of Uzbekistan** (with David King, 1994) all have pages densely saturated with printing ink applied directly, without pre-press originals or solutions. The pages become an image through what they accumulate on their surfaces from running through the press over and over again, heavy, solid, thick with the layered density of ink taken off broad surfaces of wood or linoleum, patterned with type or other elements of design. Campbell is clearly intent on coaxing a performance out of his press and pushing it toward innovative manipulation. **Ten Years of Uzbekistan** is a large format book whose pages are thickly layered with ink — they are dense, dark, and physically heavy with it. The work is taken from a 1934 commemorative album of this title designed by Alexander Rodchenko. The faces in the album were defaced by Rodchenko as the people they represented were pronounced "missing" in the course of the ensuing decade. This quality of defacement and the violence it suggests are recorded in graphic terms by Campbell's printing. The sheets are an arena of history and memory, their fabrication layers the human drama in conflicting tones of ever darkening ink. Here material serves a symbolic function, exhibiting itself to inscribe the obliterating forces of power within the passage of history. Each pass through the press contributes to the obliteration of a phantom trace of an individual existence. This is a dark book, a frightening book, but one which absorbs the viewer the way the ink absorbs light, into itself, not away, as if the ever deepening field might reward one's probing search with a final recovery of the original image.

The typographic abstractions made by Hendrik Werkman in the 1920s, many for his own pleasure as visual works, others for his journal **the next call**, were created entirely from printing elements worked into a design. Werkman called these pieces **druksels** (prints) and they were largely produced as unique works. Placement and arrangement were worked out on the press rather than in advance through elaborate designs, but Werkman did not extend this process to book printing in the way that someone like Campbell has done. In my own book, **From A to Z** (1977), discussed earlier, as well as **Twenty-six '76** (1976), much of the writing was done in the composing stick (the device used to hold type in the process of setting), and the design decisions were made on the press rather than based on preexisting layouts.

Todd Walker has combined various technologies and production methods in his highly complicated books. One such work, **O** (1983) whose title page reads "opuntia is just another name for prickly pear", was produced entirely by Walker through his Thumbprint Press. Walker uses imagery generated through several levels of electronic manipulation — first captured by a video camera, then processed on an Apple computer, and displayed on a video monitor. The translation into print was made through yet another set of photographic procedures. The result is imagery with a mosaic feel to it, multi-faceted and shimmering, as if we were seeing through the eyes of some electronic insect or were at the receiving end of a tapestry of optic fiber. Walker uses process as a means of creating effects of subtle color and image distortions which explore the processes he uses and demonstrate their capacity. Throughout the book there are images of prickly pears, and a series of text manipulations generated through programmed processes accompanies them. The prickly pear is a most unlikely object to send through a computer screen. All of its material properties seem antithetical to the electronic medium. And yet it works as an icon of resistance and transformation. An endnote on the colophon extends Walker's description of the processing of the images through these many electronic means: "the computer couldn't do any of these jobs until it taught me what it expected me to tell it to do in order for it to do whatever it does."

In all of these works a form comes into being through an exploration of production means, rather than being conceived of in advance and merely executed by a printer or binder. Many artists' books include some aspect of this attitude, though the concept of a book which is a record of its own making has, in some part, to involve the artist in the final printing as well as the writing or design.

Artists' Books about Making Artists' Books

Emmett Williams' **Chicken Feet, Duck Limbs and Dada Handshakes** (Western Front, 1984) and Michael Goodman's **How to Make an Artist's Book** (Nexus Press, 1980s) are both exceedingly droll, wry works about the making of artists' books. Goodman gives a succinct account of how to make the generic made-by-any-old-artist artist's book. His tiny work offers a critical image of the artist's book by reducing the process to a formula in which more or less any image is put with more or less any text, printed poorly, and staplebound. While this certainly doesn't describe all the works which fall under the rubric of artists' books, it has the advantage of pointing out how circumscribed the terms of originality become — certain patterns of creativity turn out to be only original in a mythic sense. Goodman, who as printer and director at Nexus Press, had the opportunity to see many artists' books come into being (and to review prospectuses for many more which did not) is aware of the many clichés showing up in the emerging artform. Goodman kindly turns the humor on himself — the "generic" photos are of himself, and he does not have his jokes at

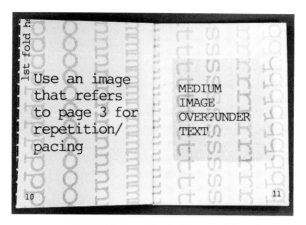

Michael Goodman, How to Make an Artist's Book, 1980s

anyone's expense but his own.

Williams' book is a first-hand narrative, the story of his being invited to Vancouver to make this book. He recounts his trip, his arrival with a book already in mind, a project which would extend other projects he had done elsewhere. He had been invited specifically to do an artist's book, "An artist's book! at that! Yes, it had to be an artist's book! The great scam. The new genre for lightweights." Williams does not escape his own scathing sarcasm as he humorously details the process by which an early morning meal at a Chinese restaurant where he consumes a pile of chicken feet leads him to transform his entire project. The telling of the story which links the events which give rise to the phrases of the title takes up the book's full space — along with the various drawings made with the appendages (duck's feet!) described. Though on one level this book is only about itself, on another it provides insights into the artist's book as process and form — which, when used creatively, can even surprise the artist out of habitual patterns of thought or approach to the book as a work of art. In the final book to be considered in this chapter, these patterns are examined in a far more theoretical fashion.

Real Fiction

There are few books which are made with such apparent self-consciousness about their production as this work by Helen Douglas and Telfer Stokes. As the title announces, **Real Fiction** forges an interchange between the structures of a book as representation and the relations to an external world. The "real" is both the literal reality of the book and the

Emmett Williams, **Chicken Feet, Duck Limbs, and Dada Handshakes**, 1984, NYPL

reality external to the book which can only be represented as a fiction (incomplete, contrived, un-"true" because it is a representation — "real" because it is an actual book). **Real Fiction** (Visual Studies Workshop Press and Weproductions, 1987) is subtitled **An Enquiry into the Bookeresque**.

In its first opening, the shadow of a page on the left hints at the shadow of a structure on the right which quotes the book form as an element of architectural space. The opening reads as book, page, wall, room. The next opening reads "there are two sides to every opening" and the type appears to float above the page casting its shadow as if on a page curled downward far more radically than the page on which the words are printed. Thus in the first two openings we have already encountered several levels of reference to the book as a space of presentation and illusion, of appearances and realities, literal surfaces and their imitation as delusions. As the book proceeds it elaborates on this alternation: comments about the book and images of a book whose pages also make a space continue to play off each other. A door appears in one of the sheets of the book pages pictured, the pages peel back, showing a photograph of an outdoor site. A brick makes its entrance, and next to it, a photograph of a brick wall which, in the next opening, has been folded around to make the shape of a wall, itself leading to a shed. These are all photographs, not real things, but the photograph is a most believable fiction of the real until its own materiality (as something to be cut, folded, framed or cropped) is brought to our attention. Figures appear in the photographic space and enter what is evidently a tiny model, mockup of a house set into the image of the pages of the open book. The text, meanwhile, speaks of spaces

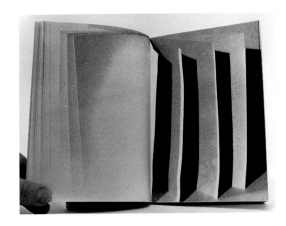

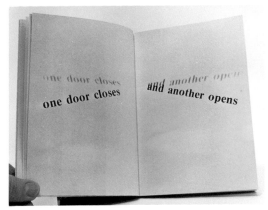

Helen Douglas and Telfer Stokes, **Real Fiction**, 1987

made and occupied which nonetheless search to be contained.

The devices of framing, internal resonance between the textual reference to illusions and the processes of making the illusion within the image of a book lay bare the mechanisms of book as process. The concept of representation, through which a book comes to "contain" things in the pedestrian sense, is made into a game of self-referentiality. Here the book is not merely about its own making, but also about its own conceiving. The work shows how a book is thought of as a space — where space means the interior pages and the conceptual boundary which gives the elements their meaning. The processes revealed here are not so much production or even creative processes as they are thought processes in which the conventions which make a book have been codified in ways we never articulate. The meaning of the book as a boundary, a point of delimitation and demarcation on the one hand, and the meaning of the book as a space, infinitely imaginable and expandable on the other hand, are explored as two aspects of the paradoxical nature of the book — any book — as a **Real Fiction**.

1 It is for this reason that I am including so few works of concrete poetry — they are only sometimes book works, far more frequently, single poems produced over a few pages or as a single sheet. The varied and imaginative page manipulations of Ferdinand Kriwet, Jiri Kolar, Bernard Heidsieck, Eugen Gomringer, Julian Blaine, Ilse and Pierre Garnier, Augusto and Haroldo De Campos to name just a few of the most renowned figures, all make significant contributions.

2 I am unable to locate any bibliographic reference for this work.

3 The text of this book was largely generated at the typecase in the process of setting. Since the restraints on what could be said in the book were set by the amount of type in the cases, this was the only way to proceed — once the letters were physically depleted the utterances were constrained by what remained. Another restraint on the work was that everything in it was to be meaningful, and so there are no nonsensical strings of leftover letters or figures set to take up space or use up type.

4 This work is co-published by Walther König (Köln), Hansjörg Mayer (Stuttgart), and Edition Stähle (Zurich).

5 There is also an earlier work, **Transformations I** (1973-74) in which Lanyon structures the pages in this way.

6 See Chapter 9 for more discussion of this work.

7 Ruther's own characterization of himself, not mine.

8 Joe Ruther, **Color by Joseph** (FM Productions, 1976).

9 These overprintings appear to be made from a positive plate process with the pattern-making elements drawn on mylar or on the plate itself — thus in contrast to Ruther and Zimmermann. Freeman combines the negative and positive plate processes in many of his works. Positive plates can offer more immediacy to an artist who wants to get the look of drawn or painted surfaces into an offset process.

10 The Hansjörg Mayer editions of these works are frequently larger editions of works Roth produced himself in shorter runs several years earlier.

Erica Van Horn, **Black Dog White Bark**, 1987

8

The Book as a Visual Form

All books are visual. Even books which rely exclusively on type, or on unusual materials, or those which contain only blank sheets have a visual presence and character. All books are tactile and spatial as well — their physicality is fundamental to their meaning. Similarly, the elements of visual and physical materiality participate in a book's temporal effect — the weight of paper, covers, endpapers or insets, fold-outs or enclosures all contribute to the experience of a book. However, it is clear that there are books which maximize their visual potential by taking advantage of images, color, photographic materials, sequencing, juxtaposition or narratives. (Though narratives will be dealt with extensively in Chapter 10, a few examples of purely visual narrative works will be examined here as well.) Many book artists treat linguistic or verbal elements of a book as visual elements; these will be discussed in the next chapter rather than included here.

The mark, the image, the photograph, the page, the sequence, the whole: a book's potential in visual terms is complex and multivalent. The production methods available to produce visual elements in a book are highly varied. All the visual artist's materials (crayons, pencils, ink, watercolor and so forth) can be applied to the pages, edges, endsheets, and covers of a book. Printing methods have their own possibilities for producing images — whether through low-tech approaches such as potato and stencil printing or more high-tech photographic and computer methods related to offset lithography, silk screen, or polymer plates. Many artists' books use direct production methods — that is, they produce images in the book **as it is made** (whether printed or produced through handwork or some combination). In other cases, images are reproduced — from either drawn or photographed originals. Since the specific qualities of production methods are integral to the effects which appear in a book, attention will be focused on the relations between image and production.

A word about the interpretation of visual images may add a useful critical dimension to this discussion. Writing in the 1960s and 1970s, the
French theorist and semiotician Roland Barthes described the ways in
which language can either anchor meaning in an image or else helps serve
a relay function to put the image into relation with other elements in a
complex structure.1 Without language to serve these delimiting functions,
he emphasized, the image floats, a site for many possible interpretations.2
Moving beyond Barthes' observations on the image into the realm of
books involves a leap in scale and complexity. In books which use visual
materials exclusively — that is, without any verbal elements — the images
often function with a loose, indeterminate ambiguity of meaning. Mutable, elusive, mobile, and difficult to pin down, they produce significance
through their relations to each other or to the other material elements of
the book: paper color and texture, scale, binding and so forth. In a visual
book it is often as much these relations as the specific images which serve
to anchor meaning. Sequence and juxtaposition can provide restraints on
the images or they can increase their potential for open-ended value —
letting the images loose into unconstrained interactions. The poetic range
of imagery in artists' books spans the full spectrum — from poignant to
humorous, banal to profound — with an added intensity produced by the
fact that images in books are almost never single images, but are bound
into a complex sequence.

Photographic and Non-Photographic Images
An image which is non-photographic is produced without any reliance
on photographic means. A good example of non-photographic printing
methods are cut stencils. These were used by Clifton Meador in **The Book
of Doom** (Space Heater Multiples, 1984) where the images were entirely
produced using hand-cut templates. Spray paint was applied directly to
the pages through the entire edition. Another example of non-photographic images are linoleum prints, such as those in Julie Chen and Nance
O'Banion's **Domestic Science** (Flying Fish, 1990). And there are hand
drawn and painted pages, such as those in Timothy C. Ely's unique books.
There is an appealing purity to the idea of images which go directly onto
the page of a book, making the volume and the edition as a production,
rather than a reproduction.3

Many artists' books are produced through offset lithography which is
inherently photographic in nature: a light-sensitive emulsion on the sur-

face of offset plates is exposed to form the image from which printed impressions are made. In this sense, any book which is produced using offset printing has a photographic component to it, but the images may be produced in any manner. A drawing, painting, etching, or linoleum cut or photograph — can be **reproduced** using offset.

Anytime a book is produced through offset printing processes, photographic methods are likely to enter at the last stage. Printing processes and their relation to the images produced will be discussed to clarify the effects of production on the final result.

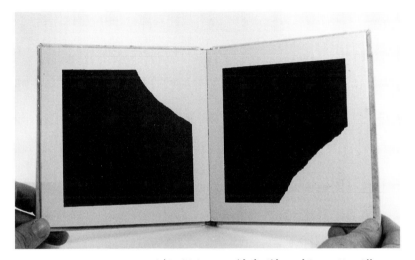

Sol Lewitt, **Squares with the Sides and Corners Torn Off**, 1974

Abstract images

The first pair of books provide an opportunity to discuss the nature of the page and its relation to the image. The nature of the abstraction in both cases calls attention to this relation, and where a page might normally be thought of either as a surface support for a graphic pattern or image, or a means of presenting an illusion, in these works the page is taken literally as an image and a page simultaneously.

Giovanni Anselmo and Gian Enzo Sperone's **116 Particolari** (1974) makes use of abstract images as the basis of its visual form similar to Sol Lewitt's **Squares with the Sides and Corners Torn Off** (MTL, 1974). In both cases the page is the full unit of the image. There is no distinction made between image and page — the image is not a drawing or element which sits on or inside the margins of a page which serves as field or support.

In **Particolari** this idea is worked out through the "partial" coloration of certain pages in a sequence which is otherwise comprised of pages which are black or all white. The partially-colored pages give them the appearance of hard-edged abstractions whose areas of white intrude into the black field or whose black forms define the limits of the white shapes. There is no iconic value to be read in these pages — no figurative referent — there is only the allocation of a percentage of the page to black ink, white paper, or some internal division of the two. The parts are literal — and fundamental — to what conventionally comprises a book — paper and ink. The pages don't reproduce an image, they are an image. By contrast, in Lewitt's book, though the "square" of the title is isomorphic with the square of the page — their visual identity is not one and the same. They are distinguished at a conceptual level. This allows a distinction between the "square" whose sides are torn off and the square which is the page to be made visually, almost like a literal pun. The pages "show" the square with its sides ripped (first one corner, then another, then a side, etc.). This "image" has been made by taking a sheet of paper the size of the page and tearing it, then using that as the basis of the masking sheet which controls the exposed area on the offset plate. The image of the square in its torn condition forms the image on the page. Unlike **Particolari**, in which the divisions are not the image of any thing, Lewitt's book gets its internal distinctions between the black and white areas of the page by using the outlines of these actual squares. Since the dimensions of the square and page are the same, however, the effect is to make the pages into those torn squares, the negative area of the sheet visually "erasing" itself from the sheet.

This may sound a bit tautological, but it is important to realize that this distinction between the literal page and the conceptual page exists and that it functions in some sense in all books — whether they are concerned with images, language, or other elements of meaning. Of course there are other kinds of abstract images which structure artists' books or appear in them. Many of Sol Lewitt's books are concerned with visual abstraction, especially those which are images of propositions like **Four Basic Kinds of Straight Lines** (Studio International, 1969). And there are books which use color in the production of images in a way which further contributes to this tension between the literal and conceptual page.

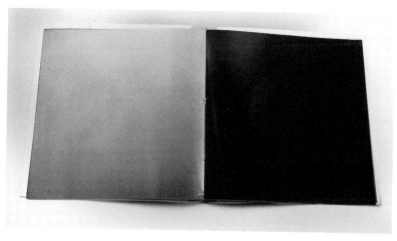

Bruce Nauman, **L.A. Air**, 1970

Color as an Element of Visual Structure

Bruce Nauman's L.A. Air (Multiples, 1970) and Maurizio Nannucci's 60 Natural Greens (Renzo Spagnole, Ed., 1977) are both quite simple in their appearance. The conceptual premise which drives each is grounded in an apprehension of what color is and how it produces meaning through visual perception. Both are produced by offset printing, though the photographic original of Nannucci's images give them a higher allegiance to the category of photographic books to be discussed below, I include it here for the contrast it makes with Nauman's work. L.A. Air is a large format work which consists of a sequence of pages on which the ink colors go from a tepid ochre to a deep rich brown through various tones of sepia, smoke, and yellowish grey. The joke is obvious. These are the colors of the air in Los Angeles and the sequence in which one encounters them in the bound pages intensifies their hue by contrast. There is no narrative hinted at — the colors don't deepen or lighten — they are like swatches taken from different parts of the atmosphere on multiple days in various light or climate conditions. Here color is again both literal and conceptual — it may be read as a representation of haze, smog, mist, and other natural and polluting elements, and also may be experienced directly, as color. The large sheet size guarantees that this experience takes place — the field of color is sufficiently large to saturate the field of vision if the book is held in a conventional manner. The page has no particular identity, it simply serves as material support, and the colors are not a photographic record of the air. Nannucci's **Greens** are "natural" because each of the sixty images in the book is a photograph of a bit of foliage. The differences in pigmentation caused by varying amounts of chlorophyll, fiber, and other plant characteristics determine the colors which make up the palette of greens. This combined with the color separation technology available during the book's production. Nannucci's colors are referential to the plants identified in the image, since they are four-color reproductions of photographs. Here the photograph is literalized — made to signify something other than the iconic image it contains — the book is not about "60 plants" but "60 natural greens" whose similarities and differences are emphasized by the finite structure of the book. Thus we have Nauman using literal color to refer outside the book, and Nannucci using color literally to make the book into a field of reference.

Karen Chance, **Parallax**, 1987

Color may also be used for far more decorative or informative purposes. There are other books which I have mentioned earlier, such as Karen Chance's **Parallax** (Nexus Press, 1987) and Kevin Osborn's **Tropos** (Osbornbook, 1988) which use color to structure their pages. Chance emphasizes the turnings which demarcate each opening by shifting color at the boundary of the page, thus letting the crease in her accordion-fold structure serve as the end of one field of color and beginning of the next. In this way, color becomes a device for making each opening a separate space within the narrative as well as within the visual field. **Parallax** was offset printed and the images were made using various aspects of the printing process. The shapes which are figures of people, animals, shadows, architectural elements, swaths of light, and other highly readable forms were often cut from rubylith, a light-blocking, film-like material used to isolate areas for printing. Rather than make these in a drawing first, Chance made them through print materials — this means there are no "originals" which exist as drawings (though there were most likely outline drawings or sketches) before the printed product. The work is produced as a print, and also, thought through as a book — it is linear and sequential, its pictorially driven narrative moves from page to page with graphic momentum. Patterns and variations of color, shading, and tone were produced using screens made from spray paint patterns, drawn patterns, and so forth so that the result is richly layered.4 In **Tropos** spot color is applied with certain runs using a split fountain as well.5 This means that the runs per page — or passes of the page through the press — can be calculated by counting the number of colors of ink — but no photographic separation of any kind is necessary in printing. Osborn's colors layer, overlap upon the pages, each contributing graphically to the rising and falling tide of activity. This work articulates its frequencies through additions and subtractions of hues and pigments rather than forging a narrative sequence or spatially explicit structure through color means.

Color can provide discontinuity or continuity. The effect of continuity was seen in **Desire** (Nexus Press, 1989) by Helen Douglas and Telfer Stokes where a single blue line — an image of fence wire which has a distinctly graphic autonomy — established links from page to page through disconnected images. Color is used to fragment images to equally successful ends in Felipe Ehrenberg's **Codex Aeroscriptus Ehrenbergensis** (Nexus Press, 1990). This offset book uses high-contrast photographic images. Its colors are flat, rich, and graphic creating an effect of great intensity and presence. With its vocabulary of skulls, roosters, cowboys, guns, and other identifiable motifs, this book has visual links to the work of Mexican folk artists and traditional poster designers. Here color serves to keep the graphic elements distinct on the page — which otherwise might flatten into a mass of collaged elements. By contrast to the conceptual clarity of **L.A. Air** or the narrative lucidity of **Parallax**, the Ehrenberg **Codex** (a self-portrait whose cultural references are clear) is chaotic. Images are layered with a spontaneous looseness, as if dumping the contents of a psyche through a rapid, unedited process of free association. Large areas of vivid color seem to underly the graphic motifs so that a rising bell tower on a yellow ground separates from the brilliant blue figure of a man waving or the magenta nipples of a large-breasted woman. These are all discontinuous images whose pastiched relations are distinguished through the discrete boundaries of color.

Felipe Ehrenberg, **Codex Aeroscriptus Ehrenbergensis**, 1990

Finally, paper can provide an element of color as it does in Erica Van Horn's **Black Dog White Bark** (Visual Studies Workshop, 1987). Printed on dark blue paper the book consists of a series of images of a black dog making a huge white bark. The "bark" moves through the blue field of the paper, a searchlight making itself "heard" through the vibrant contrast of tone. At the end the poor dog has barked itself out and lies on its back, mouth open, teeth extended into a final long white bark. The repeated sequence of the dog and the barks and the visual tone of the verbal outcry have the force of a fully realized set of symbols. There is no question that we can "hear" the dog's bark because of the contrast in paper and ink and that Van Horn has maximixed the effect of minimal printing means.

The Drawing or Drawn Line

Jan Voss's **Detour** (1989) is a tour de force use of line in a book form. Though many other artists use drawings to structure a book as a single drawing whose internal subdivisions fall on individual pages, Voss's work is about the way in which a wandering line may sustain itself through an entire work. Though not comprised of a single continuous line (on a page by page basis, the images are more complex than that) the book's premise — the detour — is the endless **diversion** of the linear movement from any terminal resolution. Rather than go clear to its endpoint, the line in Voss's book does everything it can to delay its arrival at the other end of the book. A man catches a cloud, rides on a train, visits an art gallery, wanders through a landscape which ranges from mountains to jungles to sea. Sustaining this conceit across a few hundred sheets, the book is not a book of drawings, it is a book as drawing, a drawn-out extension in time and physical space.

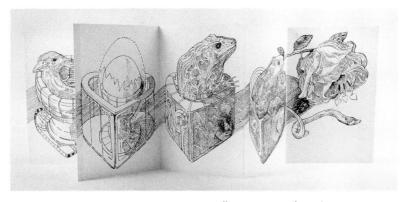

Ellen Lanyon, **Transformation II**, 1982

Other books have relied on similar conceits — the elaboration of a single image over the full length of a book. Michel Milliarakis's **Fragments Graphiques d'un livre d'images** (1975) is a sustained invention of this kind. The work is comprised of three small-scale (a few inches in each dimension), accordion-fold books in a custom case which unfold through dozens of graphic transformations. Though the movement from fold to fold is sequential and the metamorphoses of space and action rely on this forward movement, the images are not linear as much as graphic black and white production. Ellen Lanyon's **Transformation I** and **II** (Printed Matter, 1976 and Chicago Books, 1982) formalize the idea of graphic linear movement as a structure, making them both the subject matter and the means of execution.

Martin Rosz, **Zeichnungen**, 1988

But drawings can function in a completely different manner within a book. There is the tradition of the sketchbook or notebook as the basis of an artist's book. Though some of these works feel more incidental than intentional in character, they are distinctly graphic. The spontaneity of an artist's jottings, as in the case of Martin Rosz's **Zeichnungen** (Rainer Verlag, 1988), can be represented with a striking intimacy in an artist's book. Most sketchbooks do not move beyond their haphazard character (though the chance juxtapositions in sketchbooks create interesting and often unexpected meanings) and Rosz's work is no exception. A richly accurate offset reproduction of the thick, warm lines of his pencil sketches, it is nonetheless just that — a sketchbook reproduction, and it would be a mistake to read too much intentionality into its book form. While the act of drawing can be, as above, structured to form the basis of a book, the structure of a book can also be used to give drawings a particular meaning and format. **3500 Meisterzeichnungen** (1975) by Arthur Werkner (known professionally as Turi) consists of a hundred pages gridded into thirty-five small blocks each of which contains a small black and white pen drawing.6 On the title page of the book, with no verbal commentary, there is a photograph of a pen and a stopwatch lying on top of the gridded sheet. The concept is clear: these are timed sketches, rapid and instantaneous — and their "times" are recorded in a table at the end of the book. The format of the grid is respected to allow each drawing a discrete identity and also

206

overruled so that the images on certain pages coalesce into a whole. Without a book format to support them, these images would have a different character. Within the bound pages the thick pen lines have an aggressive presence, the repetitive quality of the format becomes a means of reading the images, and the stark black and white offset reproduction of the pen lines interferes very little with their character.

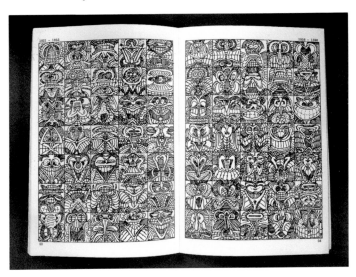

Turi, **3500 Meisterzeichnungen**, 1975

Brief Marks, another Jan Voss book (Kontexts Publications, 1979), also makes use of a grid and a drawn image. Voss's work consists of eleven sheets of white paper which have been perforated in a grid. Each sheet has a different scale of grid (with one squared-out element at the lowest extreme and five hundred and sixty elements at the highest). The white pages are interleaved with flat black sheets which visually transform the perforations into striking dotted lines. Inside each grid block — which looks like a postage stamp in a sheet — are rapid line drawings. These do not have the development of Werkman's little images — which look like cartoonish sketches and are suggestively readable. Voss's "marks" are rapidly made designs which are only descriptive of abstract forms in space. They are neat, spatially explicit, and carefully executed — not scribbles — but they are not images of anything specific. The success of this book is its full combination of elements: the interaction of the perforations with the interleaved sheet, the simplicity of the grid, and the

207

cleanness of the drawn marks (offset printed), the varying scale of the grids and the drawings, and the muteness of the whole whose only verbal contributions besides the title and artist's name are the production details on the back of the army green paper cover. Movement is achieved by the change in scale, integration by the use of the two different papers (plus cover), and development comes from the transition from large to small grids in a series which is replete and yet without any apparent closure. Though drawing is not the only visual element here, it is the manifest content which gives the formal elements a central focus.

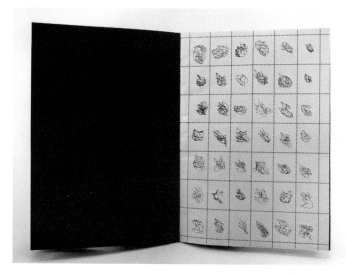

Jan Voss, **Brief Marks**, 1979

There is one last book I want to include here because it makes an unusual contribution to the idea of what constitutes a drawing or a mark. This is Clifton Meador's **New Doors** (Nexus Press, 1985), whose images were made entirely with solid and perforation rule impressed into the sheets on a letterpress.7 Made in the shape of a house icon (pitched roof, straight walls), the single signature work has no color or language or other imagery in its interior (the cover has a bright pattern printed in three colors around the title). Each page has a differently designed "door" — by which is meant an opening in the page. Because these designs are impressed with the straight or perforation rule, their lines frequently break the sheet, making their complex geometric forms read even more strongly. The work has the subtlety of a monochromatic piece and the

208

complexity of a sculptural work — while the unfolding sequence in all its variety fascinates us like that of a kaleidoscope or a catalogue of snowflakes, every turning revealing another, different, but related form.

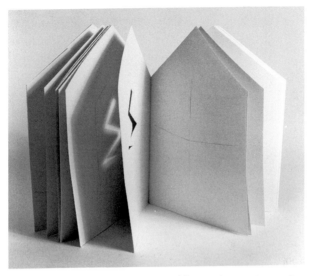

Clifton Meador, **New Doors**, 1985

Stamps and Standard Marks

The use of standardized marks for production takes various forms and the following works demonstrate a few ways these have been used by artists in making books. For instance, Ray DiPalma has made extensive use of rubber stamps maximizing their potential as a graphic production method. For DiPalma the vocabulary of rubber stamps is wide ranging. He amassed a large collection of stamps which have geometric and recognizable forms — everything from stars to airplanes, squares to men, wiggly lines and female profiles, to a whole gamut of words and phrases. In DiPalma's hands these become a drawing tool, not merely an image to reproduce. DiPalma's capacity to raise their use to an interesting conceptual level is apparent in such works as 10 Pyramids (1977). Here, DiPalma incorporates the minimalist aesthetic with its reduced visual forms and its prescriptive program for their construction into a rubber-stamp book. The book is small and consists of ten "pyramids" made with five lines each—three to describe the vertical edges of the form and two to describe the baseline. The pyramids are the manifestation of a drawing problem — the-way to create a form in the connections made from line to line (rather

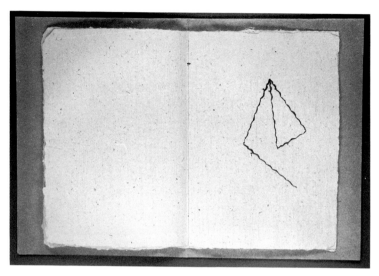

Ray DiPalma, **10 Pyramids**, 1977

than point to point) emphatically showing that lines provide the vocabulary of marks (these were actually the edges of rubber stamps). Thus the
pyramids are deliberately made with varying degrees of success — in a few
the lines meet perfectly, thus forming the seamless illusion of a schematic
drawing of a geometric form. In other cases, the lines just barely miss,
forcing the viewer to deal with them as lines on the page. It is the classic
tension, again, between literal and illusionary modes of using the page
which takes this work into the conceptual arena. In the final image, the
baseline of the pyramid's right face extends across the full space of the
page off the edge of the sheet. Base has become horizon, image has
become projection, line has become vector, and this little, inconspicuous
rubber stamp work has articulated visual and spatial complexities. Printed
in pale stamp-pad inks on textured paper, the work has a satisfying tactil-
ity, its pages turn easily, and are bound with a pamphlet stitch in a
straightforward manner. DiPalma's work has considerable range and this
is a well-realized example of rubber-stamp book work — using the modu-
lar aspect of the rubber-stamp medium and the specificity of the book format.

Leon Ferrari's **Hombres** (Ediciones Licopodio, 1984) uses standard
forms from architectural drawings as its basis.8 These forms are not line,
section and elevation conventions, but the rounded trees and plant forms,
humans in various poses, and architectural components which are pro-

duced as rub-on transfers. These mass produced images which look as if they were machine drawn, are used in design presentations. The world they represent is black and white and shadowless, featureless and repetitious, without individuation from one tree to the next or one human to another. In **Hombres** Ferrari makes a critical statement about overpopulation and dehumanization under the regimes of repetitive labor and bureaucratic organization. The standardized elements are marshalled into elaborate arrangements and then choreographed to appear to move in patterns of increasing complexity and futility. Reproduced offset from black and white originals, the book (which is about 8 1/2 x 11 inches) has a repetitive insistence to it which reinforces the effect of the images. There is a "no exit" quality to the way in which the simpler geometric patterns into which the figures are placed become increasingly complex arrangements of intersecting paths. This book work relies on this developing complexity to intensify the meaning of the standard elements which make up its basic visual units.

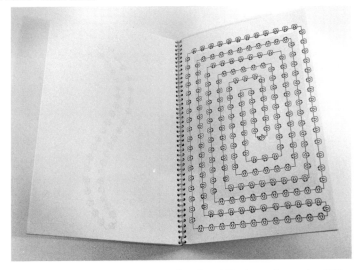

Leon Ferrari, **Hombres**, 1984, courtesy NYPL

Emmett Williams's **Guardian Angel active-passive** (Edition Hundertmark, 1985) and Dieter Roth's **Stupidogramme** (Hansjörg Mayer, 1975) are lighter in tone than Ferrari's book. Both make use of standard marks to make a visual joke. Roth's book is a parody of the verbal puzzles in which words are embedded in a matrix of letters and the reader discerns them in diagonal, vertical, or horizontal patterns. An inane exercise to begin with, these games are rendered more ridiculous in Roth's version in which the grid consists of greatly exaggerated outsized commas instead of letters. These are circled with the same careful intentionality as the units in the normal word game, but without any specific result aside from the formal grouping. In Williams's book the only graphic element is a small black circle with smaller white circles in its interior. The combination gives the black circles the look of "googley-eyes" — the plastic eyes with a loose black plastic disc in them used on stuffed animals. The humor of this quotation on Williams's part is further reinforced by the fact that he arranges these circles/eyes on facing pages in a "passive" and "active" opposition. The neat orderly arrangement on the left side is then mocked and parodied by a disorderly and badly behaved group on the right. The result is a sense of animateness, as if the "bad" forms were acting out, like mischievous children refusing to line up or sit still. With each succeeding page there are more of the little creatures, and the final page is filled to capacity. These are both black and white, offset works in which production is minimalized rather than brought into an active role.

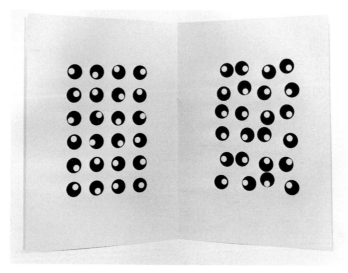

Emmett Williams, **Guardian Angel active-passive**, 1985

Visual Narratives

There are important early precedents for books which are narrative in their structure and yet use only visual images. In the twentieth century, these include the works of both Franz Masereel and Lynd Ward. In the grey area between artists' books and books by artists produced as trade books, these works established the visual parameters according to which contemporary artists like Eric Drooker compose their pictorial narratives. For one thing, both Masereel and Ward used striking black and white images printed from original woodcuts in order to create their images.9 The results of these processes are emphatic high-contrast images (though these media could be used to make more refined passages of mid-tones in keeping with the conventions of woodblock engraving, the medium lends itself to high contrast).

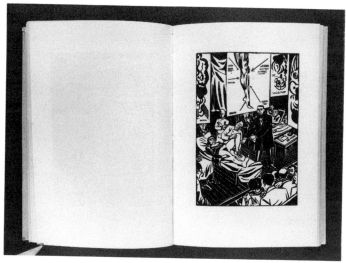

Franz Masereel, **The City**, 1925

Masereel was a Belgian artist whose works, such as **The City**, appeared in the 1920s and 1930s. **The City** (Kurt Wolff Verlag, 1925) is more descriptive and thematic in unity than strictly narrative.10 There is often a relation in the images, one to the next: for instance, the first sequence shows a man looking at the city from a distance, then trains arriving, followed by a closer look at the platform, and then a man dead in city traffic — all with enough spatial connection to permit a loose narrative reading. In other sequences we move from place to place, from interior domestic site to exterior work site, from newspaper office to streetscape, from hospital room to public square. Like his contemporary, Georg Grosz, whose **Ecce Homo** (Malik Verlag, 1923) was another striking visual commentary on his times, Masereel is as much a chronicler and picturemaker as he is a storyteller. By contrast Lynd Ward's work is clearly narrative. **Gods' Man**

Lynd Ward, **Gods' Man**, 1929

(Jonathan Cape and Harrison Smith), published in 1929, is a graphic novel.11 The turn from image to image moves the story along as a young artist tries to make his way in the world. The gaps between the images are carefully calculated to permit continuity while storyboarding the narrative. The story is a variant on the Faustian classic: the artist makes a pact with a mysterious figure who furnishes him with a charmed brush; the artist at first reaps success and then meets his inevitable demise. Though many contemporary artists have made books in which there is a visual narrative, one who works directly in the graphic vein of Ward and Masereel is Eric Drooker. Drooker's book **Home** (Communicomix, 1986), though more up to date in look and style than his predecessors, follows their conventions. Drooker's images and concerns are more contemporary, his narrative logic more open than Ward's, his critical view less extensive than Masereel's. **Home** is a dark book. It tells the story of man who loses his job and spirals downward in a terrifyingly swift passage to utter misery. The drawings have the crudeness of underground comic imagery and the starkness of their expressionist precedessors.

Narratives of a more absurd, less linear variety also find their place in artists' books. One outstanding example is Willyum Rowe's book **Nurse Duck Approaches and Enters and Leaves The Garden of Eden** (Visual Studies Workshop, 1982). This work takes full advantage of the possibilities of offset ink printing color. The combinations have been manipulated

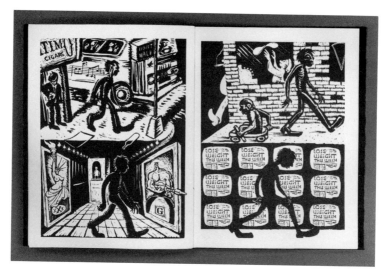

Eric Drooker, **Home**, 1986

in pre-press production to isolate and intensify areas of brilliant hue. But Rowe's book which almost shouldn't work as a narrative does so because of a few very strong structural elements. First of all there is the figure of Nurse Duck herself, a storybook figure, no doubt appropriated from some reassuring elementary school text, who approaches the reader with firm step, in her perfect uniform, carrying a large bowl on a tray and a towel over her arm. This figure never changes and every place in which she appears in the book she is the same size, scale, and Maalox-pink color. This figure anchors the other images in a narrative sequence. Whether she appears rising above the horizon of a cell wall, walking across the surface of an epidermal section, or floating in the midst of microscopic organisms, her presence renders everything else landscape and background. By cutting her off within frames, angling her fixed figure, and using the rightward directed aspect of her gaze, Rowe is able to reinforce the conventional movement of the book. In almost every spread, she moves down and across the opening so that on the very last sheet, the outer cover, she gradually disappears into a dark frame as part of swirling cosmic dust. Here the inexorable logic of the book has been demonstrated and the stasis of the rest of the imagery is free to contribute its absurd and vivid iconography to the scenes.

The final work of non-photographic images to be considered here is one of the coded narratives of Warja Lavater, **La Melodie de Tur di di**

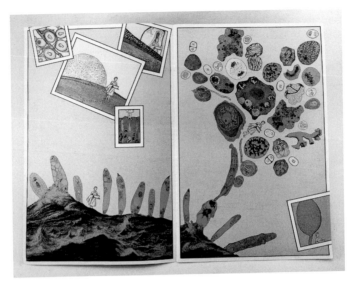

Willyum Rowe, **Nurse Duck...**, Visual Studies Workshop, 1982

Warja Lavater, **La Melodie de Tur di di**, 1971

(Adrien Maeght Editeur, 1971).12 Lavater takes a story, often a well-known fairy tale, and encodes its narrative structure into a pictorial representation. The individual characters are given a graphic identity. In **Tur di di** the main character (a youngster in a musical family) looks something like a baby Pac-man though he was invented long before. Tur di di's adventures — a coming of age story in which he finds his own voice — stretch through the accordion-fold book in brightly colored images which are just on the border between schematic diagrams and actual pictures. As in Nurse Duck, it is the stable image of the central character which promotes continuity as one follows his movements from scene to scene. But rather than move through a collage landscape according to an absurd logic, **Tur**

216

di di moves through a schematic image which is derived from the structural elements in the story. Lavater has performed a graphic translation of the narrative rather than illustrating it or drawing it in conventional iconography. Though some of the imagery is recognizable as a street scene or recording studio, even these images lend themselves to an abstract reading. In some of Lavater's works the code is sufficiently complex to require a key so that the reader can understand the meaning of the graphic elements. Lavater's skill in manipulating the book as a sequential space is particularly evident in the way elements in these pages turn the corners of the folds. A band of grey skyline can become the outside edge of a studio space or a graphic family tree become the edge of a forest by continuing into the next opening. This continuity and mutation link the book visually so as to reinforce narrative movement.

Photo Images Without Narratives
Ed Ruscha has created many works which have become classics of the photographic, non-narrative artist's book. The determinants of sequence or boundaries, and the often arbitrary decision to show "twenty-six" or "twelve" or "all" of something provide the books with basic structural principles, as I have discussed earlier.13 There are many photographers who put their work into portfolio or even book format without thinking through what actually differentiates a book from a mere collection or mobile exhibition space.

An artist whose work does attend to the concept of the book is Sol Lewitt. **Brick Wall** (Tanglewood Press, 1977), mentioned in chapter seven, uses photographic images without a narrative structure and yet with full recognition of the ways images work together when they are bound into a fixed sequence. **Brick Wall** would work as a mounted exhibition of photographs. But the fixed proximity of the images to each other, as well as their sequence, and their function in that sequence makes them work as a book. They are deliberately related, through the way in which the movement from one to the next reads as a sequence. The images — again in an aesthetic which clearly reveals its minimalist origins — are all black and white photographs of a brick wall. The texture, tone, and color of the bricks varies depending upon the time of day. The raking light of morning or late afternoon, the more direct light of midday, the muted light of an overcast moment, all have their place in this series. The result is an intensely focused and nuanced visual experience which relies heavily on

Sol Lewitt, **Brick Wall**, 1977

the turning of each page to bring the value of each image to the fore. The qualities of the wall become familiar through repetition, and its differences over time show its identity to be mutable. There is no attempt to collapse the wall and the page, as in Lewitt's earlier work with the torn squares. Here the image is clearly photographic, though the bit of wall is contextless and dislocated in cultural space and historical time, the record of the surface provides a chronology within the book's finite and sequential confines.

The nature of the photographic non-narrative book is about forging relations among a group of images through this use of the book's two major structural features — its sequential regularity and its stable finitude. Order and binding, relation and containment; these are the basic principles of the book whether amplified, resisted, or transgressed. In Masao Gozu's **In New York, February 1971 - December 1984** (1984) the finite nature of the book is echoed in the strong framing device of the page. Gozu's images are all of people in windows in New York City. All of these photographs of windows are enlarged, reduced, cropped, and printed to fit as perfectly as possible just inside the dimensions of the page. As a result, many disparate window forms are made to relate to each other as variants on the same image. The people leaning from or sitting in or behind these windows all communicate from a space behind the page into the opening of the book, which serves as the street or public space. Here space becomes curiously coded because of Gozu's insistence on the window's frontality and the viewer's continual confrontation of those fenestrated openings within the openings of the book.14 Bounded in time by Gozu's experience of the city, the photographs have no relation to each other outside their theme and this time frame — occasionally the glance of one group connects with events or gazes of figures on the facing page, but there is no attempt to overdetermine either sequence or a story.

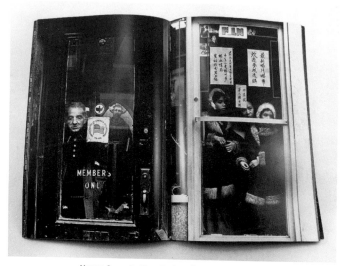

Masao Gozu, **In New York, February 1971 - December 1984**, 1984

Adrian Piper's **Colored People** (Bookworks, 1991) uses photographic images of people to a very different end. Her work plays on the pun of its title, raising and disappointing expectations of a work about persons of mixed racial heritage. Like Gozu's, her book is relatively large in format (about 11 x 8 1/2 inches) and also offset printed on coated stock, a paper particularly suited to the reproduction of photographic images. Piper's collection consists of photographs of about a dozen individuals each of whom appears individually in an image in all of the eight sections of the book. The sections are all titled by an emotion which carries a color association with it — "tickled pink," "green with envy," "purple with anger," and so forth. In each image the person photographed takes on an appropriate facial expression and onto the black and white photograph is superimposed a scribbled area in the color of the indicated emotion. The effect is a tongue-in-cheek commentary on emotions, identity, race, and color. The formal strength of the work comes from its consistency of format and the fact that the photographs do not come in the same sequence in each section, thus upsetting the predictability of their order. The photographs can readily be compared by flipping back and forth through the pages of the book. As the work is comprised of about a hundred and fifty images, this would be difficult if the piece were displayed in a gallery. Nonetheless, Piper is not particularly concerned with the book as a form, she takes book conventions as a given and makes use of them to a good end. However, this works as a thematic exposition rather than a formal exploration of the book form.

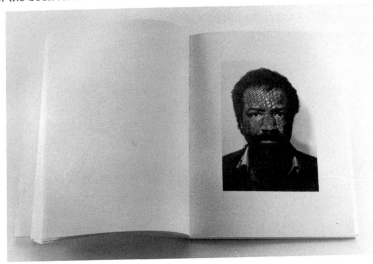

Adrian Piper, **Colored People**, 1991

Variations on the Photo-Roman

The photo-roman is well-known in many cultures, particularly in Italy, Spain, and to a lesser degree in France. It is barely known in the United States where the romance novel takes a textual, rather than visual, form. Though the ordinary photo-roman combines both words and images in a cartoon-strip like photographic sequence, the artist's book version sometimes takes the visual image as its exclusive material. The subject matter of the photo-roman in its conventional form is always romance ("photo-roman" means "photographic romance"). It is a printed soap opera. Artists' interpretations run the full gamut. Douglas Beube's **Manhattan Street Romance** (Visual Studies Workshop, 1982) self-consciously imitates the

photo-roman genre though the work displays the pastiche aesthetic of a
contemporary artist.

Douglas Beube, **Manhattan Street Romance**, 1982

In Beube's work Manhattan is as much the object of affection as the
woman whom the narrator courts. The front cover shows New York at
night, a random section of lit up highrises, against which the white drop-
out type of the title reads like a neon sign. A postcard-sized image stuck
into the center of the scene shows Broadway at night, and its dark tonal
values allow the inset to blend with the surrounding image. On top of that
inset is the torn image of a heart, its top two rounded globes marking out
a dark space, its missing point poignantly torn from the whole. The book
plays with conventions of narrative, establishing at the outset the identity
of two characters, a narrator named Max and a woman with the initial "M"
— presumably the "Marian" of the dedication. Images of two breakfast
plates on a table by the window face a postcard of a man and a woman.
Other scenes of a domestic interior, glimpses of the woman's feet and
shoes, her eye, later her face, and images of a couple in the park are the
strongest links to a narrative. There are a few blocks of text which provide
moments of insight into the nature of their relationship but there is no
attempt to depict or detail a story. The photographic elements change
scale in the pastiches — sometimes a torn fragment of a photograph is
imposed on the skyline of the city, sometimes the hand of one of the characters holds this bit of pastiche in place, so that the space of the book
moves between that of writer and reader, illusion, and self-conscious
attention to the photographic quality of the images. This is a deconstructed photo-roman which refers to the genre, but does not repeat its
conventions. The book flows because a quasi-narrative expectation has
been established, and because the structure of the pages has enough con-

tinuity to move the reader forward. The black and white photographs keep the images cool and formal with a film noir feeling.

Urs Luthi's enigmatic book **The Desert is Across the Street** (De Appel, 1975) uses the photograpic medium to create a book of suggestive but indecipherable images. Offset printed on coated stock these images are blurry, out of focus, and very dark. There is a sense of ambiguity about the space — inside or outside — and the characters — two young and very hip looking people in dark clothes and sunglasses. If there is a story in this book, it is a one of non-sequitors and abrupt transitions, more in the manner of Heinrich von Kleist than of Emile Zola. Though the book bears a strong resemblance to the **policier** (noir detective) films of French directors of the 1940s and 1950s as well as to Jean Luc Godard's parodic imitations of them (from the same period as this book). There is a path. There is a park. There is a parking garage. And there are the figures in the dark glasses. The out of focus blurriness of the images adds to their intrigue, and the passage through the book leaves one with the distinct impression of having witnessed something, though precisely what is not quite clear. Luthi's strength, like Beube's, is in taking the conventionally legible sequence of photo-narratives and deconstructing them enough to be intriguing but not so much as to lose the compelling sense that the images have revealed connections which will become clear with sufficient contemplation.

Urs Luthi, **The Desert is Across the Street**, 1975

John Baldessari is also highly skilled in this manipulation of photographic narratives. Like Luthi, Baldessari includes no verbal elements in **The Telephone Book with Pearls** (Imschoot, 1988). This is a later Baldessari book — his earlier photo-roman derivatives were simpler in format and presentation. **The Telephone Book** contains many of the

John Baldessari, **The Telephone Book with Pearls**, 1988

graphic elements which Baldessari brought into his large photo-collage works of the 1980s — particularly the odd but distinctive shapes of the cropped images and the brightly colored circles or dots used to cover faces or other important details. (**Close Cropped Tales**, Cepa Gallery, 1981, uses these cropping conventions as its premise in a series of sections titled "A three-sided tale," through "An eight-sided tale".) Baldessari's narrative in **The Telephone Book** is articulated mainly through the use of dramatic still shots. In the opening sequence there is an image of a phone caught between two different persons' hands; then the neck of a woman dancing with a male partner — again displaying pearls; and a third image in which another woman in a black cocktail dress wearing another string of pearls speaks on the phone. The sequence's structure replays the main themes of the title through a careful deconstruction of the elements — telephone and pearls — into variations on their identity. The same elements show up, but as different versions, and the assumption of their relation is strong enough to carry through the book into every appearance of phone or pearls. Male power and female objectification are presented as pictorial and cultural stereotypes — Baldessari is particularly sensitive to such cliches — and the "roles" of the gendered individuals is part of the subtext of the tale. There can be no single recuperated narrative here — the figures are always different people in new settings photographed in

223

varied ways — but the unity of thematic concerns makes a narrative in spite of the absence of any overarching story. The graphic consistency and seductive production values aid this process, as well as the references to the classic late 19th-century tale by Guy de Maupassant, "The Necklace." In de Maupassant's story a woman's covetousness causes her downful when she loses a borrowed piece of jewelry and spends her lifetime paying to replace it — only to find out after many years go by that it was a fake. The absence of clear narrative structure keeps Baldessari's tale from the tight moral closure of the original, but the final image of the book is taken from the movie version of the story, a close-up of the fabulous paste necklace glowing on the rounded neck of a 1940s movie actress.

Marcel Broodthaers, **Voyage on the North Sea**, 1973

As visual works, the books discussed here largely function without the need for language, forging a narrative sequence or non-narrative relation through formal and thematic means. In **Voyage on the North Sea** (Petersburg Press, 1973) Marcel Broodthaers takes an image of an oil painting (a reproduction of an oil painting of a sailing ship on — where else — the North Sea) and uses it along with a single black and white photograph of a sailboat as the only images in the work. He deconstructs the oil painting showing bits and pieces of it enlarged and reduced. This calls attention to details of its original production and reproduction. But it also creates effects of movement, approach and withdrawal, from the photographed boat. The book's meaning remains slightly elusive. We make a voyage in this work, moving through a rough sea of deconstructive techniques and visual pleasure, and are shown the image as information through its dissection. But the image is the book, and the book is the fully reconstructed whole of the fragmented single image whose parts are continually juxtaposed to the black and white photograph. On the one hand, this is an exposition of and about visuality, and on the other hand it is a visual deconstruction of an unrevealed proposition.

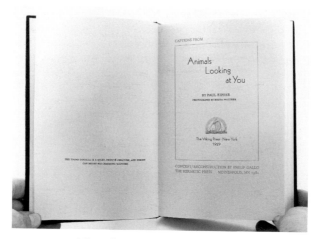

Phillip Gallo, **Captions from Animals Looking at You**, 1981

At another extreme from this work is a book with absent images. This is Phillip Gallo's, **Captions from Animals Looking at You** (Hermetic Press, 1981). Gallo's book is a reconstruction of a 1929 publication, **Animals Looking at You**, from which he has taken only the captions. Though they have no visual form whatsoever, these images exist. They are referred to, pointed to, and invoked through both verbal means and the empty blank space on the page above these lines. This is a photographic work without images present. These are images which signify fully and repletely through their absence. This is true only because they are named and invoked in verbal terms. Language in this case does not anchor, relay, or complement meaning in the image, it produces it completely. Whether or not this should qualify as a photographic work seems open to debate. But I like the idea of thinking of it that way and of ending this section on the book as a visual form with a work whose visual component is in the mind not the eye of the reader.

1 Roland Barthes, **Image/Music/Text** (Hill & Wang, 1979) especially, "The Rhetoric of the Image."

2 I'm not trying to discount the ambiguities of which language is capable either, since

artists' books are often an arena for loosening language from its pedestrian or conventional functions.

3 The idea of **production** is meant to be distinguished from the idea of **reproduction** which takes an existing image and makes it into a multiple. A **production** can result in a multiple — and any medium, offset included, can be used for the direct creation of images. But the term **reproduction** implies that the image is not made in the process of printing, but exists before and outside of that process, thus undergoing some kind of transformation in that process from original image to a reproduction in another medium. For further disucussion of this refer to the catalog **Offset**, (Interplanetary Productions, 1993) from Brad Freeman's exhbition of the same name and to Phil Zimmermann's "Offset" issue of **Exposure** 21:3 (1983).

4 Most of the book appears to have been printed in CMYK — that is four-color process, but with brighter, hotter inks than standard process inks. There are also areas of spot color.

5 The term "spot color" refers to the use of a particular color of ink, rather than color achieved through four-color process printing. In a "split fountain" ink color is added to the press's fountain of ink in such a way that a blend is made on the sheet — a range of color is thus achieved in a single run. A split fountain might have a blue on one end and bright green on the other and over the course of the run they blend in the center, any combination of colors may be used.

6 No publisher is listed: the drawings were done in relation to two exhibitions the first at the Galerie im Taxispalais in Innsbruck in 1974, the second at the Forum Stadtpark in Graz, 1975, while the credit for the book reads Forum fur aktuelle Kunst in Innsbruck. See also the Dieter Roth's **1234 Most Speedy Drawings**.

7 **Rule** refers to lengths of metal cast in varying thicknesses to produced straight "ruled" lines on a page; perforation rule is used for scoring and perforating a sheet by increasing the pressure and packing on the press.

8 Buenos Aires and Sao Paolo are listed as locations for the publisher.

9 Now, linoleum cuts, or scratchboard (a white board coated with a black waxy covering the artist scrapes away) can be used to achieve similar effects with far less labor.

10 Schocken Books (New York) issued a reprint, with brief final notes, in 1988.

11 This is the accurate spelling of the title, the implications of which are left to the reader.

12 The bird subfamily Turdinae, which includes robins, thrushes, and bluebirds, are a group of particularly fine singers.

13 See Chapter 6.

14 This is similar to Karen Chance's manipulation of space in **Parallax** — though her interpenetration of private/public spaces was done with cut holes connecting the two.

9

Books as Verbal Exploration

The idea of the book as a textual document is familiar from novels to cookbooks, instruction manuals to law books, the Bible to a myriad of other forms. In artists' books the appearance of text is malleable and liable to be subject to manipulation through formal means. As in the case of images, production means vary: calligraphy, ordinary handwriting, stencils, rubber stamps, letterpress, press-type, photographic and computer generated typography are all possible ways of putting type onto pages. Sometimes the very form of the writing is invented so that the marks are closer to images than letters and make use of production methods generally reserved for pictures.

There are artists' books which — to make a fine point of distinction — use language and artists' books which are actually written. There is no moral or aesthetic hierarchy among these but they have a different feel for language. In the first group language has an ordinariness — it is familiar, but not self-conscious, and tends to be instrumental and prosaic rather than poetic.ı In the second group language is appreciated for all its material properties and linguistic resonance. In such works the sonoric aspects of language such as rhythm, texture, timing, and also the visual aspects are brought into the book form as part of its substance. In this section the works I will deal with almost all belong to this second category.

Invented Writing: Scripts and Glyphs

There is something about invented writing which exerts a fascination. The glyphs which show up, for instance, on the pages of Timothy C. Ely's work have the potent suggestiveness of spells or incantations in an esoteric language. The marks are imbued with meaning but seem to belong to a secret realm which charges these invented signs with power and value. One is drawn into their curious forms with an intense desire to decipher, decode, and get at their elusive content. Not all of these works have occult allegiances; humor and parody are as often components of invented scripts as are serious or arcane practices.

The Lettrists, a post-1945, avant-garde group formed in Paris by the Roumanian Isidore Isou, were not only involved in the invention of new glyphic writing forms, but made this activity one of their central concerns. Isou (some of whose works were discussed earlier) was convinced that his Lettrist innovations signalled the beginning of a third phase of written communication. In his version of history, alphabetic writing and the invention of the printing press had marked the first two major phases of written language. The Lettrists' approach was going to initiate the third. Isou's idea was that Lettrism was an interrogation of letterforms as the fundamental units of communication — and he wanted to see language destructively pulverized and then reinvented through their experiments. New forms and new letters would form the basis of an entirely original written language. Isou's closest allies in this endeavor were the first two artists to join in his Lettrist movement — Maurice Lemaitre and Gabriel Pomerand. Both produced works which attempted to fulfill Isou's call for a Lettrist "hypergraphy:" Pomerand made the innovative **St. Ghetto des Prets** book in 1950 and Lemaitre created his **Roman Hypergraphique** in the same year. Many other Lettrist works by these and the host of followers Isou attracted in the 1950s and 1960s exist, though there is a mannered and derivative look to much of the later work. The reinvention of language as a reinvention of the social order, politics, culture — in short, as the means to reinvent the world — was a major tenet of the historical, early 20th-century avant-garde; the Lettrists gave it its last mainstream art-world incarnation.

I will discuss one of Lemaitre's works to give a sense of the formal character of the inventions on which the Lettrists placed such expectations. The **Roman Hypergraphique (Hypergraphic Novel)** (1950) consists of ten pages and one could easily argue that it does not quite constitute a book. But since it was named and conceived of as a "novel" I will treat it as an autonomous work.2 Lemaitre's novel — the "real and spiritual journey of a young man" — works with visual images, glyph-like marks, small icons, and letters used as graphic elements. Lemaitre tries to avoid using letters conventionally. Though the tenets of the Lettrist invention were elaborate, they were not always clear, but one of their main characteristics was an interdiction against normative usage. Lemaitre was true to this one principle, at least, and his mixture of rebus-like arrangements and

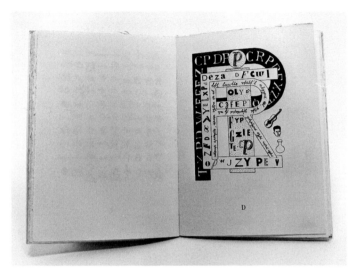

Maurice Lemaitre, **Roman Hypergraphique**, 1950

schematic diagrams interwove with his newly invented phonetic alphabet. On one page of this novel Lemaitre arranged images of the solar system, planet earth, the continent of Europe, and other particulars in decreasing scale — ending the sequence with an image of himself. There are no Lettrist inventions here, but there is a belief in the use of visual materials as primary means of communication. Another page was composed of small drawings of objects meant to be read according to the resemblance between their shapes and that of letters. This was a painfully slow way to assemble words, but a reasonably successful way of blocking their easy translation into disembodied meaning. The "letters" take so much deciphering that conventional reading is deferred. Another page used images as if they communicated sense directly — with a rising sun "meaning" the act of arising, a footstep indicating a trip, a line of waves a body of water, and so forth. Lemaitre was unperturbed by the indeterminate aspect of these images — or at least did not acknowledge them. In another image he used letters of the alphabet according to a set of substitutions and containing a buried key to their meaning. Graphically successful, Lemaitre considered this the best attempt he had made at a "mise en page hypergraphique" (or "hypergraphic page layout"). In other pages he made use of an invented phonetic alphabet, some classic images from the history of writing particularly non-alphabetic scripts, and any other graphic means he could muster. The result is highly worked, but almost

229

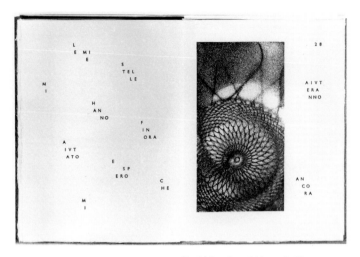

Max Ernst & Iliazd (Ilia Zdanevich), **Maximiliana**, 1964

completely unintelligible. The Lettrist desire for destruction and reconfiguration of communicative means at the basic level of the mark is well served by these attempts, but the repercussions in either the artworld or beyond were not forthcoming.

In Lettrist productions these glyphs were abundant. They appeared on the surfaces of clothing, photographs, common objects, walls, movie screens, and all the materials associated with fine arts. In the history of relations between art and writing they serve as one rather florid and prolific intersection. More elegant invented scripts exist, however, and more complete investigations of the relations between the book and writing. One book in which writing is explored as a graphic (even cosmographic) medium is **Maximiliana** (41 Degrees, 1964) which was the result of a collaboration between Max Ernst and Iliazd.3 According to the criteria of format and production this work could be considered a **livre d'artiste**, but the work of Iliazd occupies a peculiar grey zone between this genre and that of the artist's book. Books were Iliazd's sole medium. The works he produced under his imprint 41 Degrees were always collaborative projects in which he had as much responsibility for every aspect of design and production as any of the artists or writers with whom he collaborated. Iliazd designed the typography, layouts, all of the structure, sequence, and format of **Maximiliana**. He researched the text and then assisted in setting, printing, and binding the work.4 Like all of Iliazd's books this work is thought through in every single detail.

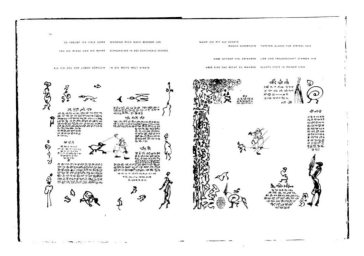

Max Ernst & Iliazd (Ilia Zdanevich), **Maximiliana**, 1964

The text of this book is taken from the writings of a 19th-century astronomer, Guillaume Tempel, who had given the name "Maximiliana" to a newly discovered stellar body. Iliazd noted the coincidence of names and used this as a point of departure for the collaboration with (Max) Ernst. Tempel, an impoverished astronomer, had written epigrammatic texts about his struggle to sustain his profession without support — a theme which found sympathy with Iliazd whose passions for books, Byzantine church architecture, ballet, and mountain terrain barely provided him with a subsistence. **Maximiliana** is a veritable catalogue of the possibilities of invented and conventional writing. Iliazd takes typography into many constellations and configurations to produce an effect of astronomical phenomena under observation. Alternating with these pages are elaborately laid-out sheets filled with Ernst's invented writings. Iliazd provided a template for each block and Ernst drew in the requisite forms. Ernst's writing displays vitality and graphic invention throughout — his dynamic lines curl and knot to form strings of signs which resemble organic forms (flatworms, amoebas, fish, and reptiles) as well as echoing the hieratic and hieroglyphic scripts of ancient or exotic cultures. The range of the book, and the structural integrity of its parts to the whole, allow it to serve as a study of the way writing functions visually — from the clearly measured lines of handset type to their spatialized form and back into the primeval origins of the Ernst inventions.

Between the artifices of Lemaitre's hypergraphic novel and the elegant

231

graphic innovations of Ernst's "writing" many aspects of glyphs and invented scripts can be considered. For instance, one can examine real glyphs, ancient or not-so ancient writing systems whose linguistic coral-laries are long-gone, unknown, or elusive. These undeciphered languages continue to exert their fascination as visual signs — an interest which often diminishes if they can be read.5

Mikal And & Elizabeth Was, **The Plagiarist Codex**, n.d.

Dagur Helgason's book, **Islenskir Galdrastafir** (Stop Over Press, n.d.) is based on a 13th-century text on early Icelandic runes and resonates nicely with the work of Mikal And and Elizabeth Was **The Plagiarist Codex** (Xexoxial Endarchy, n.d.). Both contain bits of writing which cannot be read, both present them in book form as a way of offering these images to a public which must rely on the writer's text for possible comprehension. The plagiarised work redraws its originals with a funny edge, as if acknowledging the impossibility of accuracy. The Helgason book is more flat, and circumspect and relies on the distance of cultures to guarantee its authenticity (how could I know, how would I, whether these are real runes or the product of Helgason's imagination or genetic pool?). Xexox-ial's book is subtitled "an old Maya information hieroglyph" and the images are convincing reworkings of original forms — here given new translations and new impact. Its last words are: "something post-indus-trial gives way to both words — reprint." These are accompanied by images of two scribes and an image of something else enigmatic. And this

232

is where it ends — the invented and the elusive, the esoteric and the arcane — the image of marks might represent some language just beyond the limits of our capacity to read them.

Concrete Poetry

Concrete poetry differs from early 20th-century experiments with the visual appearance of language in both its form and aesthetic principles. While Futurist and Dada artists used a variety of typefaces and formats to liberate poetic language from the constraints of literary conventions, particularly the linear format of the even grey-toned page, Concrete poets were intent on forging a unity between the visual and verbal aspects of a work. Early avant-garde experiments had a random, chaotic, and allover quality to the language and the look of the page (examples being the ransom-note typographic works of Dadaists like Raoul Hausmann and Tristan Tzara). In contrast, Concrete poetry tends to be condensed, even reductive. The forms of Concrete poetry vary, but these works are united by their desire to literally **concretize** meaning — embed its verbal complexity in a material, visual form from which it cannot be separated. In this way, Concrete poets take the concept of materiality of language farther than earlier experimenters, trying to forge inseparable bonds of meaning and presentation through visual form. 6

Many Concrete poets were interested in spatialized images or tropes, as in Eugen Gomringer's work **the constellations** (first published in German as **konstellationen**, Spiral Press, 1953) which spreads the verbal material over the page in a pattern meant to embody the constellations. Other poets made small, pictorial references in their work — the letters of the word "pendulum" swing outward from the left margin in Ernesto M. de Melo e Castro's "Pendulo," 1962, while the words of John Furnival's "The Eiffel Tower," 1966, compose a sexually charged image of that most iconic of forms along with a phallic partner depicted rising between the posts of its sprawling base. While many of these poets' works were collected in book form or anthologized, a considerable number of these works are engaged only with the page, rather than the book.

The American poet Richard Kostelanetz published many concrete and visual works in books such as **Visual Language** (Assembling Press, 1970) and **Illuminations** (Future Press, 1977). Kostelanetz characterized these "concrete" works as "emphasizing the fragmentation of language..." and asserted that its primary intention was "the elimination of conventional

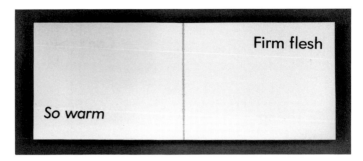

Richard Kostelanetz, **One Night Stood**, 1977

syntax." Though these two collections by Kostelanetz contain a seemingly endless number of approaches to the deconstruction of language through reductive visual means, they remain collections of works sustained at most across several pages. In **One Night Stood** (Future Press, 1977), however, Kostelanetz uses the book structure as part of his "concrete" agenda. The book is small and thick, hand-sized. There are two voices in the book, one which appears on the upper part of the right page, one on the bottom edge of the left. These voices, whose language consists only of phrases, chart the course of a one-night stand encounter whose specifics are hinted at, not rendered explicitly. The structural divisions of the book function as part of the conversation, keeping the alternation going and preserving the brevity and spareness of the suggestive remarks.

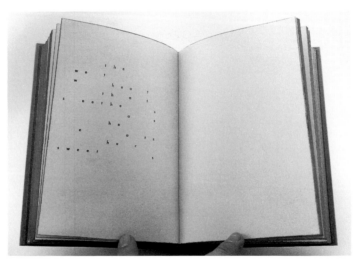

Emmett Williams, **Sweethearts**, 1968

Emmett Williams's **Sweethearts** (Something Else Press, 1968) is also fundamentally concrete in character but engaged with the book form. It is composed of a single word: "sweethearts." Through successive manipulations of the letters of this word, Williams structures a secondary text from his dissections. Page after page reveals the possibilities of deconstruction as Williams drops letters out of their sequence in the word to let it read. Part of Williams' skill is his respect for the position of the letters in the word — which is always preserved — while he pulls out phrase after phrase, as in "he wets her sweet ears." The book is the extension and exhaustion of these experiments in taking the terms of affection apart.

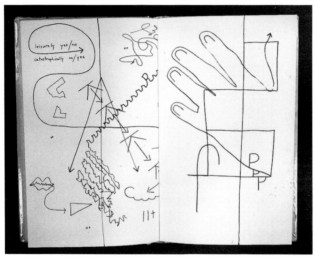

Steve McCaffery and b.p. Nichol, **In England Now That Spring**, 1979

Steve McCaffery and b.p. Nichol have a far more complex relation to language in their collaborative work **In England Now that Spring** (Aya Press, 1979). Each of the poets made an individual contribution to the book, which is comprised of three parts. In the middle section they collaborated in what are the most graphically adventurous portions. This work has more affinities to literary publishing than to artists' books, but the self-conscious attention which the work displays to the structure of a book as an extension of its poetics is important. It also serves as a particularly vivid example of the organizational sensitivity which poets frequently make use of in putting their work into book form. Both poets make use of visual configurations in their work. In McCaffery's poems "Position of Sheep" part I and II, for instance, the words "sheep" and "lamb" dot the page in imitation of their place in the landscape. In more elaborately diagrammatic works such as the "Six Glasgow Texts," the page becomes a score for action, instruction, and performance rather than a linguistic transcription.7

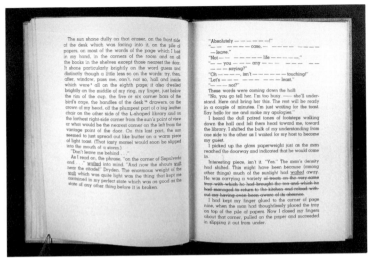

Madeline Gins, **Word Rain**, 1969

A work which makes the book form subject as well as vehicle for exploration is Madeline Gins's, **Word Rain** (Grossman Publishers, 1969). In a familiar gesture of self-consciousness, the title page of this book is a photograph of an open book, its shadowed pages showing the full curve and curl of the pages turned back from the spine. Gins codes every aspect of this book with self-referential values. From the outset the text talks about itself, its presence and presentation, its attempts to show what it is as image and producer of images. "Look at this sentence. There is nothing on it. Now look at this sentence. I see a place of desert ribbed with dunes held in place with drops of slime just above a layer of petrified tentacles. There is nothing in this sentence. I say I see a book in this sentence. Without me, it words the page; yet says nothing."

Within the text Gins breaks from her narrative about the book to provide instructions on how to read the book — and the manipulations of type on the page make use of every possible convention — lined through, blanked out, filled in with hyphens and dashes, crowding a page, putting only a single phrase in the midst of a blank turning. The image of language as an atmospheric activity (rain) invoked by the title is carried through as

236

a prevailing metaphor in a work which slips continually from literal to abstract language, and from self-reference to open-ended suggestion. The final page of the book is densely overprinted, though the normal line spacing is preserved. At the bottom of this block of mostly unreadable text are two sentences: "The body is composed 98% of water." and "This page contains every word in the book." With these two final sentences the meaning of "word rain" as an organic, corporeal, linguistic experience is brought into focus and given its most graphic representation of visual density. Gins's book is printed offset, though there is no structural reason why it could not have been letterpress or xerox since only in two places does it rely on photographic images — the title page already described and an interior page showing the thumb and edge of a hand holding the book. Everywhere else the book is composed of type and text whose visual variety is conceived within conventions rather than through their deconstruction or transgression.

Typewriter Works

Another favorite medium of poets who experiment with the visual form of poetry is the typewriter. The precision of the typewriter, especially older models, which allocated the same amount of line space to every letter, made it a versatile tool for graphic manipulation.

Minimalist sculptor Carl Andre's typewriter works from the 1960s have a strong relation to the sculptural works he was doing at the same time. Ordered, measured, regular variations on simple structural arrangements, these pieces turn the patient patterning of paper with typewritten marks into works of visual subtlety. Unlike the Nannucci's M40/1967, which derives its structure from the keyboard sequence, Andre's picks and choses among the visual possibilities of the typewriter as an austere palette of tonal marks.[8] Andre's most sustained project in this medium was **Still, A Novel**, a project whose novelistic qualities are breadth and duration rather than detailed narratives or characters.[9] The work consists of page after page of typescripted marks and becomes an image of stillness and stability as well as taking the concept "still" as a sign of endurance and extensive temporality. The various meanings of the title, **Still, A Novel**, also defend the work against expected protests, proclaiming that this minimalist project is — in spite of all its unconventional features — a novel.

The typewritten works of Henri Chopin, **Typewriter poems** (Edition

Henri Chopin, **Typewriter Poems**, 1982

Hundertmark, 1982) and Bernard Heidsieck, **Poèsie Sonore** (Edition Hundertmark, 1984) are far more chaotic and visually fragmented than Andre's carefully gridded pages. Heidsieck's pieces were meant to score a performed work or at the very least to perform on the page. The distribution of words and syllables are sometimes accompanied with instructions for their rendering in voice or for other factors such as signs, breathing, or the use of simultaneous enunciation. Such works are far more easily produced by typewriter than through other means since the physical placement on the sheet can be precisely figured simply by positioning the carriage. In letterpress such elaborate spacing requires considerable justification, a process far more time consuming and arduous than in the typewritten medium.10 Heidsieck's poems stretch the full space of the openings in this small book. His attention to the whole work as a series of movements is clearly rendered in the position of blocks of type and the progression from page to page. The straightforward character of Heidsieck's work is quite different from Chopin's book which is comprised of reproductions of typewriter works. Chopin's pieces, mainly using the graphic rather than the alphabetic characters of the keyboard, have been painted, stained, and played with as images before being reproduced. They float in murky clouds of unclear grey matter reproduced on grey paper, the perfectly structural blocks of typewritten marks blurred and partially obscured by the fluid passages which have been layered onto

238

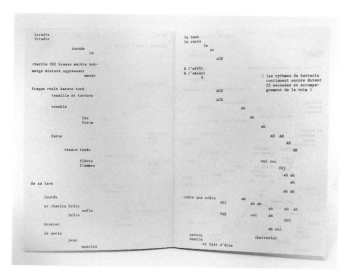

Bernard Heidsieck, **Poèsie Sonore**, 1984

them. The contrast between these organic, liquid forms and the regular pattern of the typewriter has its own aesthetic effect — the emphatic distinction of organic and mechanical forms — but unlike Heidsieck's book, Chopin's is a collection of miscellaneous parts rather than an integration into a whole.

Steve McCaffery's two part work **Carnival** — **The First Panel: 1967-70** (Coach House Press, 1973) and **The Second Panel:1970-75** (Coach House Press, n.d.) — is made using a typewriter. But to call it a typewriter work would be to suggest that its identity should be constrained to its mode of production, which is far from true. **Carnival** was conceived within the tradition of theoretical poetics which derives its impetus from the early avant-garde work of Mallarmé and Kruchenyk, Mayakovsky and Marinetti, as well as the major mainstreams of experimental Anglophone verse in the work of Ezra Pound, Louis Zukovsky, and Charles Olson. For McCaffery, poetics are a form of symbolic intervention, a means of creating a subversive, or at least alternative, space of language as a form of spiritual regeneration and expansion. McCaffery defines his work as a form of "counter-communication" and **Carnival** is its graphemic (using script, letters, and other visual text elements) expression. The work is comprised of standard typewriter sheets which are all part of a single, large-scale composition. There are sixteen pages in the book, which is not bound (the sheets were perforated in the original binding so that they could be removed and

Steve McCaffery, **Carnival: The Second Panel**, 1970-75

assembled). **The First Panel** used the typewriter exclusively, **Panel Two** extended to xerography, rubber-stamp, hand-lettering, stencils and other forms of letter production. The result was a five-color original (repro-duced in the Coach House edition in black and red) in which "language units are placed in visible conflict, in patterns of defective messages, cre-ating a semantic texture by shaping an interference within the clear line of statement."11 For McCaffery, the typewriter is not only a tool, but a machine with a complex historical and cultural past. He links it to early 18th century poetic forms with which its invention was contemporary (rather than to the 19th century world of mechanical reproduction and commerce with which it is more generally associated). The typewriter's capacity to participate in poetic order as well as its subversion is empha-sized in McCaffery's working out of visual linguistic form, a kind of "semantic patchwork," in which "blocks of truncated sense ... overlap, converge, collide without transition..."12 In book form, one encounters the field as a series of discrete units, each of which contains material from its proximate neighbors in the whole work to which they belong. McCaffery is attentive to the boundaries of the page, even as he overrides its limits in forging connections from panel to panel. But each individual sheet manages to hold its own as a visual work, each is remarkably different

240

Charles Bernstein, **Veil**, 1987

from the others, and each has a remarkable range of richness in its variation of visual, as well as poetic, tone.

In Charles Bernstein's **Veil** (Xexoxial Editions, 1987) language "veils" and covers itself in a process of overprinting. The original poems were produced using IBM Selectric typewriter elements (regular and italic). The texts, like the final page of Madeline Gins's **Word Rain**, are densely overprinted to form the veiling effect of the title. The language layers into a translucent screen which cancels the possibility of reading, but does not entirely obliterate text. Words seep through, in some places almost legible, and the veil between meaning and reading seems always on the verge of lifting. The words themselves veil the page and the progression of the pages is towards greater density. The end sheets of the book use enlarged extracts of passages blown up, reproduced photomechanically, and printed to reinforce the graphic quality of their manipulation. The typewriter's presence is overwhelming here, quite at the opposite extreme from the work of another artist, Davi Det Hompson.

Hompson's approach to the use and presentation of language is as flat, dull, and deliberately levelled as possible. His are not works which fall flat, but works which are made to be flat and affectless. Hompson has developed this monotone verbality into his characteristic style in the pamphlet book, **Understand. This is only temporary** (Hompson, n.d.). In this work, an enlarged typescript has been printed onto 8 1/2 x 11 inch sheets which are folded and stapled into the book. The statements are blank, enigmatic, and brief such as: "You should uncover it immediately." The result is a suggestive series of statements whose relation to each other and to the book are vague, but held together through the punch line on the final page, "I didn't know you could type." Many of Hompson's books use this format, which he has endowed with a particular value through continual use. Clive Phillpot, who has a sympathetic relation to Hompson's work, feels that Hompson continually calls attention to the fact of language's visual form through these works. "Because written or printed words stand in for spoken language it is easy not to see that reading is a visual activity," Phillpot writes.13 Though it may be true that Hompson's language is acutely verbal, the contrast of Bernstein's work is significant here since Bernstein obviously takes it as a given in **Veil** that the language he is using is written and graphic, not a transcription of an utterance while Hompson makes minimal use of the visual potential of the typewriter.

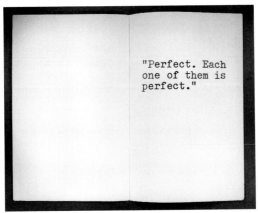

Davi Det Hompson, **Understand**, n.d.

Found Poetry

Found poetry is a favorite form of both contemporary writers and the makers of artists' books. In both cases what is stressed is the richness of language as we encounter it in the world with all its strangeness, irony, and idiosyncracy. A major figure in the synthesis of found poetry and the book form is Bern Porter. Porter's works are numerous, beginning in the 1950s with his publication of **Found Poems** (later republished by Some-

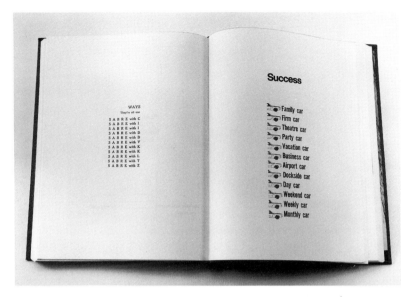

Bern Porter, **Found Poems**, 1972

thing Else Press, 1972). Writing of Porter's work in his annotated bibliography of Something Else, Peter Frank stated that "Porter is to the poem what Duchamp was to the art object, a debunker of handiwork fetishism and exemplary artist-as-intercessor between phenomenon and receptor."14 Porter used every available non-literary source for his work though it is often his skill in cutting or collaging these bits of found language together which provides their impact. All of his books, from **Found Poems** to **The Book of Do's** (Dog Ear Press, 1982), and **Sweet End** (Dog Ear Press, 1989) are compendia of found work selected according to theme. Porter's talent is his capacity to manipulate the sequence and timing of these pieces. They are not merely shoved into the book in a haphazard manner but given a textual progression and nuanced graphic relations in their page to page juxtaposition. The commentary which Porter's poems produce on the spectacle of contemporary life is pointed and sharp. One edited headline reads "10 reasons why we do faster, more," while below this, numbered from 1 to 10, are ten repetitions of the statement "We do our own" with the work "fabrication" appended to line 6 of the series. Porter's works are a critique of consumer culture . This is made clear in the imperative voice used in **The Book of Do's** or the pieces collected on the theme of death, funeral rites, and burial in **Sweet End**.

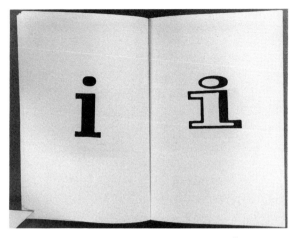

Ann Noel, **YOU**, 1982

By contrast to Porter's complex and multilayered eclecticism, Ann Noel's **You** (Rainer Verlag, 1982) has a classical feel. It is minimal, clean, and very focused. Where Porter's books are large in format (8 1/2 x 11" pages) Noel's is compact and thick, a bulky satisfying tome to hold, printed on yellowish paper perfectbound in a paler yellow wrapper. The title, **You**, of the work is the only occurrence of the second-person pronoun in the work, the contents of which consist of several hundred instances of the letter "i" each in a different typeface and style. Enlarged photographically so that they all have a consistent scale, the letters embody the individuated character of personal identity. Each "i" is a self, a persona, an image, as a single first-person pronoun in graphic form. Fat, thin, slanted and straight, outlined and bold, decorative and austerely plain, Noel's graphic spectrum never repeats itself. The beauty of the work gives the book a seriousness in spite of its obvious humor. The repetition and variations of the "I" has as much resonance with minimalist and formal aesthetics as with cultural issues or identity politics.

A highly synthetic, labor-intensive work of found language is an early book by Emily McVarish, **being the letters / the parts of speech / The Psychopathology of Everyday Life** (1990). This was produced without a press or printing equipment using the local xerox store, cutting knife and paste pot in an edition of thirteen copies. It is an epistolary novel which recounts the trials of "first person" in a desperate and hopelessly inept attempt to communicate with "second person." This drama of grammatical characters is synthesized from an actual grammar text and from Sigmund

Freud's **The Psychopathology of Everyday Life**. The letters they exchange are contained in envelopes, themselves bound to make the pages of the book. The first letter maps the distance between them. An opening line reads: "So there you are in Los Angeles and similar places, between the monkeys and the angels." While a closing line states: "As for me, I roam the house, looking for signs of the broken edges where this subject (you) has been. [....] 'Mind' and philosophical literary things shuffle and pretend to succeed in disguising the loss." And so they do shuffle and pretend, these literary things, these phrases cut and pasted into new almost seamless arrangements recycling the words of the rule makers into a story of broken communication. Though the book had production problems — it is already falling apart at the spine, its inadequate paste no longer holding, the smeared edges of the title plaquette stained with the marks of inept gluing — the book has a power to it which derives from the artist's convictions. With all of its faults, this work survives as a complete world unto itself, filled with dramatic intrigue and closeted secrets extracted from sources and transformed in their new context.

Emily McVarish, **being the letters...**, 1990

The final work of found poetry here is a visual, photographic collection rather than a strictly typographic one. Nathan Lyons', **Verbal Landscape / Dinosaur Sat Down** (Visual Studies Workshop Press, 1987), is a collection of photographs of language found in the landscape.15 Lyons' skill is in the strict ordering of elements within the book so that they flow from one to the next and back. Offset printed as duotones, these photographs preserve much of the material richness of their found originals — handprinting, professional signmaking, or amateur stop-gap measures in varying states of decay or preservation are all included. Peeling paint, fading letters, or worn masonry add to the evocative feeling of the language. For instance, in one image, "Mural goes here" appears in roughly spray-painted stencil-form letters on the base of a huge expanse of concrete freeway support, and in the next decorated letters cut out of paper droop selectively in a store window, transforming the original word "SIGNS" into "SINS" through this accidental wear. In all four cases (Porter, Noel, McVarish, Lyons), the "found" poetry is visual and tactile as well as linguistic in character (though McVarish has cut her text so closely together that the marks of appropriation disappear). The physical form of the books permits the display of this distinct aesthetic sensibility — from Noel's tight format and formalist attitude, to Porter's large, floppy works of dense compilation, and Lyons' photographic specificity.

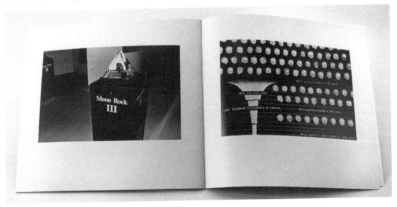

Nathan Lyons, **Dinosaur Sat Down**, 1987

Page as Field or Frame

The precedents for using the page as field or even pictorial frame in which verbal elements take on some of the qualities of an image can be found in the work of Filippo Marinetti, the Italian Futurist, whose "words in liberty" took the old tradition of pattern poetry into a new relation with avant-garde language and poetics. Marinetti's publication **Les Mots en Liberté** (Milan, 1919) used the basic structure of pictorial images — horizon line, illusion of depth, and schematic diagrams of spatial relations. Russian and German Dada and Futurist poets made other typographically experimental works, but there are only a few pages in them which actively made use of the page as a pictorial image. In the latter half of the 20th century there are many concrete poets who have used the visual form of language to investigate the relations between visual and verbal imagery. Since much of this work has been limited to individual pages, poems, or wall pieces rather than book form it doesn't contribute much to this discussion. There are, however, some works which both attend to the book as a form and make use of the page as a field. Very few of these are pictorial in their organization or reference though many are highly self-conscious about the structural elements of the page.16

Robert Barry's **Come On** (Imschoot Uitgevers, 1987) and Giovanni Anselmo's **Lire** (Imschoot Uitgevers, 1990) have some elements in common. Both are small-format works with very little language in them — Anselmo's text consists entirely of the one word "lire" ("read") which is presented in varying sizes on the page. This focuses on the word and its basic meaning as an instance of the act of reading. Since "lire" is also the monetary denomination in Italy, the meaning of Anselmo's text and its relative sizes has other suggestions in it as well. Barry's book is more complex since its verbal range is broader and the graphic means more varied. It consists of single phrases, like the title phrase, pitched at the margins of the book as expletives or exclamations. These are simple works, which use a small amount of language and conceptual investment to make a book whose parts integrate a moment's reflection on the nature of the book with its linguistic content.

Two artists whose work offers more sustained investigation are Keith Smith and John Crombie. Smith's work has been mentioned before in various contexts. Both of these artists make interesting use of the book as a linguistic form. The difference in media in these two works serves to differentiate aspects of the representation of language in book form. Smith's **Snow Job Book 115** (Smith, 1986) was an early experiment with a Macintosh computer. It shows its age — or rather, displays its historical moment of production — at every turn. The type is full of the "jaggies" — an effect of early electronic printers' inability to deal with the visual manipulations of type size, scale, and spatial arrangement. The text goes through every possible acrobatic manuever available on the computer at the time — it bends, twists, writhes, and floats over the pages, ending in a final "meltdown" moment of disintegration. There is a play between the "snowjob" of the title — with its implications of hoodwinking — and the references of

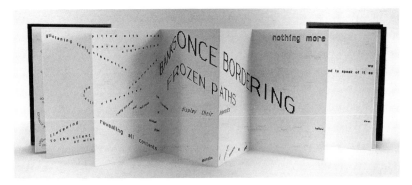

Keith Smith, **Snow Job**, (Book 115) 1986

the text which are strictly focused on real, literal snow. (Smith lives in Rochester, New York, after all and has an all too intimate relation with snow.) In **Overcast/Outcast** (Smith, 1986) Smith takes these manipulations a step farther. While **Snowjob** is almost entirely graphic — a flat pattern on the page — **Outcast** develops dimensionality with its verbal materials. The thematic concerns of the book — homosexuality identity in contemporary culture — is well served by the sleight-of-hand complexities of representation and dissimulation.

Crombie's **Spreading the Word** (Kickshaws, 1987) was printed letterpress with the type set by hand, rather than printed offset from computer or photo-generated type. As a consequence its graphic "moves" are made within the vocabulary of that medium (straight lines of a single size of type put into discrete horizontal rows). In graphic and spatial terms, the two artists are equally successful, showing that neither medium restricts or determines their possibilities. Crombie's book lives up to the sexual innuendo of the title, and the movement of the lines of type into and through each other's space (not obliterating each other as in Bernstein's **Veil**, but interpenetrating the discrete margins in which they are suspended) is further eroticized by the content of the words. Phrases like "come puss come" expand and contract through the use of varying sizes of type so that the text refuses to stabilize on the page. This mobility gives the illusion that the language hangs in space as well as moving across the screen or field of the page. This illusion is amplified in Crombie's work of a year later, **So** (Kickshaws, 1988). Here the text is structured as a maze. Lines weaving a story turn the corners of the pages and wrap around the book in an interlocking structure through which the reader may pick a varied course. The

248

reading requires that the pages of the book be turned through several times in sequence in order to follow the logic of the sentences. These do not follow down the page, but move through the whole book front to back and then around again. This produces the sensation that the text is a moving, writhing mass of language, in spite of its well-behaved letterpress decorum.

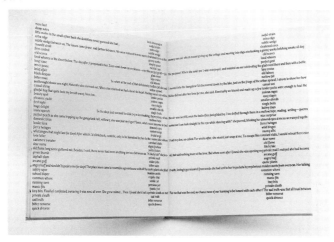

John Crombie, **Spreading the Word**, 1987

Scale and Progression

There are verbal works which use dynamic transformations, either of scale or of a progressive sequence, as aspects of linguistic meaning. One such work is the collaboration **Sheherezade** (Zweig and Anderson, 1988) produced by Janet Zweig and Holly Anderson. Here, the theme of the embedded narrative takes graphic form.17 The story of Sheherezade, the woman whose life depends upon her narrative ability (Sheherezade is condemned to death by the Sultan, but he is so enthralled with her story-telling ability that he allows her to live as long as she goes on intriguing him with a tale), is shown as a movement from one story to another as if they were literally embedded in each other. The typeset letters of the name "Sheherezade" are gradually enlarged to fill the page. As they do so, one realizes that a body of text is sitting in the counter (open white space) within one of the letters. As the scale continues to increase, one is able to read that block of narrative, which continues to enlarge, fill the page, and then reveal the next block of text. Each of these blocks of text contains a story which in turn gives rise to another narrative. Each ends with a segue into the next tale, naming it, and moving the story one layer deeper: "But the older ones know that truths are buried in the story 'Blood Beach.'" The text action takes place on the right page while on the left a tiny female figure in the outside lower corner of the page appears to put on and throw off a hooded garment. The book works as a flip book — moving through it rapidly one sees the visual progressions on each side of the opening. But one can also read through it at a slower rate, gradually becoming engulfed in the text, then passing through it into the next.

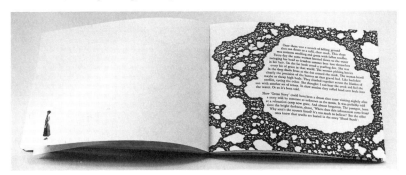

Janet Zweig and Holly Anderson, **Sheherezade**, 1988

In **Father's Garden** (Campbell, 1989) Ken Campbell uses text rows as garden rows. Eschewing cuteness or preciousness in this work, however, Campbell's duplication of form becomes a means of demonstrating the complex negotiations of the emotionally charged relation of parent and son. The body of a text printed out on a page is obliterated by geometric solid forms which cancel its legibility. A phrase, a few words, or, occasionally, a full line of text escapes from this cancellation. As the pages turn, the blocking effect is displaced from one area of the text to the next so that over the course of the book the entirety of the work is revealed. In Campbell's own words, he uses the typographic page "as a garden of exits and entrances." The sheets are dark, the printing muted, and the work feels like a garden coming just barely alive in early spring. All of the graphic means are from the typesetter's case — printer's ornaments and borders, and rules as well as type. The progression of the book has an order to it which is similar to that of hoeing or planting, though the sequence always cancels as much as it reveals. "Our father's juice flows everywhere" is one line, an image of paternal omnipotence or organic pantheism, or perhaps a combination of the two. The rhythms of **Father's Garden** are created in the process of repetition and revelation which

250

structure the sequence and timing of the book; but this is not merely a formal exercise — the work is charged with personal meaning.

Ken Campbell, **Father's Garden,** 1989

In two letterpress books which I wrote and printed, **Through Light and the Alphabet** (Druckwerk 1986) and **The Word Made Flesh** (Druckwerk 1988), I was intent on using contrasts in scale as a way of introducing hierarchies of meaning and forms of movement into the printed text. **Through Light and the Alphabet** disintegrates linear reading by the addition of a new typographic element on each successive opening. Once a typographic theme is introduced, it is sustained, so that by the time the book is finished, there is a complex multilinear text on the page. The differences in typographic scale allow these to be read at different rates but prohibit their ever being read all at once. In **The Word Made Flesh** a red field of six-point letters (in a precise Copperplate typeface) serve as a linguistic ground against which the manipulations of the main text, printed in black, are defined. The typographic complexities stall the reader and the visual scale of the elements forces the reader to put letter combinations together to puzzle out the words. The letters of the title phrase are spelled out one to a page in sequence so that the book's unifying element is provided by huge, darkly inked, wood letters. In these works the manipulations of typographic size play a role in the gradual revelation of the text, not only at the level of the page but also throughout the book.

251

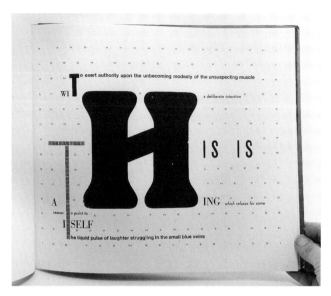

Johanna Drucker, **The Word Made Flesh**, 1988

One last book which deals with scale, though it is a work of poetry rather than an artist's book is Joe Elliot's **Poems Meant to be Centered on Much Larger Pages** (1993). The title is the punchline of the book but its conceptual implications are quite resonant. One question is whether the relation between page size and meaning is a linguistic issue, a poetic issue, or a book production issue. The lines fit very well on their pages as is, but Elliot seems to want his poems to be treated to a more deluxe presentation — with the wide margins, heavy paper, and elegant typography accorded poetic texts in luxurious volumes. Or he could be suggesting that they need more visual space to breathe, to come into their own as poetic works. Whatever Elliot's actual desire, the book transforms the reading of these poems into an examination of them in relation to their material form in this small, xeroxed pamphlet of ordinary white paper with its bright yellow cover. One wonders how much "larger" the page would have to be to accomodate them suitably. They become works about the book, and the reference to the book, though not part of the poems per se, is an aspect of their thematic identity.

In Conclusion

As a book which sums up many of the issues raised by books as a form of verbal expression, Ruth Laxson's **Wheeling** (Press 63 Plus, 1992) rewards inquiry. It is a passionately original work, born of pain and personal vision, put together with excruciating but careful labor in a page by page investigation of language as image and meaning. Laxson did all the production work except for the offset printing and her working through of design and conceptual problems is evident on every page. No words are used without a good reason — everything is meant, placed, and positioned for a purpose. The book is the product of several different print media, and though the bulk of the text was handset type printed letterpress, offset and silkscreen printing were also used. The result is a hybrid complexity, each page is at once a poetic statement and a graphic composition. Wheeling is a quintessential artist's book.

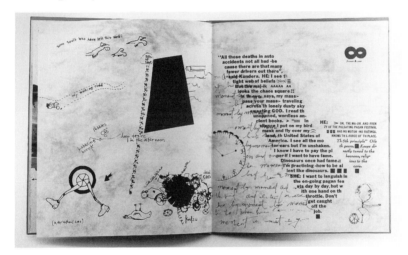

Ruth Laxson, **Wheeling**, 1992

Wheeling is almost square in format, about 8 x 9 inches, bound in grey boards, and separated into three signatures. The endsheets, also grey, wrap from the inside of the boards to the space between the signatures. Cut into the shape of a wheel, their curved form rises from the spine into the space of the book. These round, grey wheels are perforated in a pattern which gives them the visual echo of a tire. This icon is the major motif of the book whose themes range from automobile lore to the destruction of culture, while telling the underlying story of a death in an accident. There is no overt narrative, no detailing of an incident. The movement of the language from topic to topic allows an open framework for the text comprised of free associative language, thought, and research. The scope of the work is broad. From fragments of personal reflection and recorded conversation it moves out to consider problems of population, energy, and the fate of the planet. The wheels which are the automobile motif are also the wheels of fate, the wheels of a cosmos meshing gears.

The first and last signature were printed on a "frost" paper, the interior signature on a speckled paper which has the warm textural character of recycled fiber.18 The cloud patterns on the frost help the shaped areas of complex typography to float in the first and last sections. Patterns of wheels and circles are the basis of the typographic design. In the first opening of the "Preface," an imperfect quirky spiral which has the look of a broken watch mainspring or another mechanism which has been crushed, damaged, or run over sits on the left page. Made of the phrases — "stop," "look and listen," "go," and "rpm mph" — this form could be the diagram of a driving test or a route followed at the outset of a trip. Facing it on the right page is a perfect circle of type surrounding a solid block of text. The language is suggestive, combining references to the invention of the wheel with an image of Sisyphus — and the concept of the Omega force with the image of the circle in nature.19 Each succeeding page amplifies these themes, linking them with driving as an act of movement through time and space and a result of complex mechanics, gears, and drivers. A list of categories of people who do and don't drive is interwoven with the bent curve of a Doppler effect and so forth. All these are rendered in typographic forms whose curves and circular forms continually reinforce (and reinvent) the image of the wheel.

Wheeling's many compelling details would support a much more lengthy description and analysis, but none of that would substitute for the work's effect. This work forms a totality, one which includes a wide variety of elements such as photographic images (of wheels and cars) and a pop-up automobile on a stretch of curved road accompanied by texts on the "birth pangs of the car culture in America." There is one set of pages which are sewn into the spine and can only be read from the sides and bottom. There are shaped texts resembling cars. There are layered, overprinted pages in which letterpress text sits on offset text. And there are black-ink silkscreen scribbled images whose roughness makes a striking contrast with the formality of the type. The work's visual complexity is sustained by its verbal density - - Laxson's writing is as layered and polyvalent as the pages. The verbal exploration clearly drove this book, bringing its design into being as a fulfillment of its language. The book is filled with echos, repetitions, and resonances so that at every point one is aware of other aspects of the work — within which each linguistic and visual moment takes its place.

1 I am not making a distinction between prose and poetry, but between ordinary and imaginative uses of language.

2 It was published several times, the first time in the **Revue Lettriste**.

3 See Chapter 3 for a discussion of Iliazd (Ilia Zdanevich) in the context of Russian Futurism.

4 By the time of **Maximiliana** Iliazd was not doing the presswork on his books, or even all of the typesetting, but he did often make final adjustments to the forms of set type to make the final result correspond more closely to his carefully gridded out mockups and his vision of typographic balance.

5 There are some wonderful books on decipherment and its history; two of my favorites are Erik Iversen, **The Myth of Egypt and its Hieroglyphs** (Princeton University Press, 1961) and Maurice Pope, **The Story of Decipherment** (Thames and Hudson, 1975). But it is a peculiar feature of exotic scripts that their capacity to intrigue diminishes as their legibility increases.

6 I listed some basic references to concrete poetry earlier, in Chapter 3. Emmett Williams's **Anthology of Concrete Poetry** (Something Else Press, 1967), is one good source. The Ruth and Marvin Sackner Archive of Concrete and Visual Poetry catalogue is replete with references to their multi-thousand volume collection of this work. Marjorie Perloff's **Radical Artifice** (Chicago, 1992), David Seaman's **Concrete Poetry in France 1910-1960** (UMI, 1981) and the huge **Poesure et Peintrie** catalogue are also good resources.

7 These were originally performed at the Sound and Syntax Festival in Scotland in 1978.

8 See the discussion of this work in Chapter 7.

9 The only copy of this work I have seen was at Paula Cooper Gallery in NYC.

10 This is one of the places in which computers aren't necessarily advantageous — the manipulations of the typewriter are so specific to its physical form and production that duplicating these spatial techniques in electronic media often takes far more labor than when one can simply move the carriage to line up with a particular point on the paper.

11 Steve McCaffery, "Introduction" **Carnival**, "The Second Panel: 1970-75" (Coach House Press, n.d.)

12 Ibid.

13 Clive Phillpot, "Some Contemporary Artists and their Books," **Artists' Books: A Critical Anthology and Sourcebook**, p.119. A similar contrast could be said to exist

between Heidsieck and Chopin's pieces since Heidsieck is attempting to make the visual a transcription or prescription of spoken or performed language and Chopin's text has no oral corallary.

14 Peter Frank, **Something Else Press, An Annotated Bibliography**, (McPherson and Company, 1983), p.42.

15 A book designed to go with an exhibition, but not as a catalogue.

16 Hamish Fulton's **Song of the Skylark** (Coracle Press, 1982) is a good example of an abstract use of the page as a pictorial reference.

17 The term "embedded narrative" refers to the development of one story within another, as in the image of Chinese boxes, each serving as the container for the next in a long sequence.

18 Laxson lists these in her colophon as Graphica 100 Frost and Beckett Enhance.

19 As king of Corinth Sisyphus had been cunning and greedy and was thus condemned in Hades to push a huge stone up a hill towards a summit from which it always rolled back down, and he had to start uphill again.

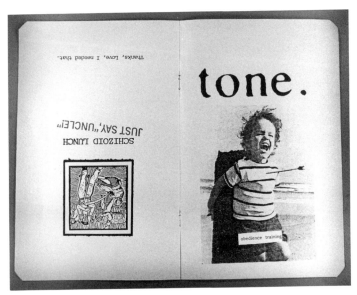

John Edwards, **Mono Tone**, Don Milliken, **Schizoid Lunch**, 1980s

IO

The Book as Sequence:
Narrative and Non-Narrative

Finitude and sequence are two fundamental structural elements of a book. The limits of a book — its finite parameters in space and time and its demarcated physical boundaries — are so basic that only within dematerialized conceptual propositions or electronic space can they be suspended. The use of sequence varies from book to book. Even fixed sequence need not apply universally — it can be argued that certain "books" which are made up of sets of cards or loose elements still belong under the definition of a book form.

Janet Zweig and Holly Anderson, **This Book is Extremely Receptive**, 1989

The way in which sequence is articulated gives each book its unique identity. A sequence can be made to move very quickly — the flip book is the extreme of this, but there are other sequences which have either very little resistance or else a great deal of momentum and thus move rapidly. In **This Book is Extremely Receptive** (Sheherazade, 1989) Janet Zweig and Holly Anderson incorporate the image of a turning satellite dish as a flip-book motif on the lower right corner whose momentum is graphically reinforced by images of sound waves. The typographic text appears to move very quickly through this field, also generating the sensation of a

257

fast moving book. In other cases, the jump from one page to another or one turning to another can be used to slow the movement. Internal flaps, gates, or other devices such as those in Margot Lovejoy's **Labyrinth** (Center for Editions, SUNY Purchase, 1991) tend to keep a reader in a page rather than moving **through** the book. There are books in which there are contradictory sequences — to read all of the narrative of John Crombie's **So** (Kickshaws, 1988), for instance, one has to turn through the pages several times. In a standard scholarly book the ongoing reading of the text is interrupted by the need to refer to footnotes at the end of the chapter or volume. In a reference book, such as a cookbook, telephone book, or dictionary, sequence is designed as a system of order rather than to promote linear movement — sequence participates in the distribution of elements into an organized system where location helps provide access. And in a work like Sol Lewitt's **Brick Wall** sequence is mainly a matter of time, which makes the temporal extension of the work into an experience of reading.

Margot Lovejoy, **Labyrinth**, 1991

Since both visual and verbal explorations of the book form have already been discussed in previous chapters, the works detailed here are hybrid forms which include both language and images. The complexity of many of these works becomes apparent when the structure which makes them work as books has to be analysed and described. Sometimes the simplest formats can be the most elusive to define and yet the most effective. In other cases there are many elements of a polymorphous work which all contribute to a book's effect. Though I have not devoted an entire chapter to the book as a material object, it should be stated that the properties of paper, board, and binding can work against or in favor of sequence design. It is particularly unfortunate to have to fight with a book whose pages have been bound unintentionally against the grain, or whose sheets fall out of the adhesive of a perfect binding as it is read. Though I don't believe in a standard of craft as an absolute criteria in bookmaking, the ignorance (or ignoring) of basic structural principles can undermine a book which might otherwise be engaging and successful.1

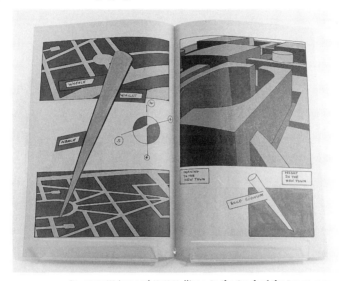

Lawrence Weiner and Matt Mullican, **In the Crack of the Dawn**, 1991

Reliance on Conventions

The popular comic book form is a highly functional combination of visual and verbal means. The conventions for separating the two or allowing them to integrate are all carefully coded, and the skills of the many artists who have engaged with comics as a commercial, personal, or underground form in the 20th century have provided a rich legacy from which book artists may draw. **In the Crack of the Dawn** (Mai 36 Galerie and Yves Gevaert, 1991) is a comic-book collaboration between conceptual artist Lawrence Weiner and a younger artist, Matt Mullican. Both Weiner and Mullican have worked with abstract concepts in their art, while Weiner has also made the artist's book one of his primary media. Mullican's work has often engaged with the determination of meaning, particularly of standard signage or graphic marks (such as the signs used on packages to indicate fragile or explosive). Not surprisingly their engagement with the comic-book form is much about the nature of the form itself. The self-reflexive theme of **In the Crack of the Dawn** is the nature of place within a book. The texts continually refer to the "out there" and "out here" of the places which are in the page and beyond the page, while the images manage a precise but abstract repetition of these themes. Maps, schematic diagrams, and drawings about specific places are put into the conventional blocks and bounded strips of the comic. The work's sequence, which cannot be accounted for in a narrative, is in large part the result of the convention of comic-book format. The work also shows how those conventions came to be so functional.2 The simple horizontal divisions of the page accord with the habit of left-right reading, guiding the eye along a path of spatially related but conceptually jarring leaps from block to block. And the linear character of language, its logical flow sentence by sentence, helps the reader to move forward. It is the formal logic, rather than the thematic logic, which allows this conceptual investigation of space within the (comic) book to work. Offset printed in vivid color, the book handles like a comic book as well, and the fact that it almost "passes" is part of its success.

The left to right movement can be relied upon unless there are instructions (or obstructions) which disrupt the reader's expectation. The most basic narrative can be generated from relying on this movement — as in 116 **Particolari** of Anselmo and Sperone discussed earlier — or in the peculiarly effective book works of Ida Applebroog. Produced mainly in the 1970s, Applebroog's books are small, apparently simple works. Their dimensions hover around five inches — palm-sized — and were offset printed from her line drawings. The images are easily read and show one or more characters involved in a single action. In **But I Wasn't There** (Dyspepsia Works, 1979) the image is of a woman sitting in her bed. Applebroog's graphic style is somewhere between a cartoon and a caricature, a biting drawing and a bland one. The figure in the bed just sits. The single image does not change, but is repeated through one turn after another. Then there is a blank spread and the comment, "But I wasn't there." This is followed by several more turns showing the image, another blank spread, and a final restatement of "But I wasn't there." The effect of the repetition of a non-changing image in a sequence in which the interjection of a verbal comment seems to carry significant emotional weight is curious. One wants to reread the image against the language, to see it differently, even to see it change. It resists, and this then returns an emotional charge to the statement — which has the same quality of inscrutable flatness as the images. The repetition in this work makes the sequence a rapid one — the pages can be turned quickly, in search of a resolution. But the resolution does not **come**, it is, in fact, **embedded** in the very repetition which seems to move so rapidly towards an end. If the image didn't repeat, if it changed, or if language accompanied the appearance of each image, then the entire effect would be different — it is this interplay between static but repeated elements which constructs the sequential effect in many of Applebroog's small books.

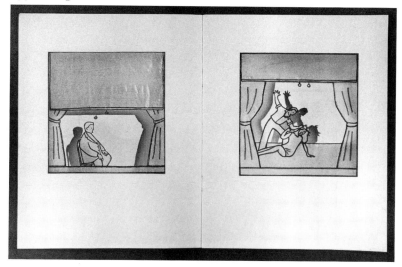

Ida Applebroog, **But I Wasn't There**, 1979

Applebroog's work is an example of a deceptively plain sequence which is actually quite complicated. By contrast, the somewhat generic work, **Pain Beau** (1979, no publisher) by Stephanie Brody Lederman, is far more conventional in its articulation of narrative sequence.3 Lederman's book is equally small in format to Applebroog's and her imagery is just as static. She used a single rubber stamp image of a man in suit and sunglasses as the only visual element in the work. This repeats throughout, on almost every page, while the text provides insight into the pained account of an unsuccessful relationship. The book is ephemeral in its production, it may have been offset or xeroxed, and has no conspicuous material properties. The pages turn quickly in following the statements which give the details of the progress and disintegration of the relation-ship through a series of descriptive statements on "him." The book is not quite narrative — we do not get a story or development, merely details which permit us to surmise what has occurred. Where Applebroog's image becomes highly charged with repetition, Lederman's serves as a point of reference. As an iconic motif the man leads us to believe that he somehow resembles the "him" of the statements either literally or metaphorically, just as the title provides a sense that he is French, and that the pun on the word "pain" ("bread") links the "beautiful pain" of the events to this well-dressed foreign male. But where Applebroog maximized the effects of sim-ilarity, turning, and the blank spread to break the repetition before taking it up again, Lederman proceeds in the same manner from page to page, always with a statement and the image. In this case repetition becomes predictability, and the sum total is an accumulation, rather than a resolu-tion (enigmatic or not). The book's structure is not really pushed to par-ticipate in the construction of the piece — whereas Applebroog's book relies on the breaks in its bound sequence as part of its meaning.

Jan Voss, **Wartelist**, 1984

Jan Voss's **Wartelist** (self-published, 1984) makes a useful closing work in this section since its entire structure is based on repetition and exten-sion. Voss's book consists of a cover sheet. Both the outside and inside of this sheet are printed and then it is folded to form a basic pamphlet. The outside title and colophon are printed (on front and back respectively) in grey ink. On the inside of the cover sheet is a scene. On the left page is a person waiting at a bus stop by the side of the road; on the right side there is a bus arriving. Into the spine fold of this sheet any number of copies of a second sheet can be inserted. On this second sheet there are only images of the road, always the same road, an empty swath of grey asphalt through a field of green grass below a bright blue sky. Printed in three colors, black, yellow, and blue, the image is quite simple and the edge of the road is designed to line up with the bit of road on the inside front cover. When you purchase **Wartelist** you can purchase as many interior sheets as you like — thus shortening or extending the wait the person at the bus stop has. The additional sheets are all sections of road and landscape so that the book's length becomes an experience of waiting. One turns through page after page of empty road where sequence is both duration and distance. **Wartelist** calls attention to sequence as a fundamental feature of artists' books.

Gilbert and George, **Dark Shadow**, 1974, NYPL

Photo-Narratives with Text

Narratives using photographic means supplemented by a text range from the sequentially literal (mapping every step of an event or story) to the more abstract, fragmentary, or enigmatic. The English art team, Gilbert and George have produced a number of books in which they play with the literal relation between text and image in the telling of a tale. **Dark Shadow** (Art for All, 1974) is typical of these works. The layout is absolutely flat-footed — there is text on the left facing an image on the right. The text is set in a large-sized roman face (about 14 or 16 point and

263

thus slightly reminiscent of a child's book face) widely leaded and perfectly justified. The flat-footedness is shown immediately as a conceit —
each page contains exactly enough words to end the section on the last
line of the page, thus making perfectly even blocks of text. The images are
of Gilbert and George, dressed in collarless grey suits, black shoes and
socks, black ties, white shirts. Their conservative upper-class formality is
represented in an equally conservative domestic setting where they are
shown having cocktails. **Dark Shadow** plays with its conventionality quite
self-consciously, and there are many instances where the exaggerated
rhetoric of the dramatic prose is placed next to a banal image of a cocktail
in a glass, or a hand with a cigarette. Dark shadows do appear in these
photos, but they have more the quality of slight neurosis combined with
an attempt at dramatic lighting than of real threat or violence. Like the
rest of their art and performance work, this is at once serious and ironic,
there is humor in the tone, but the story of dissolute drunkenness and
ultimate self-destruction is far from light. The regular structure of the
image and text in continual alternation makes this an easy sequence, one
which moves rapidly and in which the narrative prose provides much of
the momentum. Compact in scale (about 6 x 9 inches) the work is offset
printed on heavy enough text stock to feel solid and substantial, reinforcing its appearance of reliable quality.

Gilbert and George's format might make it seem that the structure of
narrative, especially prose narrative, is so strong that it will always carry
a book, but this is not true. There are plenty of instances of works (which
will remain nameless) which use a photographic image and prose story
without achieving movement or sequential flow. In Gilbert and George
just the right amount of text has been put on these pages, and the typographic color of the text (as well as its large size) allows it to move at a
good pace. Duane Michaels's **Take One and See Mt. Fujiyama** (Stefan
Mihal Books, 1976) is also linear in form but the tale it tells is even less reli-
ably straightforward than **Dark Shadow**. Gilbert and George's photographs were clearly stills, set-up shots designed to punctuate the narrative. Michaels's photographs have the appearance of being more spontaneous, yet their snap-shot-like appearance is at odds with their contrived disjunction of normal imagery or events. They function more like
frames excerpted from a filmic sequence than as independent images.4
There are four short narratives in Michael's book all of which rely on both
photographs and captions. The captions are handwritten under the

images and have all the characteristic immediacy and intimacy of personal jottings. The milieu has an alternative lifestyle (circa 1970s art student) feel to it — the black and white images show young people in rather spare apartments engaged in drugs, sex, and a complex social life. The narratives are slightly absurd and transform the ordinary into the extraordinary. A dull afternoon of reading becomes a nightmarish sexual encounter in which the close-up of an erection in white cotton underwear provides the title image to the book ("Mt. Fujiyama"). A fetishized glove provides the means for an intimate encounter, a tongue transforms into a penis, a naked man dreams of a pair of boots — these are stories which hover between dream and drug experiences and in which the actions in the photographs become ironic and significant through the accompanying language. The stories are short and the photographs establish characters, objects, identities of time and action sufficiently to carry the sequence forward. Enough trails over from frame to frame to provide continuity.

Duane Michaels, **Take One and See Mt. Fujiyama**, 1976

Such concepts of continuity can be taken to extreme. In Peter Lyssiotis's **Three Cheers for Civilization** (Champion Books, 1985) the frame to frame continuity with which he structures the narrative is often inscribed visually as a single striking feature. In the title tale he relies on repeating the extreme angle of a steep uphill street in every image while in "The Great Wall," he reasserts the graphic continuity of a line of (disconnected) brick fences in parts of Australia to connect them visually in a parody of the Chinese original. Lyssiotis's narratives have their own humor and interest, but they also have the feeling of works run on a relentlessly linear track.

Two other books which make use of photographic imagery as the basis of a narrative structure are **Royal Road Test** (Mason Williams and Edward

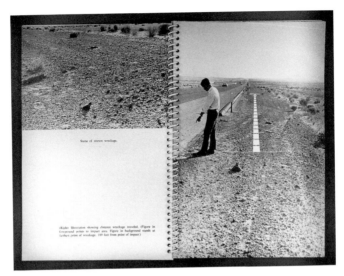

Ed Ruscha, Patrick Blackwell, and Mason Williams, **Royal Road Test**, 1969

Ruscha, 1967) and **Crackers** (Heavy Industry, 1969). **Royal Road Test** was a collaboration produced by Ed Ruscha, Mason Williams, and Patrick Blackwell. Spiral bound in yellow glossy cover stock bearing only the title words (with "Royal" in the logotype of the typewriter manufacturing company) the book at first looks like a manual for an office machine. The work's tongue-in-cheek tone is announced in its opening epigram: "It was too directly bound to its own anguish to be anything other than a cry of negation; carrying within itself the seeds of its own destruction." This statement (referring to the typewriter), printed alone on a glossy page, is followed in the next turning by a full page black and white photograph identified in its caption as the "Royal (Model X) Typewriter." In perfect imitation of published results from a scientific test, the book goes on to provide data: time, date, place of the test, and the results of throwing the typewriter from a moving car. "Test site area," "scene of strewn wreckage," "point of impact," and other neutral descriptive statements accompany the black and white documentary photos. There is no narrative here except that of the accumulating data and yet the book moves along with a rhythmic flow. The seductively clean quality of the glossy pages and the nicely printed half-tone images as well as the deadpan humor of the entire work give it a coherence. However it has neither the dramatic effect of Applebroog's work nor the cultural and psychological resonance of Gilbert and George's.

Ed Ruscha and Mason Williams, **Crackers**, 1969

Crackers, in which Ruscha again collaborated with Mason Williams, is a straightforward narrative told in photos. "Crackers" is the only word in the book, though the Williams story on which the narrative is based "How to derive the maximum enjoyment from crackers" is printed in extremely small type on the inside back flap. **Crackers** works because it is a story — albeit a fairly dim-witted misogynistic one in which the joke of the book is at the expense of an unsuspecting woman. The narrative is like a machine which moves from image to image while the main male figure moves through a series of different spaces involved with a single continuous action (the making of a huge salad in a motel bed). One peculiar aspect of this work is that the orientation of the images goes from vertical to horizontal without any particular regard for the effect of these changes on the structure of the book. Also black and white, the images have a vague "noir" quality to them, but there are ways in which the choices made about the images and their relation to each other doesn't work. Not only is there the problem of changing orientation, but there is also a disregard for left to right movement within the images so that they don't always successfully connect across turnings. In addition, the timing of the images has not been carefully calibrated — the camera dwells on each scene (perhaps because it as been set up with considerable effort) in a manner which is repetitive for no reason. The book is caught between an excess and an economy of means which seems incidental. The beauty of the book is in its stable page after page of single full-sized images — the photos always fill the frame and bleed and are printed on an appropriately slippery coated stock.

267

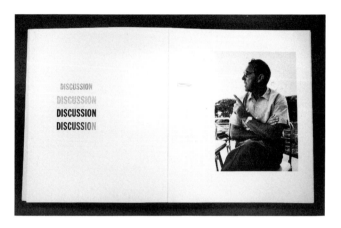

Todd Walker, **Three Soliloquies**, 1977

These narratives all have a single story line, movement, and sequential structure. In **Three Soliloquies** (1977) Todd Walker created three photo-essay narratives which experiment with narrative relations. The first is a series of photographs from 1961 linked and captioned to indicate their common theme: the transformation of California into its (then) contemporary condition. Here the linkages depend on formal connections between the images (horizontal patterns, diagonals, contrast) and the captions. In the third essay, uncaptioned photographs from 1967 form an intimate portrait (or possibly a male objectification) of a young nude woman. But in the middle section, "Discussion" from 1961 there is a very different organization and movement through a sequence of images. The first photograph is of a man pointing left and looking left though he is on the right side of the page. This contrast causes the reader to look back into the earlier page for the object of this man's intense focus. The gesture is counter to the forward movement of the book. The fuller scene is supplied upon turning the page — a table outdoors with remains of lunch or cocktails at which the man is seated in active conversation with two women. The third image, facing the second in the opening, shows the women's faces (tight, disgusted, even angry) and the man's gesturing hand (not his body or face). Then the figures get separated into individual photos — a woman responding, the man pointing and speaking, then both gesturing toward their bodies, then close-ups of their faces through a sequence of several more turns. The result is that the sequence pulls us into the emotional intensity of a discussion about which we know little but its scene and graphic gestures (physical, facial, bodily). Printed on one side only of folded sheets whose loose ends are bound into the spine, the images have a fine photographic quality — well shot and offset printed by Walker — and yet an immediacy.5 The sequential relation here is key and the use of the book as an arena in which the opposing tensions of a conversational exchange can be separated across the spine integrate the sequence into its physical setting. This is not so much a linear narrative as it is a sequential investigation which zeros in on its subject in order to show the emotional complexity of the scene and uses the book's physical features to reinforce this.

Complex or "Polysemiotic" Narratives
Not all narratives are linear or simple. The complication of a narrative form can occur at the level of the text/image relations or within the struc-

ture of the book. Roland Penrose's **The Road is Wider than Long** (London Gallery Editions, 1939) is an example of the ways an ostensibly straightforward text and image relation can produce multivalence. Penrose's work is clearly within a Surrealist tradition, its narrative twists and sleights of hand belong to literary history as much as to the interrogation of the artist's book. But the book has some features which show up in later artists' books and these need to be traced back to their precedents. This story of a road trip through the Balkans uses black and white images and blocks of poetic prose to create a dreamlike and disturbing account. For instance, an image of a hugely laden cart is accompanied by the phrase "Leeches eat their bones." Penrose's narrative of a journey is interrupted and thwarted by the irruption of illogical pronouncements, disorienting the reader and causing the images to be reread against their suggestive implications. (Strains of this Surrealist illogic are what inform Michaels' work as well as Gilbert and George's.) The work's surface linearity is fractured by these breaks in narrative continuity, and the text/image relations do not duplicate each other. Instead, they become more than a simple sum of parts, a unique synthesis.6

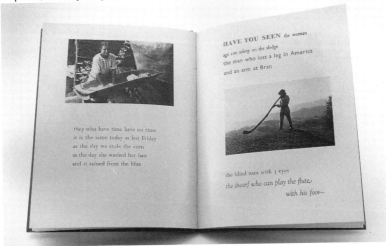

Roland Penrose, **The Road is Wider than Long**, 1939

More recently, however, the possibilities of multiple narratives or of narratives which intermingle and layer different aspects of a single story have found more complex formal expression in artists' books. One of these is Dick Higgins's, **Of Celebration of Morning** (Printed Editions,

Dick Higgins, **Of Celebration of Morning**, 1980

1980), a book to which he gave the descriptive subtitle, "a polysemiotic fiction." This is a complicated work, one whose fixed bound sequence suggests only one of many possible readings. Both within the pages and in the appendix there are suggestions for alternative readings of the work whose initial presentation is ordered according to chronology. The pages are elaborate collages of drawn, photographed, typeset, handwritten, and other elements, often linked by diacritical marks such as dramatically curving arrows. The language and images in the book center around a young man, Justin, whose "worlds" or activities and thoughts are obsessively recorded. The book is chronological, tracing his activity through a year — from first glance and meeting through relationships and implied self-destruction. The texts and images are curiously difficult to locate in a particular point of view — as though the author were polymorphous, rather than the presentation of the subject. At times Justin appears to be the object of amorous interest and at others to be an object of study, his body serving as the basis for drawings no more erotic than the instruction manual of a swim-stroke or life-saving technique. This seems to be both a specific and a generic portrait simultaneously, cancelling any easy allocation of information to one or the other reading. Is this a profile of a "young man" or a study of "Justin?" The work addresses the interest of one generation for the peers of its children, and all that this displaced focus implies (oedipally, erotically, and self-reflexively). As a visual, graphic work it is

271

highly complex, its many fragmentary parts unable to be easily reconciled into a unified whole. There is no linear path, no singular reading, and the elements play off each other in a continual montage producing the "poly-semiotic" effect.

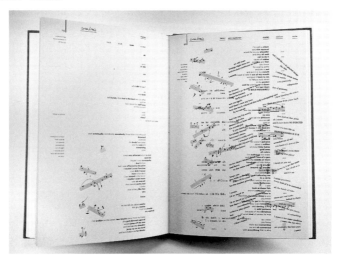

Warren Lehrer, **I Mean You Know**, 1985

Warren Lehrer's work, including I **Mean You Know** (EarSay Books and Visual Studies Workshop, 1985), often has such visual and graphic complexity though its means and ends are quite distinct from that of Higgins. Lehrer's work could be discussed as a verbal exploration as well as a conceptual space for performance. As Lehrer states in his introductory remarks, the book "is a play of voices that celebrates the music of thought." Lehrer uses graphic layouts and formats to "delineate the varieties of orchestrations and juxtapositions of voices within a musical score format." This approach is reminiscent of the work of Ilia Zdanevich (Iliazd) whose **dras** or plays used the page as both a score and a performance site. Lehrer's intentions are similar — the book can be used as a script or understood as a performance. There are seven characters in the book, each of which is given a distinct graphic identity (Zapf bold and italic, century schoolbook roman, univers, and so forth).7 Their voices, each granted a column down the page, interact with each other in an ongoing play of overlapping and simultaneous commentary while the description of action or stage directions are delineated in six-point type in the left margin. The overall effect is both orderly and chaotic — the structure of the book is clear, and the visual identity and relations of elements unmistakable — but the pages have the look of a hectic scene of complicated action. The dubious effect of communication — a certain doubt about the possibility for success in the expression and reception of meaning — is part of this work in which speech resembles noise and music as much as it resembles written text. While the movement through the book is linear and progressive, the movement through a page is polyvalent and spatial, rather than unidirectional — the two don't so much work against each other as work in relation so that meaning moves forward and outward like soundwaves in a musical piece. This is an interesting effect to achieve with the linear sequence of a bound book. The "polysemiotic" narrative offers the reader numerous possible readings by the nature of its internal formal presentations, as well as its thematic interweaving of themes, characters, and points of view.

Documentary Narratives

The compilation of documentary material can provide the evidence of a narrative, rather than its synthetic linear unity. Martha Hawley's **Notebooks** (IJ Books, 1979) does this with rather limited graphic means while Dennis Wheatley's works, such as **The Malinsay Massacre** (Rutledge Press, 1939), are elaborate exercises in production. Hawley's book is a mystery, one which never quite reveals or resolves its dilemmas. **Notebooks** is written as a multivoiced work, one in which different individuals each give their own account of events. Small in size, designed to look like a paperback novel, the work contains a section of black and white photographs whose relation to the text ranges from complementary to oblique — either presenting information to fill out a character or providing clues unobtainable within the written text. Extracts from diaries, taped interviews, handwritten records, and official police drafts all have a place here, and within the restricted format which Hawley allowed herself, even the graphic forms have variety. One nice touch is the inclusion of an index — a gesture which transforms the textual material of a fiction into the verbal file of an actual crime. There is no meta-narrative or synthetic narrative in this book, the book's pieces have to be fitted together by the reader in order to figure out what has occured. Hawley's work has a conceptual hole in its center — it deliberately cycles around an empty place in which there is no identifiable event or originating cause for the text.

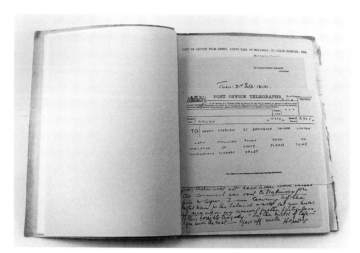

Dennis Wheatley, **The Malinsay Massacre**, 1939

Dennis Wheatley's works make use of a similar approach to the recounting of a narrative through evidence or documents without benefit of any overarching text. But **The Malinsay Massacre** is distinguished by its rich material values in production. Where Hawley must rely on the distinctions between individual voice and the format conventions of various documentary modes, Wheatly remakes his documents and produces a full file of maps, charts, letters, reports, diagrams, photographs, drawings, newspaper clippings, and other evidence. Though the writing and conception are not much different than those of a run-of-the-mill murder mystery of the same date (Agatha Christie or Georges Simenon come to mind), the book has a completely satisfying visual and tactile quality. If one reads Hawley's book in a continual search for the absent center, one goes through Wheatley's book with endless delight in the diversity of the pieces presented as evidence. It is not just the narrative elements which contribute to this book, but the graphic quality of letterheads from Malinsay Castle, or the incidental columns included in the clippings of "The West Highland Bulletin." The solution to the crime is not provided by the author or any of the "characters" — though the final pages contain some key questions for solving the mystery. Sequence and narrative are bound up with discovery and disclosure and depend upon keeping a reader interested in the book's game.

Jean Le Gac's **Le Recit** (Edition Hossman Hamburg, 1972) is a far more sophisticated version of the Wheatley approach, though Le Gac does not reproduce individual documents per se. Rather, the bits of evidential material are presented so as to give them the "look" of their "original" sources. Le Gac has taken snippets and fragments from various newspapers and journals and then altered them so that they always include the the name "Florent Max." This rubric becomes the key point of unity — all the textual references are forced to congeal around it because of the strength of the proper name. Some of the "messages" constructed are personal, and the continual displacement of "Max" into the public discourse of the newsprint page creates a curious tension in mapping "his" movements and activities. The contingent nature of textual meaning is clarified in this process. The documentary approach, rather than guaranteeing the authenticity of the narrative, seems instead to undercut its possibility.

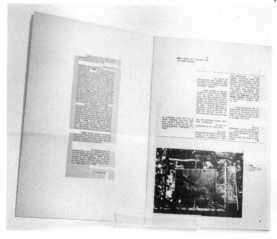

Jean Le Gac, **Le Récit**, 1972

Non-Narrative Visual Sequences

Sequence can function meaningfully outside of narrative structures. In the works which are discussed here relations are forged in a page by page sequence which gives the images or words a meaning through that juxtaposition and movement. Some of these rely on or result in a story. Sequence works as a framework within which each element or page make a contribution and has a place. A number of books which rely on sequence as a structural principle have been mentioned earlier in other contexts: Barbara Schmidt-Heins's 1949-1979 (1979) a chronological self-portrait in single photographs, Ann Chamberlain's Family Album (1991) with split facing pages making a transition from mother's image to father's through the movement of the book, or the externally determined sequence of **Every Building on the Sunset Strip** (1966) by Ed Ruscha. The irrefutable logic of certain kinds of sequences, such as photographic panoramas or chronological ordering, can be extended to other forms of encounter. The logic of movement through space, for instance, structures Stephen Willats's **Stairwell** (Coracle, 1970). Following a school-building stair-case from top to bottom, then recording the whole from a sequence of positions in which Willats always looks both up and down, the photographer creates a document whose banality is transcended by its formal resolution and its pathetic richness. By this latter phrase I mean that the residual signs of use and wear — graffiti, dirt, bare bulbs, and so forth — get important attention here as graphic presence. Captions which accompany the images merely reinforce the spatial specificity of the experience ("The long groan of wind" or "A jet plane zooms overhead"). The book embodies a manual of looking as a self-conscious act. It has the same effect as the "making strange" prescribed by early 20th-century Soviet theorists such as Viktor Shklovsky, for whom such defamiliarizing processes had a political effect since they were meant to reawaken the complacent consciousness to the conditions of lived experience.

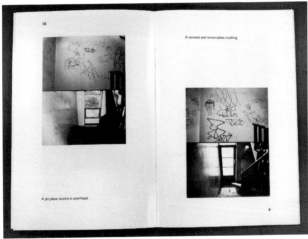

Stephen Willats, **Stairwell**, 1970

But a non-narrative visual sequence can be generated arbitrarily, or at least without a preexisting external order on which it depends. **Black Holes** (The Drill Press, 1979) by Kingsley Parker is one example of this. Like George Gessert's **Dust and Light** (Green Light, 1987), Parker's book has an

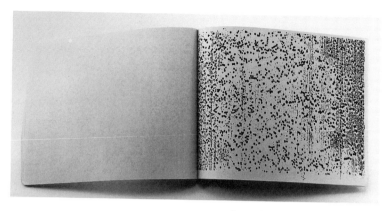

George Gessert, **Dust and Light**, 1987

inevitable graphic logic to it. Both are progressions — Gessert's from the merest specks of dust on the glass of a xerox machine to increasing density and darkness, and Parker's from the smallest dark specks on a sheet of paper to increasingly large ones. The "black holes" which are distributed across the speckled sky map of Parker's first page (spray paint? flecks off a toothbrush? random pen pricks? a visually degraded sky chart?) progress from tiny points of darkness to large, round black spaces. These loom on the sheet towards which we appear to move at warp speed. Sequence is everything in this work, making the sense of scale a factor in the reading of these forms as astronomical phenomena. Parker's work is printed and the sense of gradual movement is an effect of his drawings. This is unlike Gessert's book where the xerox process has been manipulated to form the sequence of visual events.

Sequence works very differently in Guiseppe Penone's **Svolgere la propria pelle** (Sperone Editore, 1971). This is an excruciatingly close examination of the skin of a number of different individuals. Using a small pane of glass as a means of flattening the flesh, Penone photographed skin on the head, face, shoulders, torso, abdomen, legs, feet, and fingers. Each small photograph was then put into a grid of six on a page. The strong visual links across the edges of the grid unify the image on each page into a close-up of some part of the anatomy. This vagueness is part of the work, which manages to stretch and extend its "body" through the full length of the several dozen pages which comprise the book. Sequence becomes a matter of examination, study, a slow and painstaking process of collage and rereading, rather than a matter of movement. The "corpus" of the work is fragmentary and polymorphous, and curiously affectless — that is,

277

there is no surplus of information or display of aesthetic conceits. The effect is a documentary flatness in which sequence is the only logic: the sequence of examination and reconstitution of a bodily unity. The book is dark, either on account of the photographs or the quality of the offset printing, and this gritty graininess lends it a low-budget and slightly-disturbing quality. The sequence of the body drives the book's photographic order, and the reassembly of the body drives the visual reading restoring closure to the fragmented and flattened forms.8

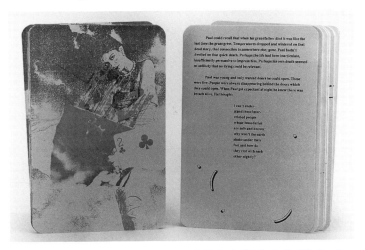

Peter Beaman and Elizabeth Whitely, **Deck of Cards**, 1989

Almost and Not-Quite Narratives

There are structures which work against narrative — and which also push the limit of the book as a form — which nonetheless demand a place in this discussion. One such structure is the "deck of cards" approach to the book. There are numerous examples — I can think of several from within the literary community, for instance — one of my favorites being Robert Grenier's **Sentences are Like Birds** (Tuumba Press, 1980s). Several such works will be discussed briefly here beginning with Peter Beaman and Elizabeth Whitely's eponymously titled **Deck of Cards** (Beaman, 1989) and Carolee Schneemann's **ABC** (Schneemann, 1977). Beaman and Whitely and Schneemann's works are similar in that they rely upon narrative conventions (the idea of unified place, time, action, and characters) as a way for their parts to be read in relation to each other. Shuffling Schneemann's deck of cards and rearranging the dialogues and conversational exchanges among the three major characters (Anthony, Bruce, and Car-

278

olee) makes and remakes a story. The color-coded cards (for quotes, dreams, or reported language) provide variety, and the narrative created depends on whether one reads long sections of speech or reverie in the pattern of the whole. The book is funny, pointed, biting, and unstructured, yet produces an effect of a collaged report of interactions, rather than a coherent account. Schneemann's box is cloth bound, with tie closing, gold stamped on the cover — all in the spirit of fine binding.

Beaman and Whitely's project comes packaged in a box with a clear plastic cover — like those used to sell greeting cards. One side of the Beaman and Whitely cards — which are oversized, more like book pages than playing cards — is printed with images. These repeat, rather than each bearing a unique picture, and thus seem to have a lower potential for storytelling than the text side of the cards. The texts are printed in several colors and typefaces, but the major characters, Paul and Dora, Richard, Enid, and Bob appear with regularity. Certain cards contain dialogue without naming the speakers, allowing this exchange to be fed into any of the possible imagined relations among named individuals. Other sections are more descriptive and proselike — such as "Paul thought of Dora — her skin rampant with moments." These are hypertext before the computer — works whose potential for linking and branching is structured into the way the blocks of prose break and offer possibilities for recombining. They rely on their finite book-like nature to produce their endless-seeming variety of sequences, and yet it is sequence and narrative which are the conceptual frameworks which give them their definition.

Jim Pomeroy's **Apollo Jest** (Pomeroy, 1983) and Brad Freeman's **Long Slow Screw Alphasex Book** (Varicose, 1990) both rely on fixed sequences. The cards of **Apollo Jest** are numbered sequentially and their subject is the interrogation of the Apollo moon landing. Real or staged? Actual or merely a Hollywood prank? The cards are printed in off-register red and blue, these create a three-dimensional illusion when looked at through the red/blue filter glasses provided in the package. The effect of staring into these space scapes and reading the black captions displaying and dispersing skepticism about the nature of the events depicted in such a contrived manner is quite strange. The sequence of the work moves through many sites and locations in a global and even orbital reach. Loose and unbound, the deck relies on being read in a fixed order. Freeman's **Long Slow Screw** is an "alpha-sex book" comprised of cards drilled through the center and threaded onto a long stove bolt. Reading involves unscrewing

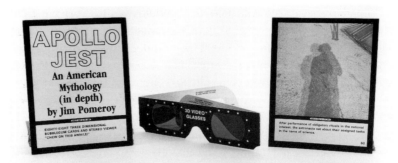

Jim Pomeroy, **Apollo Jest**, 1983

the cards from their fixed sequence and then laying them out to make a single image. The cards fit together, the photograph printed on each side of them functions puzzle-like to become a full image, while these are over-printed with words relating to sexual activity. Each card gets its share according to its initial letter ("lips," "labia," "lover," or "breasts," "but-tocks," "boobs," and so forth). The work can be taken in one slow sequence or rearranged and read without the constraining hardware, though it is this feature which takes the work's relation to sequence into a unique physical form. The timing of the movement of pages is a direct result of their manipulation — the time involved in getting them to be threaded off the central screw.

Brad Freeman, **Long Slow Screw Alpha Sex Book**, 1990

Not all indeterminate sequences or uncertain narratives are the result of physical variations on the book form. Barbara Cesery and Marilyn Zuckerman's, **Monday Morning Movie** (Street Editions, 1981) uses an accordion-fold structure to present a series of vignettes. It is the nature of the relation of these vignettes which calls narrative conventions into question. The book works through double-panel sequences, each of which contains a scenario for a filmic rewriting — events from the "real" life of the characters is combined with the storyline of a cliche script ("James Cagney," "World War I," and "World War II" for instance). Though the scripts are intercut with individual poetic reminiscences, bits of material from family albums, and other personal memorabilia, the panels seem to only relate to each other thematically. There is little sense of movement or continuity from panel to panel and the repetition of devices and conceits from section to section is the only unifying element. The end result is that this work functions less as a book than as an album, a collection which feels incidental rather than structural or intentional. It should work as a book, but doesn't quite.

By contrast, Gary Richman's **Dr. Dogwit's Inventory of Provisional Alignments** (Blue Book Issue, 1985) and **Teaching a Carolina Dog to Say "Mama" Part One** (Blue Book Issue, 1983) shouldn't work as books and yet do. Both are highly intriguing. **Dr. Dogwit's** uses a simple format, image facing text. Each is divided into three horizontal strips on opposite pages. In the image strips a sequence of images (generally four to a line) from photographic, illustrational, and clip-art sources presents one aspect of the elements to be "aligned." The chunks of text which occupy the same band of space in the facing page are produced in enlarged typewriter face, all caps. Across the pages are sprinkled white stickers, round dots with dog footprints on them. Here the provisionality of the "alignments" is far stronger than their convincing relations, and yet the effect of the whole is a prodigious invention of meaning. This is not the slightly warped dislocation of Roland Penrose's finely tuned Surrealist narrative, but the far more random, chaotic, free-for-all combination of elements which seems to be generated from the chance encounters with information characteristic of post-war media saturated society. What are we to make of all of these highly specific pieces of visual and verbal information? Their relations to each other, in the inevitable "meaning effect" produced by reading, feel increasingly and skillfully overdetermined as one moves through the book. The work's manic intensity is displayed in its limitless diversity,

281

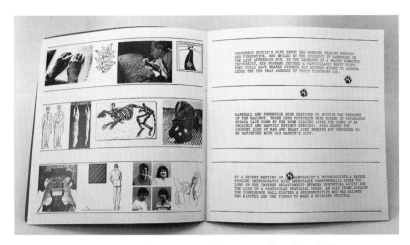

Gary Richman, **Dr. Dogwit's Inventory of Provisional Alignments**, 1985

while puns and coincidences of image and language occur at every turn. It feels as though the synthetic text had been generated in order to provide unity to the images, which would otherwise remain unrelated. Writing is serving here as a tissue of unity sutured together against improbable odds. For instance, a visual sequence of 1) two army men, 2) two pigs hung up after slaughter, 3) an excavated animal skelton, and 4) a dog with a ball is faced by the following text: "Marshall and Frederick were destined to survive the trenches of the Maginot. Those less fortunate were buried in variegated strata laid down by the Wurm glacier (over the bones of an ungainly and happily extinct species). Fido sensed the crunchy ribs of a beast just beneath but pretended to be satisfied with his master's gift." Richman's prose stretches to include whatever four images show up in any line. Both of these books have no narrative logic and no sequential linkages, but manage by their sheer inventiveness to sustain a reading momentum.

Final Note
The artists Helen Douglas and Telfer Stokes use sequence and narrative forms generated from within, for, and as book structures in a number of their works. In other words, they collapse the realm of book form with the structure of narrative and sequential form by making the two mirror each other in various visual and phenomenological ways. **Chinese Whispers** (Weproductions, 1976), for instance, moves through long sustained sequences of photographs which approach an outbuilding at Deuchar Mill

282

where the two artists work. As in Michael Snow's **Cover to Cover** (Nova Scotia School of Art and Design, 1975) there is a deliberately cinematic character to the movement. We move into the interior space and witness the construction of a corner cupboard whose dimensions are precisely the same proportion as the pages of the book. The cupboard space then becomes both the represented space and the literal space of the openings. A kettle, bread box, hotplate, timer, and other elements take their places on the shelves until attention to a seed packet changes the direction and color of the visual narrative. The book is neither story nor document but a spatialized narrative of the book as a place — domestic, artistic, located — but open-ended. This is a place into which things may be put and/or positioned and whose sequential construction is revealed rather than covered-up. This work has a deconstructed feel to it, a literal taking apart of its means as the means of its making.

Telfer Stokes, **Passage**, 1972

By contrast, the short sequences in Stokes' **Passage** (Weproductions, 1972) comment upon this literalness in other ways. In one sequence a hole is shown slowing burning through the paper. In another opening a pair of badly worn mocassins are shown on facing pages or a sink is viewed from above, dry on the left and with water running on the right. In yet another sequence a sandwich is made one step at a time, the slice of bread filling the sheet as various substances (butter and jelly) are smeared on it, covered, and eaten. A candle melting on a kitchen table ignites a container of salt in a series of half a dozen turns. In each case the sequences are passages, moments of transition from one state to another, recorded as events within the structure of the book.9 For Stokes sequence is made clear in this literalization, one in which images demonstrate the logical consequence of transitions. This makes the book's turnings dynamic, giving them the power of transformation or, at the very least, showing that they participate in its presentation.

It should be clear from this discussion that sequence and narrative are related, but not redundant, elements of book structures. Timing and movement in a book can be constructed from visual, verbal, and material components as well as their combination. And the relations between stories, the conceptual and literal spaces of a book, and its finite structure are almost infinitely variable depending on the imaginative vision of the artist rather than the limitations of the book form.

1 There are books whose passionate vision is so strong that their craft problems are simply a moot point and I personally prefer these to the well-made and vapid, vacuous, objects which unfortunately are more common.

2 See also **The Logic of Comics**, Stephen McCleod. (This reference came from a young man who attended my lecture at SUNY Purchase in March, 1995, whom I don't know by name, but who might remember his comment and who deserves to be thanked.)

3 The term "generic" applied to this work isn't meant negatively, just descriptively.

4 This kind of sequential relation is even stronger in Michael Snow's **Cover to Cover**, discussed in Chapter 6, where the attempt to replicate a filmic narrative in book form is highly developed.

5 Unfortunately this book was perfect bound and after fifteen years, it is coming apart. A cautionary tale.

6 This is Renée Riese Hubert's thesis in **Surrealism and the Book** (University of California Press, 1984).

7 The first sustained example of this approach to "character" in type which I know of is the version of Eugene Ionesco's **Bald Soprano** designed by French artist Robert Massin in 1963.

8 It is not exactly clear what Penone's motivation was in using the flattening sheet of glass — whether it had to do with the book form and the desire to establish a parallelism between picture plane of the page and the flat plane of the glass over the flesh or not.

9 There are jokes on the work of other contemporary artists in this book, i.e., that of Ruscha, Weiner, and Baldessari. One of the final sequences in the book is a take-off on a sequence done by conceptual artist Joseph Kosuth whose pieces "One and three"

explored relations between words, images, and objects as aspects of something's identity. ("One and Three Chairs" contained the dictionary definition, a photograph, and an actual chair.). Stokes' piece, "One and three positions" consists of four (the sum total) images of three frames each in which a milk bottle is placed on its side, upside down, and upright.

Brad Freeman, **Overrun**, 1990

II

The Artist's Book
as an Agent of Social Change

The books discussed here are conceived of as agents of political persuasion and as vehicles to advocate a change of consciousness or policy in some area of contemporary life. The concept of what constitutes a political work of art varies from artist to artist and there is much formal, aesthetic, and thematic variety in activist works. Many of these books function by revealing or commenting upon an existing situation in a way which offers a critical reading. These works are often narrative, descriptive, and embedded in personal experiences of individuals — and their agenda is to point to conditions of injustice, oppression, or discrimination. Others of these works provide information which is impersonal in nature and meant to be subversive or enlightening. Some deal with people living at the edges of society, powerless or marginalized. And finally there are activist works which use the book as a platform for social critique or as a means of advocating directly for specific policies.1 But these books are self-consciously artists' books — they make use of elements of production to communicate their position in a way which invests heavily in aesthetics. Manipulation of images, text, and attention to format, layout, and binding all play a part in these works. The question of whether or not such works are effective in achieving social change belongs to the larger debate about the efficacy of art as a political instrument in contemporary culture. Expressing a point of view, making a vision or voice or position heard, and contributing to the ongoing discussion of politically charged issues is all part of the arena of public debate in which politics, ideology, and aesthetics overlap. These books foreground that aspect of their identity and are often produced primarily with a political motivation.

Personal Documentary Sensibility
Stephen Willats' book **Cha Cha Cha** (Coracle, 1982) integrates a personal point of view and a documentary sensibility. Focusing on the gay

Stephen Willats, **Cha Cha Cha**, 1982

British punk scene and a club called the Cha Cha Cha, Willats makes a strikingly formal presentation of texts and images. The pages are divided, top and bottom, and each place takes on and maintains a specific identity through the course of the book. The top left page is the place for Willats' own narrative, the bottom left contains a photograph. The theme of Willats' texts are the fears, paranoias, and difficulties of being publicly perceived as gay. The anxiety of moments on the street, of being followed, threatened, or harassed are interwoven with a narrative of life "on the scene" of gay subculture. The text on the facing page, lower left, always belongs to a speaker whose photograph appears above it. The background of each page is black, the right is white, so that they make a striking graphic contrast, and the photographs which portray the costumed, pierced, decorated, and elaborately made-up figures on the right have an equally dramatic character to their self-construction. The graphic tone of the book is repetitive and formalized which allows the impact of the photographs and narratives to be maximized. The book resembles an album of private souvenirs and snapshots but has the identity of a documentary text infused with a personal viewpoint. There is no didactic message in Willats' piece, only a presentation of a particular segment of lived experience to which his work provides us access we might not otherwise have. Judgement and response are left to the reader who is given information which would not circulate readily (except as fashion) beyond the initiates to that scene.

Martha Rosler's book, **Service: A Trilogy** (Printed Matter, 1978) is clearly activist and documentary. **Service** is a collection of three different accounts of the experiences of women working in domestic service in the United States. All three are immigrants but each has different aspirations and her own background through which to process her experience. The book's structure is derived from postcards the women wrote to Rosler to describe the events of their lives. The temporal dimension of the work is collapsed in the synthetic final narrative, but the sequence of difficulties which these women encounter in trying to obtain payment for their work, support for their families, and their struggle with the basics of survival from a position of relative powerlessness are evident. The course of these women's lives and the choices they make within their restricted circumstances communicates with considerable poignancy and first-person voices give the narratives compelling conviction. The book is small, postcard-sized, not illustrated except for its black and white cover photograph of a woman working in a kitchen. Though Rosler introduces no commentary text, her editing and presentation demonstrates her proactive stance on the regulation of domestic labor. **Service** is a call for change.

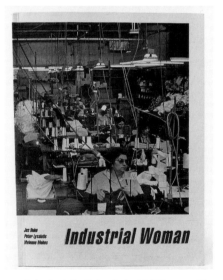

Duke, Lyssiotis, Mehes, **Industrial Woman**, 1986

Industrial Woman (1986) is a collaboration among three individuals: Jas Duke, Peter Lyssiotis and Vivienne Mehes. It was produced by the Industrial Woman Collective from a photographic exhibition of the same title. This book "portrays a cross-section of some of the problems and experiences of working women in Australia." Drugs, maternity leave, sexual harassment, working on the line, health and safety, migrant women, and repetitive stress syndrome are titles of sections in the book. Each section contains photographs of specific women working. They are identified in their workplace and the nature of their job and their time in the industry in which they work is given. The text in the book is translated in every section into Turkish, Greek, Maltese, Spanish, Vietnamese, Serbian, and Croatian, all languages spoken in the workplace in the Australian factories in which these women work. The intended audience for this book is clearly not just the artworld. This book has a more straightforward documentary character than the work of either Rosler or Willats. Its binding and format are indistinguishable from that of a trade book and it no doubt was meant to function as one. But there are collages and typographically manipulated phrases on the pages which announce each section, as well as other editorial decisions, which make it evident that an art audience was also targeted as a likely interested readership. The book is clearly a cross-over book, one which takes advantage of the potential of books to be a widely distributed and readily available means of providing information. It makes very little intervention into or interrogation of the book form, rather, relies on its conventions to produce an effective communication. While much of the information in this book is compiled data, tying the specifics to individual women and their situations pushes the details into a personal realm where the effects of what is being described are grounded in testimonials of actual experience.

Bill Burke's **They Shall Cast Out Demons** (Nexus Press, 1983) transforms the documentary through his own personal experience. This work is so intimately imbricated in Burke's own vision of the medical profession which is the subject of the book that there can be no claim at all to neutrality in the work. The dedication, in handwriting on an otherwise blank page, is the only piece of Burke's own writing in the book. "Dedicated to my parents who, when I was five, told me we were going to church but took me to the hospital for a hernia operation instead." The other blocks of text either come from the Bible or from a book about the experience of the human body from the perspective of a surgeon: Richard Selzer's **Mortal Lessons** (Simon and Schuster, 1976). Burke uses photographs in a collaged sequence of single images but the effect is a book full of movement and action. In Burke's book the distinctions between the practices of

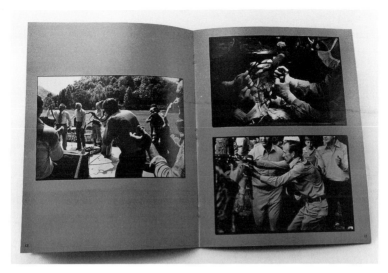

Bill Burke, **They Shall Cast Out Demons**, 1983

Western medical teams performing neurosurgical procedures and the activity of shamans among Hmong tribesmen in Laos or the activities of various Christian fundamentalists in ceremonies with rattlesnakes and copperheads are all interwoven as aspects of a single theme: medicine and faith. This calls into question the habitual terms which separate these subjects into different categories. Each image is intensely vivid, from those which show dramatic scenes of a brain open and exposed during surgery to those of an animal being slaughtered. The intensity of the spiritual drama of medicine and its grounding in cultural belief systems is continually reinforced by these images, and Burke's sardonic dedication to his parents remains as an invitation to see the blurred boundaries among these worlds. There is no obvious political agenda, no call for change of policy, in this book as there is in **Industrial Woman** and **Service**. Because of the personal aspect of Burke's work and its private revelations he demonstrates the non-neutrality of the documentary form while posing issues of cultural prejudice and belief. If Burke advocates anything it is that one suspend received patterns of thought about the body, the spirit, and the healing process. The power of this book derives from the strength of the photographic juxtapostions and Burke's attention to the structural effect of sequence.

Joan Lyons' **The Gynecologist** (Visual Studies Workshop, 1989) also has a medical theme but here a personal text is central to the book's struc-

Joan Lyons, **The Gynecologist**, 1989

ture. Lyons's narrative recounts her dealings with her male gynecologist who has been "for years" suggesting surgery to remove her uterus, ovaries, and cervix as a solution to various female troubles. The power struggle Lyons recounts is all too familiar to women who contend with the pressures of the American Medical Association in its generally white and male embodiment. The story is about power and the asymmetrical way in which cultural structures grant authority over an individual body. In this sense the book has much in common with Burke's disclosure of the cultural biases underlying the construction of medical authority. However, Lyons's sensitivity to book structure is very different aesthetically from Burke's aggressively suggestive arrangements. The Gynecologist is small and printed on warm, rich brown paper with black and opaque white ink. Lyons maximizes the effect of the color of paper through her design, manipulating it to function as a third tone in the palette which includes the two inks. The book's formal values echo the books of 17th- and 18th-century printers with large margins, small text blocks, and relatively large well-leaded type. This design complements the images in the book which are reproductions of woodcuts and engravings from medical books printed in the last five hundred years (the earliest is from 1495). Medical ignorance is presented as the basis of decisions about women's lives: authoritative drawings of the way the uterus was supposed to be structured range from cornucopia forms to those resembling rubber thimbles.

Lyons has aestheticized these into borders, images, endpaper designs so that the book swarms with rich visual material loaded with condemning information. Point by point, decision by decision, this book and Burke's articulate sequence through carefully nuanced structures — but whereas Lyons establishes a strict format, Burke varies his opening by opening. The overriding message of **The Gynecologist** is seductively presented, Lyons's resistance to pressure vindicated, and her "Afterword" contains a strong feminist assessment of the AMA's attitude toward women's medicine. There is no question that this book, with its images of calipers, intrauterine apparatuses, and bizarre images of the female anatomy serves to inform women and thus give them back, if not control over their own bodies, at least support for negotiating with rather than submitting to medical authority.

Two other books which have interesting parallels with each other on a completely different theme are Larry Walczak's **American History Lessons** (Walczak, 1979) and Brad Freeman's **SimWar** (Varicose, 1991). Both deal with the boyhood image of masculinity in relation to the American military. Both deal with contemporary issues of war and unreality, the concept of the "game" as a military culture. Walczak incorporates photographs from family albums: images of the artist as a child playing Davy Crockett and wearing a coonskin cap are juxtaposed with images of the historical figure. This juxtaposition of historical myth with childhood fantasy continues when pictures of him playing soldier, lining his toy militia up in the wrinkles of the bedclothes, are contrasted to photographs of military equipment, personnel, training, and battle formations. The "lessons" are clear, the saturation of boyhood with the military image as a romanticized masculine ideal. This ideal is normalized through games and fantasies, reinforced through the telling of history and only later questioned, pulled out of the psyche, and examined. Personal information also runs through Freeman's **SimWar**, though part of its focus is the more recent Gulf War of 1991. Rather than analysing historical myths Freeman's book contains an autobiographical narrative and a parallel set of images. As a teenager Freeman, the son of a military officer, spent time in a military hospital during the 60s recovering from an accidental injury. The hospital was receiving American soldiers wounded in Vietnam. The reality of their experience completely transformed his adolescent view of war and any images of heroism or glory were utterly dispelled by the grim realities. This narrative runs along the bottom of the pages and against a black

Larry Walczak, **American History Lessons**, 1979

background. Above this are frames which echo the shape of a television screen in which appear images from video war games, Flash Gordon films, wounded soldiers, and the Gulf War images of battle which were regularly broadcast on television during the conflict. By this juxtaposition Freeman reveals the sense of unreality which popular culture activities communicate about war and its effects. The "simulations" prepare children to participate in warfare, blurring the boundaries between on-screen activity and the news reports displayed on television broadcasts. Walczak's work is in the style of a children's book — type laid out next to black and white images in imitation of a text while Freeman visually engages the reader with the paradoxes of what is presented. Both books use the personal position as a means of criticizing militarism within an American context and each also uses materials from outside their direct personal experience to frame that critique.

Brad Freeman, **SimWar**, 1991

Impersonal Information

Patricia Tuohy's **American Information** (1982) is one of the most straightforward books of information which one could imagine. It is the size of a small travel guide and is jammed with entries covering every aspect of American life. Every aspect of American life — or at least every aspect which seems to carry some link to the image of America as a mythic notion: the history of the pledge of allegiance, the story of Robert Oppenheim, and lists of the number of rivers, roads, and miles of highway in the United States. However, this is not a standard almanac and it profiles a selective image of national identity through its process of editing. Whether "information" itself can have a national identity (what is "French" information, for example) or is merely a factor in constructing that identity, Tuohy is at pains to provide the means whereby data can be construed as contributing to an image of American life. The book is not so much flat or neutral as it is poker-faced in its attitude, providing a large compendium of data with an unstated purpose. This book is more of a document than an agent of change. It serves as a foil against which supposedly impersonal information can be reexamined in other artists' books.

For example, Hans Haacke's revelation of information is never without a clear agenda. **Der Pralinenmeister (The Chocolate Master)** (Art Metropole, 1982) is based on a portrait of Peter Ludwig first exhibited in seven diptychs at Paul Maenz Gallery in Cologne in 1981. Like many of Haacke's exhibitions since the late 1960s, its intention is to reveal information as a means of disclosing and analyzing the structures of power. In particular, Haacke is interested in the way corporate capitalism is complicit with forms of repression in the cultural arena. The texts of the seven pairs of posterlike images reproduced in this work are translated into English and printed on pages which alternate with the photographs of the originals. The work covers many aspects of the business and personal life of Peter Ludwig. The first panel gives biographical information about Ludwig's position — as head of the firm of Leonard Monheim (a company he entered when he married Monheim's daughter). His art collection is extensive, and information about its loaned works, which are exempt from property taxes, and his place on the boards of various galleries and museums in Europe and the United States is presented. The facing page details the treatment of workers, mainly women, in the factories which produce his line of "Regent" chocolates. The women are underpaid, overregulated, their private lives supervised and interfered with, and their

Hans Haacke, **Der Pralinenmeister**, 1982

working conditions and pay is substandard. The juxtaposition of these revelations about Ludwig's art activities and the conditions of the industries from which he derives the wealth which funds his multi-million dollar collection continues. Ludwig's denial that there are cultural politics in the artworld becomes increasingly shrill as the book proceeds. He repeatedly insists that art manifests the highest aspirations of culture and that his collection was motivated by the desire to preserve German culture from foreign investors or sales which might disperse it. Haacke's techniques are designed to display contradictions and leave them unresolved, which he does. The extension of the process used in this analysis also resonates outward. The reader is left with the sense that if these are the machinations which lie behind a chocolate magnate's image, they are also those which would be revealed in a study of the heads of automobile, electronic, pharmaceutical, and other corporations — and this is the impact Haacke wants. This book is neither innovative nor structurally complex, instead, Haacke uses the book form to reproduce information and circulate it widely. In this respect it is closer to the sensibility of **The Industrial Woman** than to **SimWar** or **The Gynecologist**.

Another work by Martha Rosler, **Three Works** (Nova Scotia School of Art and Design, 1981), is not only a complex documentary but also a critical investigation and commentary on the nature of the documentary pho-

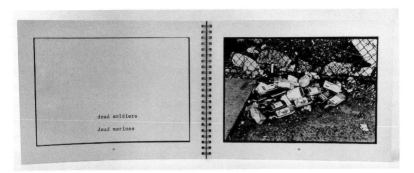

Martha Rosler, **Three Works**, 1981

tograph. Rosler's work takes apart the category of **impersonal** information, thus demonstrating its basic fallacies. Rosler is intent on showing the means by which documentary photographs produce their meaning and how such meanings are changed through context and use. The book contains three sections, the first a piece on Chile, the second on "The Bowery in two inadequate descriptive systems," and the third a long essay and study on documentary photography. Each makes very different use of the book's horizontal (8 by 11 inch) format and the coded material of heavily coated paper used for publishing photographs.

The first piece interweaves accounts of current events and human rights violations in the political climate of Chile just following the assassination of former government minister and economist, Orlando Letelier in Washington D.C., in September 1976. Rosler's use of material gathered in interviews, conversations, and research follows the conventions of political journalism and makes its impact through those means. In the second work on the Bowery, however, the conventions are taken apart. Language and photographic image are separated dramatically, each placed on the page within a hard heavy black border. And the attempt to describe the lower end of The Bowery in New York City through either system is shown to be "inadequate" for several reasons. First the two systems never seem to match up to each other. The black and white photos carry aesthetic value, the words have a poetic effect, and neither adequately describe the situation because they are fundamentally outside of the realities of the lived experience of the Bowery. Representation is fraught with problems, Rosler is asserting, because it cannot adequately show these realities and because it speaks for and displaces the people for whom what is shown is a lived experience.

297

These issues are taken up more explicitly in the critical essay which forms the final section: "in, around and afterthoughts (on documentary photography)." Here Rosler discusses various famous (and not so famous) documentary photographs and their relation to the circumstances in which they were produced and used. Rosler's argument is that many photographic works produced by "reformers" were as much about the preservation of the status quo as they were about changing or improving the condition of those photographed. The balance of power which positioned the underclass or disenfranchised individual was not changed by the document, and often the few changes sought in actual conditions merely quelled or prevented social unrest. For instance, Rosler gives details about the ways in which the story of Florence Thompson, the woman whose image became Dorothea Lange's "Migrant Mother", has been systematically excluded from the photograph's history and use (not to mention from any profits it generated through reproduction). Rosler examines Lange's interactions with the woman at the time the photograph was taken, the response of later critics and historians, as well as Roy Stryker's own agenda in demonstrating the power of American workers to triumph over adversity through determination and hard labor.2 Rosler's book thus progresses from a documentary type of piece (but one which acknowledges Rosler's role and her relation to the events described rather than a neutral voice claiming authoritative objectivity) to a deconstruction of documentary techniques through creative and critical means. Rosler's awareness of the codes of photographic publication give this work its effect since its physicality neutralizes its artistic character through simple layout and format techniques.

Critical or Analytic Works

Finally, there are many artists for whom a book creates an opportunity to focus critical attention on contemporary culture. Miles de Coster and Paul Rutkovsky have both produced works which address consumerism and media images. De Coster's book **Television** (Nexus Press, 1985), like his earlier work on money **Iconomics** (Nexus Press, 1984), is graphically complex. Elaborate printing of background patterns and photographic images appropriated from television history accompany a text which discusses the development of television formats and mythology. De Coster's work was heavily researched and elaborately scripted. From this informed point of view, De Coster analyses television as the most recent extension

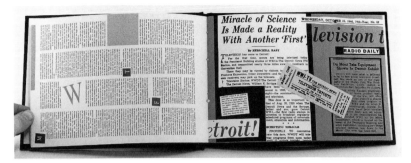

Miles DeCoster, **Television**, 1985

of the long history of communication media (images of cuneiform writing and other artifacts provide a visual point of reference for earlier systems). Printed in three colors, red, blue and black, the book maximizes their potential through the use of screens, separations, and other design manipulations.3 A blend of history and creative writing, of documentary evidence and original insight, De Coster's work is synthetic and analytical. He is critical of television as a commercial industry and as a cultural product, though his in-print versions of on-screen images also display his fascination with the medium. Rutkovsky's **Get More** (Visual Studies Workshop, 1986) is more savage and wild in format than De Coster's book. Produced on a Macintosh, again in the early days of low-resolution printers and jaggy type and images, Rutkovsky's rather crude collection of images and statements (limited to phrases a word or two in length) serves as an

Paul Rutkovsky, **Get More**, 1986

299

indictment of what he calls "the buy or be sold environment." Rutkovsky's equation of economic status with survival continues his investigation of the commodity condition of contemporary life begun years earlier in **Commodity Character** (Visual Studies Workshop, 1982). In **Get More** the computer's identity in this cycle of spectacularization, reification, and commodification is explored. This feels more like a scrapbook of early imagemaking experiments on the Mac than a work with developed sequencing or structure. The damning tone of Rutkovsky's title message is enhanced by the book's technical primitiveness.

Peter Lyssiotis, **The Products of Wealth**, 1982

The thematic focus on the ideology of contemporary life takes many forms in artists' books. All three of the following books use a variation on the structure of the photographic portfolio to build their critical commentary. The first of these is Peter Lyssiotis's **The Products of Wealth** (1982) which is a small eight-page pamphlet of black and white photocollages which have been reproduced. The images juxtapose affluence and destitution, violence and materialism, wealth and misery. Again, the use of the book format is determined by its relatively inexpensive capacity to reproduce material which can circulate widely — the messages in the images are clear, and though the book is not a substantial publication, it presents a media-based gestalt, a reading of the cruel paradoxes of late capitalism. The second book is more developed as an object and a work: Scott Hyde's **The Real Great Society Album** (Bayonne Publishing Company, 1971). It is composed of Hyde's photographs, multiple exposures (done in the camera

Scott Hyde, **The Real Great Society Album**, 1971

and darkroom) which reveal contradictions similar to those pointed out by Lyssiotis. But Hyde's imagery is limited to America in the years of and immediately following Lyndon Johnson's presidency (the title is taken from the phrase Johnson used to describe his domestic programs). Lyssiotis's work, by contrast, feels global, displaced from specific locations, and terrifyingly without history — as if the images exist in an eternal present of social horror. Hyde though using a straightforward portfolio format, pays attention to sequence: the relations among images are structured formally as well as thematically so that the book moves forward in a series of unfolding linkages. Lyssiotis's pages remain static and self-contained.

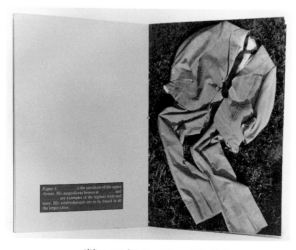

Clifton Meador, **Great Men of the Modern Age**, 1982

301

Clifton Meador's **Great Men of the Modern Age** (1982) is slightly more enigmatic than the other two books discussed and his conception derives more intimately from the structure of the printed book. If Hyde and Lyssiotis use the page as a field for the presentation of single images, Meador makes his pages in the book design process. Meador's work alternates texts and photographs of clothing laid out to make a dummy figure in the grass, each configuration accompanied by a caption on a facing page which identifies the "type" depicted: "warrior", "trendsetter", "scholar." The imagery is inseparable from the printing process — screen pattern and stripping have been used to construct the design of type and imagery not merely to reproduce an image. What these works share is their use of material culture and its capacity to produce meaning through the "stuff" of clothing, guns, dishware, automobiles, and gendered bodies. Their common theme of the "great" society foregrounds the "winner-take-all" morality of contemporary capitalist culture.

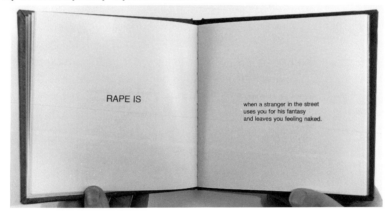

Suzanne Lacy, **Rape Is**, 1973, NYPL

Sexuality, mores, and forms of violence and prejudice are topics which have been well-served by various artists' books. A crucial early work in this vein was Suzanne Lacy's **Rape Is** (Women's Graphic Workshop, 1973) which expresses the political sensibility of the first wave of the 1970s women's art movement. Designed to raise women's consciousness through showing the range of behaviors which constitute rape, rather than obfuscating and concealing it behind layers of false moralization and judgement, Lacy's book was effective and groundbreaking. As an artist's book it communicates compelling issues directly. The cover of the wrapper bore a paper seal the reader was required to break in order to read

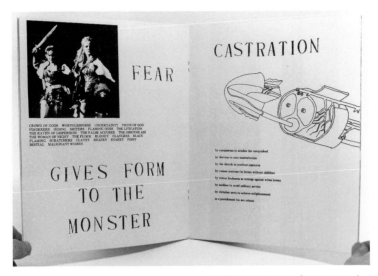

Linda Neaman, **Sex and Monsters**, n.d.

the book, and the end sheets were printed in a solid, deep, blood-red ink. Each opening has the statement "Rape is" on the left page while on the facing sheet is a description of situations women find themselves in on a regular basis — from physical to psychic and emotional harassment. The theme of sexual behavior and social prohibitions or phobias is at the center of Linda Neaman's, **Sex and Monsters** (Hallwalls, n.d.). Neaman's book is not as graphically clear or politically direct as Lacy's. It contains a blend of new age occult earth-mother graphics, popular culture images of Hollywood amazons and starlets, and texts which inscribe aspects of sexual phobias from various identified sources in a hodge-podge intended as consciousness raising. The work's major intention is to show the ways in which eroticism is demonized and sexual repression internalized and turned into anger or other destructive emotions. Suggestions of the eternal feminine, or mythically feminine, ("in the rites of Malekula, the monster Le-hev-dev, as a negative power of the feminine, is also associated with the spider") intersperse with other texts and images which display aspects of sexuality from biological and physiological functions ("In 1677 Leeuwenhoek discovered spermatozoon") to social and cultural events (photographs of a woman accused of "murder in self defense"). Sex and Monsters resembles a workbook, its large black and white pages and its page by page treatment of themes gives it a self-help or instructional-pamphlet look — no doubt exactly what Neaman intended.

303

Scott McCarney, **No Mo Pro...** 1992

Scott McCarney's **No Mo Pro Mo Ho Mo Pho Bo** (Visual Studies Workshop, 1992) is a good example of an artist's book motivated by topical concerns. McCarney's work is both a response and a protest, a means of reg-
istering anger and of using it for education and lobbying. The small pamphlet consists of a heavy weight paper cover, printed with an image of
Patrick Buchanan (right-wing pundit and former press secretary to Ronald
Reagan) and the title. Inset into Buchanan's face, just over his mouth, is a
photograph of two men kissing. Buchanan appears "to speak" their kiss, to
embrace it, and to be silenced by it simultaneously. Inside the pamphlet is
a single sheet of folded paper stapled to the spine. Bright pink, it opens
into several quadrants, each with a quote from a political conservative
with a prominent public profile — such as Donald Wildmon of the American Family Association, accompanied by a homophobic quote taken from
various sources which McCarney identifies in his colophon. Underneath
these texts and images are "negative" images of men involved in erotic
acts.4 The graphic characterization gives these an elusive character and
underscores their stigma within the public arena of right-wing and funda-
mentalist Christian rhetoric. As a small pamphlet, folding down to less
than 4 by 5 inches this is an ephemeral and topical use of the book format
to make a timely point in the spirit of 18th- and 19th-century satirical pamphlets.

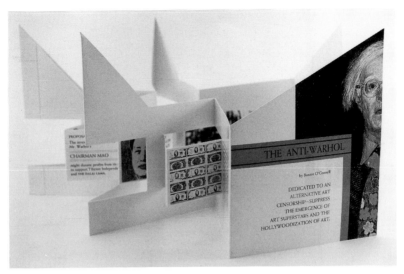

Bonnie O'Connell, **The Anti-Warhol Museum**, 1993

Bonnie O'Connell's **The Anti-Warhol Museum** (Nexus Press, 1993) makes use of a complex structure as the basis of a critique of artworld politics. In particular, she takes aim at the blind eye which cultural institutions and art stars often turn on the issues of contemporary injustice and suggests that the resources generated in the artworld be recycled to serve a broader community. The accordion-fold book is cut so that the work stands up in a star shape with panels both inset and out-thrusting. Each panel contains one part of a proposal for "The Socially Responsible Disposal of Warholia." The well-known icons of Warhol's work — from Coca Cola bottles to Campbell's soup cans and images of Chairman Mao — are juxtaposed with specific suggestions such as: "Insitutions or collectors holding versions of Warhol's Soup Cans should sell them to fund programs that will Feed the Hungry." A panel following the soup can imagery makes a succinct statement on the number of American households dependent on food stamps and statistics on the demand for food assistance to the homeless. O'Connell's work uses the striking graphics of the commercial art world and a modified book structure to question the values embodied in the Andy Warhol quote with which the book opens: "Money is the moment to me, money is my mood."

The Activist Book Examines Censorship

Janet Zweig's small publication **The 336 lines currently expurgated**

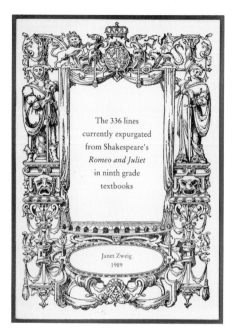

The 336 lines
currently expurgated
from Shakespeare's
Romeo and Juliet
in ninth grade
textbooks

Janet Zweig
1989

Janet Zweig, **The 336 lines...**, 1989

from Shakespeare's Romeo and Juliet in ninth grade textbooks (1989) is an activist artist's book which deals with issues of censorship. Her subject matter is the mutilation of the text and its reconstituted appearance as a seamless published work meant for junior high school instruction. The most successful acts of censorship are those which efface the marks of their own activity. This is acknowledged by Zweig, and she is reinserting those marks of erasure into the pristine form of the edited versions of classics which are used for teaching purposes. The lines which are expurgated read strangely out of context, and the prurient minds which found in them nuances likely to excite teenagers to blush, giggle, or respond to their mild, archaic sexual innuendos were clearly more informed (and possibly less experienced) than the students who would have read these snippets aloud. In an age in which AIDS is a major fact of life, the idea of keeping the sobering words "Prick love for pricking and you beat love down" from the eyes of sexually aware and active teens seems old fashioned and naive. Zweig is not so much intent on paying particular attention to these censored phrases as she is in showing how odd it was to do so in the first place. Replacing them within the original text seems to defuse their stigmatized charge — but it also returns sexuality to an inte-

306

gral place within Shakespeare's text and the textuality of adolescent life. Zweig's point is that books themselves are a site of ideological and political contest. The first page contains a brief note on "Directions for use." It says: "Xerox this book so that the words are printed on only one side of the sheet. Cut out the lines and replace them in your textbook where they belong in the play. Pass the book on to another student." Zweig is stating that the material of the book, its printed textual form, can be used as a stage for effective activism. Here the book is the agent for social change as well as a site for intervention.

1 There are independent presses dedicated to alternative publishing whose work often resembles or overlaps with some of the works which will be discussed here, such as South End Press in Boston or the New Press in New York City. The main difference between the works of these presses and that of the artists whose books are featured in this section is in their format and structure. Artists' books use complex or creative solutions whose expense, aesthetic component, and often personal inflection distinguish them from the works of presses which feature straight text, photographic images, or instructional drawings.

2 Roy Stryker was the director of a program established in 1935 to make a rural photographic survey within the Farm Security Administration, which was part of F.D. Roosevelt's 1935 Resettlement Administration.

3 The book calls for a comparison with Philip Zimmermann's **Interference** which is far more successful graphically. De Coster's design sensibility has a commercial booklet-ish aesthetic to it while Zimmermann is able to generate an original effect from pre-press screen manipulations.

4 This use of a negative to code the homoerotic as an absent or inverted space in American culture is a feature of the paintings and photomontages of the late David Wojnarowicz in his work from the 1980s.

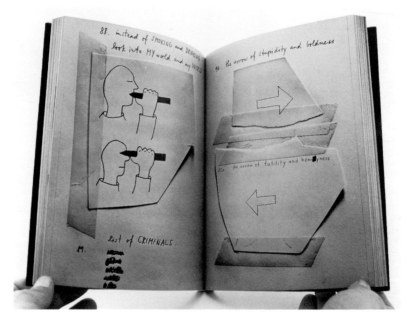

Dieter Roth, **246 Little Clouds**, 1976

12

The Book as Conceptual Space
(Performance and Exhibition)

The focus in this chapter is the book's ability to function as a conceptual space. This is done either by presenting a conceptual piece or by using the book conceptually to duplicate a function normally served by a real space of performance or exhibition. Two books which call attention to a book's identity as a conceptual space for performance are Richard Kostelanetz's **Inexistences** (1978) and George Maciunas's **Flux Paper Events** (1976). Kostelanetz's work, subtitled "constructivist fictions" is a blank book. Completely blank. Its paper pages are the realization and expectation, projection and possibility, of the fictions invoked in its subtitle. In the spirit of Russian Constructivist Kasimir Malevich's attempts to grapple with the "unrepresentable," Kostelanetz gives the impossibility a particular conceptual expression. Rather than being realized through specific forms (which, it is implied, would always be inadequate) the fictions are realized merely as form.[1] This is a conceptual gesture, one which returns the reader to the book as an object and space of potential rather than a vehicle for limited exposition or particular representation.

Maciunas's **Flux Paper Events** make a very different space out of the material form of the book — one in which the book serves as an exhibition of ways in which its pages can be made into "events." These are conceived of as the manipulation of the book's pages through various means — each of which affects the page's capacity to move, turn, or lie flat. The corners of the sheets are turned down or torn off, the paper punched through, scored, perforated, and folded, there are paper clips attached — in short, Maciunas runs through the vocabulary of banal things which may befall a sheet of paper and makes this the subject of his work. Depending on one's reading, we have moved here from the sublime to the quotidian, or the profound to the trivial. In any case, both of these artists have demonstrated the identity of the book as a form in which concept and material integrate.

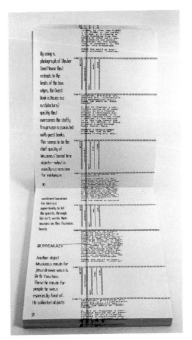 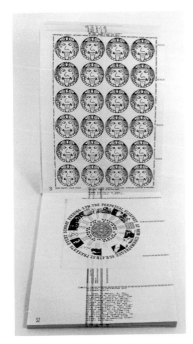

George Macuinas, **Fluxus & the Face of Time, (The Electronic Bank)**, 1984

Books of Performance

Performance as a mainstream artworld phenomenon began in the late 1950s and early 1960s when the conceptually based works of French New Realists, particularly Yves Klein and the Italian Piero Manzoni, the French Lettrists, and the international group called Fluxus were all engaging in innovative work. The Fluxus group became most renowned in this area of art activity, and the first documented Fluxus event occurred in Germany in 1962. Fluxus and earlier performance work can be traced to the influence of John Cage, whose experimental pieces with Merce Cunningham and others at Black Mountain College in the 1940s anticipated and initiated much of this later work. Cage's influence over late 20th-century art was as important and far-reaching as that of Duchamp was for the earlier half. Both were artists who reconceptualized the parameters of what constitutes the work of art. Building a sensitivity to the aesthetic component of everyday life was a fundamental aspect of the aesthetics of John Cage. The implications of much of Marcel Duchamp's conceptual work were still being integrated into mainstream art in the 1950s and 1960s, as was the work of the Dada artists whose sound poetry performances and other works had been reissued in the 1951 anthology edited by Robert Mother-well (published by Wittenborn Schultz). It is against this background of the continual rediscovery of early avant-garde performance work and later experimental activities in New York, Paris, Berlin, and elsewhere that performance art came into being.

But among performance artists, the Fluxus group are distinguished for their interest in printed matter and alternative publications such as — ephemera, mail art, and artists' books. The Fluxus group sought to erase the boundaries between art and life by making works out of the ordinary materials and events of daily existence — as in the Maciunas **Flux Paper Events**. In the anthology **Fluxus 1** (Fluxus Edition, 1964) edited by George Maciunas, a key figure in the movement, the exploration of the book as a familiar form allowed it to be significantly transformed.2 This book is bound with bolts and the pages are a series of manila envelopes which alternate with printed pages. Each envelope contains a work by a different artist, and each is materially specific. Artist Joe Jones's envelope contains a typewriter ribbon of his "favorite story;" Ann Halprin's envelopes contains a coded drawing of a path, titled a "landscape event" and a paper boat; Yoko Ono's envelope was titled "self-portrait" and it contains a piece of mirror smooth silver mylar. Table napkins, performance scores, a stocking, and other ephemera contribute to the work, and the paged sequence of the envelopes lets the reader's relation to the book unfold in time and space. Here the book is the performance as well as containing it, and the work achieves the Fluxus goal of making the audience member a performer through the structure of the piece. One does not "read" this work, but enacts it.

Many Fluxus artists were drawn to the book as a form. Not since the period of Russian Futurism were as many artists sharing an artistic sensibility so involved with the book as an immediate form of expression. Of the many examples, two particularly well-known ones demonstrate the ways these works were structured. George Brecht's **Water Yam** (Fluxus Edition, 1964) is a boxed set of cards, each of which contains a set of instructions for one or more performances. The instructions are directions for turning water on or off, honking a car horn for a specified period of time, using decks of cards passed around a group of performers, and other ordinary activities rendered extraordinary by having attention paid to them. As a book, **Water Yam** has a very open structure, there are no set sequences and no rules for its reading or use. Yoko Ono's book **Grapefruit**

(Wunternaum Press, 1964) is similarly composed of sets of instructions. Page after page describes performance works: "Wall Piece I: Sleep two walls away from each other. Whisper to each other." Another example is titled "Painting to see a room." "Drill a small, almost invisible hole in the center of the canvas and see the room through it." Such works were (and still are) the basis of Fluxus aesthetics. Whether bound books or loose cards, these instructions were meant to make the art experience available to anyone willing or interested in participation.

George Brecht, **Water Yam**, 1964

Book as Performance

Richard Tuttle's **Story with Seven Characters** (1965) makes a very different kind of performance space out of the book form. For Tuttle the book is not a performance score, it is the performance. This book is printed from seven glyphic characters each a sign which looks like a letter or punctuation mark but isn't. The book is produced on a dull, earth tone paper. The characters are printed letterpress with a minimal amount of ink so that the paper tone shows through. As typographic marks, these characters are heavy enough and bold enough to hold their own on the page. As figurative "characters" in the drama of the book they acquire personality and idiosyncracy through repetition and sequence. The continual rearrangement of the seven signs "reads" as an effect of interactions which are continually in transition. The result is that the book is both the space of and record of this supposed interaction. The work functions as a

Richard Tuttle, **Story with Seven Characters**, 1965, Spencer Collection, NYPL

closed system, one which provides meaning to the elements by giving them an arena in which to define themselves and each other.

Warren Lehrer and Dennis Bernstein's **French Fries** (EarSay and Visual Studies Workshop, 1984) combines elements of both of these aspects of book of and as performance. On the one hand, like two of Lehrer's other books (**Versations**, 1980 and **I Mean You Know** 1983), **French Fries** is both a score and a performance. The page is given the identity of a theatrical space, one in which the placement and movement of typographic elements is a schematic diagram of the action in the piece. But, on the other hand, the works have served as the basis of actual performances. **French Fries** is a graphically elaborate work. By contrast with Tuttle's minimalist subtlety, **French Fries** is a carnivalesque-pop-art-amusement-motel-and-theme-park of visual and typographic devices. The two artists made observations of events transpiring at a fast-food hamburger place. There is a large cast of characters each of whom has their own verbal and graphic style. The page is a carefully scored place of interaction, brightly colored and dense with activity, stage directions, and commentary. These texts are intercut with materials drawn from a series of interviews Lehrer and Bernstein conducted on the topic of potatoes, thus emphasizing the theme of french fries. The characters are explored in some depth and towards the end of the work there is a mini-gallery of the "book" each of these characters is writing (or would be) as an appropriate expression of their personality and identity. The graphics are elaborate and the book makes maximum use of the three colors of ink in the printing through

Warren Lehrer, **French Fries**, 1984

highly complex stripping and burning techniques in the making of the plates.3 The book's theatricality is formal as well as thematic, it functions as the basis of a dramatic enactment.4

Janet Zweig's **Heinz and Judy** (Photographic Resource Center, 1985), in contrast, could not be performed except as a book. The book is deceptively simple looking — it appears at first glance to be a black and white production with spot color added in additional runs. In fact the work was printed by a four-color separation process so that there is considerable range of color and depth in the tones. The central imagery in the book is a shadow play between two characters. These shadow interactions appear to float in an indeterminate space which appears to be either behind or above the page. The shadows appear to be cast onto the curtain of the page from behind and yet other aspects of the page structure contradict this possibility. The shadows are of two pairs of hands and two profiles, a man's and a woman's, which are almost life-sized. These gendered images interact with the irrational violence and action of the scripted text. The main text is an excerpt from a classic Punch and Judy play while a second text poses an interrogation of the gender roles exaggerated in the first. The secondary texts are taken from psychological studies of the different ways young girls and boys assess situations which pose moral dilemmas. (The "Heinz" of the title is featured in one of these dilemmas in which he is to be punished, rewarded, or excused for an action which could be widely interpreted.) These dilemmas may involve a conflict between obeying

Janet Zweig, **Heinz and Judy**, 1985

authority and taking initiative, acting generously or acting cautiously —
and the assessments of appropriate action tend to split along gender lines.
While the Punch and Judy excerpts are printed onto the page, these secondary texts appear to be on slips of cream-colored paper sitting on the
surface of the pages (they cast shadows onto them). But they also receive
the shadows of the acting hands and faces so that the sense of the page as
a curtain is transformed into that of a surface onto which all the shadows
fall and onto which another paper has been placed. Aside from the textual
richness of the work, the sheer graphic complexity of the piece continually makes reference to the spatial illusions sustainable on the page.
There's yet another set of marks on the pages — these appear to be scribbled or drawn in wax crayon and sit right on the surface. In one example,
the words "I wrote in this book" in yellow and orange seem to have been
added by a juvenile graffiti artist. Mimicking theater imagery and conventions in the use of the page, the work is also aware of the conventions of
the book. The play of versimilitude and illusion refuses to stabilize — the
ambiguous shadow play is performed within the book without whose
pages there would have been no arena of activity.

Book as a Conceptual Work

There are conceptual works which come into being only in the book
form which serves as their record and their embodiment such as Jan Dibbets's **Robin Redbreast's Territory/Sculpture** (1969) and Maurizio Nan-

315

nuci's **Star/scrivendo camminado** (Hinwil, 1978). Both of these involve systems of mapping and diagramming elaborate geographic spaces through a conceptual device. Dibbets' work shows the range of a robin by charting its movements among five posts used to create a design on a particular area of land. There was no actual work outside of Dibbets' record — the flight of the bird through the air leaving no other material trace — and so the work is the concept and sculpture. Nannucci, in contrast, imposed the form of a star on a neighborhood around the Musée des Offices in Florence; he then walked repeatedly through the area according to the route this form charted on the map, thus "writing" a star on the city's topography. In both cases the book was the record of a conceptual proposition and neither duplicates the movements being studied nor precisely provides their visual or spatial gestalt. One learns the shape of the movements through these displaced means, produced in an attempt to get at or make the configuration involved.5 The book is the completed piece — not its documentation.

Marcel Broodthaers, **Reading Lorelei**, 1975, Spencer Collection, NYPL

Two books which focus on the relations within the book are Davi Det Hompson's **Hook** and Marcel Broodthaers's **Mademoise** (discussed earlier). Marcel Broodthaers often makes use of the book as a space for the creation of a conceptual work which does not exist beyond the boundaries of its finite form. **Reading Lorelei** (Yvon Lambert, 1975) is deconstructive in its techniques and yet located within the structures of a book.

Broodthaers uses the basic binarism of a book's opening to juxtapose two columns of imagery. The love poem "Lorelei" by Heinrich Heine is the central text, but the images are reproductions of 19th-century chromolithographs of leisure spots on the Rhine which face equal sized, equally placed images of people watching television. These are all images which have been used for publicity purposes and the discrepancy between the nostalgic image of the Rhine in the chromolithographs and the packaging of that nostalgia as a consummable experience are part of the point of Broodthaers' juxtapositions. Typical of Broodthaers, the ultimate meaning of this work remains somewhat elusive, though the slow investigation of the area of the Rhine near the Lorelei Rock takes place through the movement of the book. Here again it is the book's fundamental principles of finitude and sequence, as well as binaristic juxtaposition which Broodthaers takes advantage of.

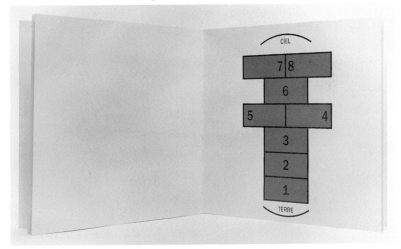

Lawrence Weiner, **La Marelle or Pie in the Sky**, 1990

Many of Lawrence Weiner's books are self-contained conceptual works realized only in book form. Critic Robert C. Morgan has written about a number of Weiner's works and uses the apt term "concrete systems" to describe their propositional format.6 The books take various forms, from graphic to linguistic, but in **Ducks on a Pond** (Imschoot Uitgevers, 1988) there is an overt suggestion of performance. Subtitled "Towards a Theatrical Engagement," the book is an analysis of the movements of a group of ducks on the surface of a pond. Their grouping and regrouping is schematically charted and analysed and from this a diagrammatic score is created. This can be read as a score to be performed, or it can be read as the performance itself wherein the book is the project and record. Bits of photographic imagery are interspersed with notes suggesting movements for the reinterpretation of the score. Like Dibbets' **Robin Redbreast**, Weiner's work uses aleatory aspects of a natural event to make a deliberate pattern (the robin's territorial parameters are only a chance pheonomena in relation to the human boundaries in the landscape within which they are noted). This piece works within the compact format which characterizes most of Weiner's books — the archness of this conceptual humor would be difficult to sustain in a larger work. Broodthaers's more elaborate books (both **Lorelei** and **Voyage on the North Sea**) though equally conceptual, make use of a material dialogue between production and reproduction of images to sustain their larger scale — their use of graphic devices expands to fit the larger pages while Weiner's work is readily contained in this smaller scale.

Weiner's **La Marelle or Pie in the Sky** (Le Nouveau Musée Villeurbanne, 1990) is a good demonstration of this point. The visual elements are striking orange and red graphics. **La Marelle** (the word means "hopscotch" in French) takes the moves of a hopscotch game and reads them as a cosmic metaphor. The collapse of the two into a single trope is facilitated by the game's assignation of the term "earth" for the starting spot and "heaven" for the finish written into the game's numbered grid. The phrases are as diagrammatic as the images, and in their bright red block letters pose questions about the disposition of the stones used to mark one's place in the game. The spaciousness of the layout, the brightness of the ink on the thick paper, add a sense of substance to the conceptual nature of the work. This is clearly a book work, however, the use of repetition to mark one's movement through the analysis of the game and the regular structure of sequences allow the conceptual conceit to be realized: the book is the enactment of a cosmic hopscotch through its pages. Both of the Weiner books use the book as a space for the realization of conceptual works. Again, these are not reproductions of pieces or texts which accompany another work, they are the works themselves.

Sjoerd Hofstra's **A Study in Averages** (ZET, 1990) has much in common with the books by Dibbets, Weiner, and Broodthaers. The book contains a series of pages on which the floor plans of individual apartments within a huge complex have been reproduced. Each individual plan is subject to the same set of measurements and calculations: the distance from the corner of the kitchen to the corner of the livingroom, from the edge of the bathtub to the door of the bathroom, from the front entry to the rear hall closet. These calculations, which have an air of the absurd, are processed into beautiful geometric diagrams analysing the space. The implications of the analysis are simple: the concept of "average" has been used to determine the minimal space for accomodating a human life within the spatial conventions of a Western European middle-class condominium or apartment lifestyle. The final averages are imposed on minimal black and white photographs of the actual rooms, but the vagueness of the images and the complexity of the diagrams do not allow the photographs to be read as real spaces: they remain as much a projected average as the rest.

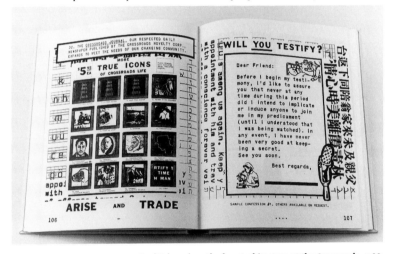

Paul Zelevansky, **Shadow Architecture at the Crossroads**, 1988

Not all uses of the book as a self-contained conceptual system are as abstract or analytic as the works just discussed. An interesting contrast to these are the books of Paul Zelevansky, **The Book of Takes** (Zartscorp, 1976), **The Case for the Burial of Ancestors** (Zartscorp and Visual Studies Workshop Press, 1981), **Shadow Architecture at the Crossroads** (CNC, 1988). Zelevansky's works contain an entire universe of references, forms, narratives, codes, and information. The three works are intimately related, though each is distinct in form and functions independently. Off-set printed from originals made with rubber stamps, presstype, type-writer, and other low-tech graphic items, the books make striking use of the potential of these media to translate into tones of black and white. Zelevanksy also exploits the structures and conventions of book form to

319

their fullest: the momentum of the narrative is interrupted and fleshed out with other information, visual material, jokes, puns, a rich array of graphic elements which continually expand the world which Zelevansky is creating in the book. On the one hand, these are closed systems, ones in which the significance and meaning of the elements, is generated entirely from their relations to each other. On the other hand, as Zelevansky says of his work "the edges of the page" are "the proscenium which contains the play" but "the screen is porous between us."7

Zelevansky's **The Case for the Burial of Ancestors** is a rewriting of the biblical book of Genesis, but the world is described in book metaphors: "there are the four edges of the known world which serve simultaneously as physical, formal and spiritual guideposts."8 The full development of these metaphors as well as their narrative exegesis continually sutures the concept of the book with the particulars of the story. For instance, a "Bindery Wall" separates the old and new worlds, and the main characters are the people of the book (the Hegemonians) whose geographical domain is described in great detail. **The Book of Takes** uses the concept of graphic and linguistic coding to make a system of signs which articulate a non-linear novel with these "takes" within a highly formalized book structure. **Shadow Architecture** contains an equally developed cosmos, but shifted into a more apocalyptic frame — a sense of dark urgency permeates the book, a sense of a world gone awry, at the "crossroads" which cries out for attention. In all of Zelevansky's work the book becomes an entire place, a universe of meaning produced from interlocking signs. The books are parallel universes structured according to the rules of a symbolic language. They are continually referencing books as metaphors as well as using the conventions of the book to elaborate their significance.

Book as Exhibition

Early 20th-century publications of visual works provide a precedent for using a publication as a form of exhibition. These include such renowned publications as Lazar El Lissitzky's **Kunstismes**, the reproduced imagery in the Russian **The World of Art**, Wassily Kandinsky's German **Der Blaue Reiter**, and a host of others such as Alfred Stieglitz's journal **Camera Work**. These proved the value of the journal or book as a form of exhibition space, one capable of circulating images and aesthetic ideas to a wide audience in an accessible and affordable form. In the 1940s, French writer and cultural minister Andre Malraux wrote the essay "Museum without Walls" in which he suggested that changes in the capacity for reproduction of images would soon make museums an outmoded form. Malraux felt that the publication of artworks or their availability in the form of printed postcards, slides, transparencies or other techniques would have a democratizing effect. The "museum without walls" was a utopian vision of cultural property loosened from the grip of institutions, curators, elite collectors, or private patrons. While it may be that the age of electronic media will finally realize Malraux's vision, in the interim many artists have found ways to realize the concept of the museum or gallery within a book form.9

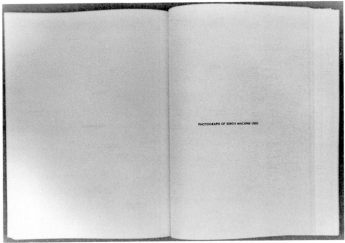

Xerox Book, 1968

A well-known early example is the exhibition catalogue published in 1968 by Seth Siegelaub as the sole site for an exhibition of conceptual artists. No other exhibition took place — this was not a situation in which a book served as a catalogue. Instead, the book publication **was** the exhibition, it was record and site of the conceptual undertaking. The untitled work, known as the **Xerox Book** (Siegelaub/Wendler, 1968) included the work of seven artists: Carl Andre, Robert Barry, Douglas Huebler, Joseph Kosuth, Sol LeWitt, Robert Morris, and Lawrence Weiner. Each of them contributed a section to the work, much of it of a highly self-referential and conceptual variety, minimal in its visual and graphic means: a xeroxed set of lines, a bit of dust, a simple statement about the page being a "photograph" of the xerox machine.10 Germano Celant's description of Douglas Huebler's piece provides an example: "Huebler... takes the page as the work's context and conditions perception through a series of logical interventions. They gradually alienate the reader from perceiving the page as an arena, and place him in the desired thought process, determined by the artist. The first page is denoted only by the dimension 'An 8 1/2" x 11" sheet of Paper,' which is denoted by a series of points, such as 'A Point Located in the Exact Center of an 8 1/2" x 11" Xerox Paper.'" Each of the artists attempted to use the xerox medium and the imperfections of its reproduction techniques in their individual sections. The book is consistent with the direction of these artists' work at the time, though the idea of a conceptual exhibition had itself already become an artworld convention by this period. (For instance, Yves Klein and the New Realists in the late 1950s had initiated such ideas as showing a bare gallery in an exhibition of "immateriality" and so forth.)11 But the use of the book as the literal and physical site opened new possibilities.

Stephen Steinman, **Art on Other Planets**, 1980, NYPL

This idea need not always be so extremely conceptual as it was with the Siegelaub work. For instance, Stephen Steinman, **Art on Other Planets** (Nexus Press, 1980) is about as far from the self-consciousness of the Siegelaub group as possible. Steinman's book offers itself as an exhibition of art which has been placed on other planets. Produced in color offset from collages, the book contains such images as Botticelli's Venus placed into the landscape of the planet Venus, or a space station on which a gasoline station from Edward Hopper's painting has been collaged against a deep space sky. If these images seem facile, they are nonetheless a playful use of the book as a space to display an exhibition which presumably stretched the full extent of the galaxy. Steinman's is a classic in a genre of the book as gallery or museum — this idea is very close to that of the book as portfolio or mobile exhibition to be discussed below. Steinman's work is distinguished from these by a specific sense of the cosmic scale of the topography of the exhibition space that he has collapsed into the book.

Barbara Bloom's **The Reign of Narcissism** (Wurttembergischer Kunstverein, 1990) accompanies the fetishistic exhibition of the same name and incorporates every element into a miniature portable version of the exhibition.12 The book is a collection of texts, images, and photographic reproductions of the many objects through which she posed her investigation of the terms (particularly the gendered terms) of artistry and identity in Western art. Using her own profile image as a basic icon and pattern she had all manner of things fabricated — from chocolates to textiles, cameos and wallpaper, statuettes and decorative medallions — in order to make an environment in which the artist's image was everywhere. Presented as a handbook to the collection, the book functions as a minigallery and compendium. The fact that the work reflects upon the nature of the collection and catalogue gives it an extra self-reflexive dimension. Bloom makes one aware of a catalogue's conventions through the book's obsessive character, and as a consequence, it is fully self-sufficient.

Bonnie O'Connell's, **The Anti-Warhol Museum**, discussed earlier, is not so much a museum as a politically charged piece. If it echoes a museum in its formal properties, that is only to give it an extra graphic power for its social agenda. Joni Mabe's **Museum Book** (Nexus Press, 1988), in contrast, is a completely manic book as museum production. The work is offset printed (on one side only) on heavy coated stock in a riot of colors and images. The tone of the book is part outsider artwork and part scrapbook. Composed from Mabe's vast collection of stickers (animals, birds, flags, stars, praying hands, automobiles, leaping trout, crosses, children in Swiss mountain outfits, Santa Claus, flowers, Easter seals, angels and saints, hearts, kittens, ducks, Holy Bibles) and her clipping files, the book is a museum of southern United States popular culture. Elvis is the major heroic figure here, right along with Jesus, and a few lesser luminaries: Tammy Wynette, Hank Williams, and John F. Kennedy. The texts in this book are found on documents which form part of the collage: "Healing through prayer cloth" a spread from a tabloid journal on the "Jim Bakker Sex Shame" or testimonials from believers who have been healed through

Joni Mabe, **The Museum Book**, 1988

a miracle of faith. The "museum" is, on the one hand, wildly heterogenous and, on the other, quite deliberately focused on "country" culture. The characters are primarily from the country and western music scene, and their legendary status is on display. Mabe is not uncritical and though her editorial point of view is eclectic she includes quotes like: "After his third divorce Jerry Lee Lewis was asked if he knew any more about women now than he had known two decades earlier, he said 'Yeah. Pussy is pussy.'" This sits in the midst of a page bordered by an old (cantankerous looking) tortoise sitting next to a man who has pulled his pants down, the hair on his thin chest tangling a medallion while his limp genitals echo the shapes of the tortoises' head and arms. There are dozens of other images on this page (and on all the others) so that any simple reading is virtually impossible. This is a museum of graphic material, much of it kitsch, camp, contemporary, mainstream, and yet quintessentially from a popular culture in which five and dimes, church activities, and gift shops contribute the major aesthetic components. The book is literally the museum — no exhibition preexisted the book and these elaborate collages have no other existence. The sense that this is the space of display and collections which are permanent, ordered, and preserved gives the book its museum status.

Francois Deschamps's **Small Oddities** (1989) is a handdrawn pamphlet book which purports to present a "collection of emblematic objects by Joe Vinal." Pretending that the "collection" (which exists only as these drawn

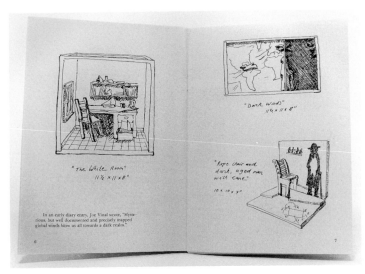

Francois Deschamps, **Small Oddities**, 1989

presentations) was the result of Vinal's own methodical investigation of the properties of ordinary objects, Deschamps presents them here within a book which serves as a tiny conceptual museum. Unlike Mabe's work, which is the museum **de facto**, **Small Oddities** lets you know that it is functioning as a museum and then proceeds to act as if the book were invisible and the presentations were as immediate, dimensional, and real as in an actual museum. Each page displays several objects whose measurements are given, their titles lettered out, their specific characteristics and properties described in brief. As a faked collection of faked objects, Deschamps's book depends on extending the conceit of this appreciative examination of the oddity of Vinal's fragmentary and disintegrating objects. Vinal, who supposedly made all of the objects, wrote of them "I feel that objects are events — events in very slow motion. Made of once-living wood which is dried, cut, glued and nailed, these things will inevitably crack, splinter, crumble and decay. I try to show this in the work." The book is a museum of Deschamps' imaginative sketches of these ideas, his exhibition of attempts to realize the "oddity" in suggested form.

Book as Portfolio or Collection

The works discussed above present themselves as a space of display and they structure relations of elements within them through that concept; the book forms to be considered in this section function more literally as albums or portfolios.This type of book does not try to compensate for the fact that it serves to present a group of work — images, texts, photographs, collages. Nonetheless, the books included here all have a degree of self-consciousness about the book as a form. This self-consciousness can manifest itself as attention to production, as in the gradual layering of ink on the pages in Joe Ruther's **Victorian Album** (FM Productions, 1970s). Not nearly as deconstructive as his other works, such as **Down and Dirty** (1980s) (whose title refers to the printing process as well as to Ruther's own verbal meanderings), the book nonetheless invokes the concept of the album as a means of presenting erotica. The format of the book keeps text and images separate, the verbal presentation is made in regular blocks with a schematically pornographic border while the images display Ruther's penchant for press and darkroom manipulations.

Another work of photographic experimentation which takes a very different technical apparatus as its point of departure is Paolo Gioli's **Spiracolografie** (nd, np.). Gioli's small book reproduces even smaller photographs which he made with a lens made from a button (which he held between thumb and forefingers so that it let light pass through onto the surface of a strip of film held into contact with the button's hole). The resulting images are extremely distorted, as if taken through a peephole from some remote distance, but their thematic concerns are as erotically suggestive as Ruther's. In both cases, the concept of the album as a private repository of images meant to be shielded from public sight is operative. "Album" carries the meaning of both concealment and display in their work, which serves as a site for privacy and fantasy.

Using the book as an album or exhibition often takes a more strictly visual and straightforward form. There are many examples of such works. Dieter Roth's **96 Piccadellies** (Eaton House and Hansjörg Mayer, 1977) simply presents a collection of 96 images of Picadelly Circus in London, each of which has been altered in a different way. This is an album. The regular format of the cards, their arrangement in rows, their neat but uninflected presentation are all album codes. Any particular effect of their sequencing is minimal — they are merely presented. The dense compression of the work in the book structure reinforces its thematic unity. This kind of exploration of a theme gives Lyle Rosbotham's **High School Students** (The Writers' Center, 1984) and Nancy Linn's **Madonna and Child** (Awhile Publication Co., 1984) their strength as book projects. Rosbotham's work is highly formal. The photographs of high school students

Lyle Rosbotham, **High School Students**, 1984

he made against white studio backdrops disconnect them from anything but their own body language, clothing, and general appearance. They are both generic and specific, each seems to represent a type and yet each is highly individualized. There is a poignancy to the images of these adolescents, with all of the discrepancies between desired adult identity and teen awkwardness still showing. Rosbotham's presentation is neutral — it is not charged with the kind of pathos which attaches to Christian Boltanski's **Classe Terminale du Lycée Chases** (Kunstrerein fur dei Rheinlarde, 1987). That book is comprised of photographs of high school students he extracted from the yearbook of the Jewish Lycée Chases during the Second World War. By contrast, Rosbotham's work offers an open visual text, which can be read any number of ways, rather than against a particular scenario of projected destruction. Nancy Linn's photographs use a madonna motif as a framework for photographing women in a parenting program at Bellevue, the psychiatric confinement facility in New York City. By contrast to both Rosbotham and Boltanski, Linn makes context a visible aspect of her photographs. The conditions in which these women and their babies live and are photographed can't be separated from the photos themselves. Linn's book does not have the aesthetic formalism of the other two artists' works, however, her pages bespeak the complexity of circumstances in which her subjects are involved. What all of these works share is a concept of "book" which is based on its conventional form and the idea that through thematic unity a book may establish its identity.

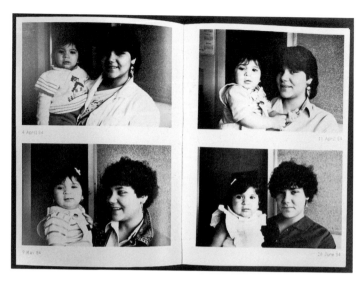

Nancy Linn, **Madonna and Child**, 1984

Maurizio Nannucci's **Lives Here** (1987) is a book of photographs which he compiled over a ten-year period. They are all photographs of the entry-ways to the homes of artists he has known, and the book serves as a port-folio bound by thematic unity which has the extra gossipy interest of being about artworld figures. But in an earlier book **Vero/Falso** (Allerheiligen-presse, 1981) he used the techniques of photo-reproduction to comment upon the distinctions between illusion and deception, representation and falsehood. Each of the openings of the book contains two images, one of which is granted the status of "true," the other "false." This status is deter-mined by the degree of dissembling involved in the image. A drawing of a hand, for instance, is considered true (it is a real outline of an actual hand) while the broken off hand of a bit of marble statuary which faces it across the gutter is considered false — it is a copy of a copy, after all. The Pla-tonic rigor with which Nannucci judges these images is played out against our understanding (and denial) of the fact that what we are presented with here are photographs, all of which deceive to the same degree. By nuancing levels of representation, Nannucci plays a sophisticated game of contrasts and comparisons, and the formal relations of the facing images, each one of a true/false pair are continually working through the struc-ture of the book.

Ernst Caramelle's **Forty Found Fakes** (Thomas Way and Company, 1978) does not use the book form to the same extent as Nannucci, but his

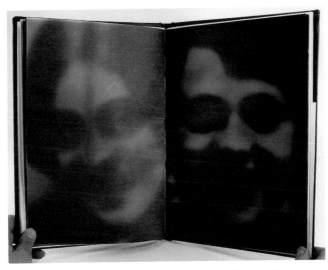

Christian Boltanski, **Classe Terminale du Lycée Chases**, 1987

collection of "fakes" comprises a rich album of artworld look-alikes. The photographs are all of "found" versions of recognizable signature style artworks by mainstream artists: a striped awning imitating Daniel Buren, a chunk of construction material resembling a Richard Serra, a line of stones resembling a Hamish Fulton walk piece, and so forth. It functions as a complement to Nannucci's **Lives Here** as a compendium of artworld injokes. Though one often "finds" these things in the world, their careful presentation in the form of a book work gives them the status of a formal commentary they lack in the casual encounter, while their parodic quality foregrounds the characteristic features of the artworks to which they refer.

The last book to be discussed within the paradigm of the portfolio is Caryl Burtner's **The Exorcism of Page Thirteen** (Gates of Heck, 1993). This is a work of found text/image/numbers. It is a compilation of around seven-hundred and fifty "13's" clipped from the pages of a variety of books. Each is different. Each brings with it whatever incidental information is attached to the one-square inch dimensions of the "exorcised" pieces. These standard, gridded pages of fragments have been photographed and reproduced in four-color printing as exact replicas of the originals. Bits of text read across the spaces between these squares suggesting a pastiche connection. And the possible forms for the number "13" plays out in its endless visual variation. This portfolio of work compiled from the materi-

329

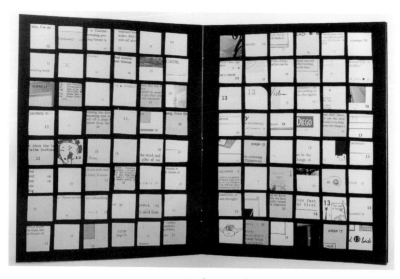

Caryl Burtner, **The Exoricism of Page Thirteen**, 1993

als of books, it seems like a good endpoint to the discussion of book as place of exhibition and display. The final square on the final page has been cut out of the thick coated paper and placed into a window cut in the cover. The two holes echo each other, but also refer to the process of "exorcism" which Burtner performed on her library collection — removing the squares which comprise these works with a surgical care and precision. Because of the gallery of flat images in which they are presented, none of these page excerpts seem to refer to the inevitable fact that they are only one side of a story in which the page "14" has had to suffer unwittingly and innocently simply because of its place in the numerical sequence of pages. The flat faces of these exorcised scraps gives them a false image of autonomy, as if they exist on the surface of this album. Our cognitive knowledge of their two-sided identity as a page is overwhelmed and repressed by their literal presentation as "only" page "13's." They have been reduced to images of those pages in a book which maintains its visual, material relation to its sources while inevitably eradicating the artifactual reality of their form. In this sense, the book as portfolio is always one step removed from an original work except where it functions as the sole or primary place of those presentations.

In Conclusion

Francois Deschamps's, **My life in a Book** (Visual Studies Workshop

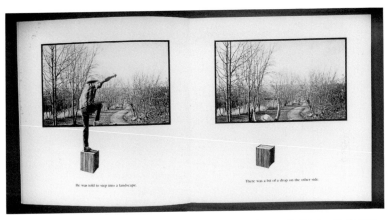

Francois Deschamps, **My Life in a Book**, 1986

Press, 1986) takes the conceptual space of the book as a premise for a fictional and graphic exploration. Deschamps's work is a narrative with a surreal logic — but it is a logic. The frontispiece image depicts (a pinecone) (+) (an apple) (=) (a pineapple) with the objects representing themselves. Deschamps's attitude toward the ordering of his story seems apparent in that first image — and the book proceeds to fulfill its promise. It begins: "One day he awoke and found himself in a book." This text is accompanied by the image of Deschamps falling out of the spine of the book and into the space of the page. This literalization of book as space continues throughout the work as Deschamps plays on the ways in which representational strategies of illusion conventionally mask their peculiarities. After appearing on the first white page, for instance, he is "told to step into a landscape" and is shown climbing over the edge of a photograph. The photograph was taken from a high angle, and Deschamps "drops" on the other side of the frame so that only his hat and raised hands are visible. Such changes in scale and play with the character of pictorial surface, drawn images, and narrative delusions are the substance of the work. In one image a fortune is held up to be read against the background of crumbled cookie crumbs, it reads: "Your life will be safer and much less exciting than you ever dreamed possible." The point is not only to mock the fated seeming narrator, disappointing his expectations of an adventure, but also to point out the basic discrepancies between the intensified terms of narrated tales and the realities of life.

The role of books as a cultural force, one which provides fantasy images of reality and provides false or at least romantic expectations of existence is subtly critiqued here. Visual puns and jokes continue and as in Deschamps's other works his deft humor and its play between convention and revelation make the work succeed. At the end the narrator lights the book on fire to escape, immolating the prison of representation which confines him. For Deschamps the space of the book is ultimately too confining, its tropes and conventions too limiting, to contain his existence.

1 This all puzzles me slightly since it seems that this is a "suprematist" fiction, not a "constructivist" one: suprematism was a movement initiated in the work of Kazimir Malevich to investigate anti-illusionistic form in visual art; constructivism is associated with Vladimir Tatlin's integration of abstract art with industrial or applied arts. Kostelanetz's work seems more concerned with the aesthetics of the former movement rather than the agenda of the latter.

2 The book was reissued in 1984 through ReFlux Editions in a perfect facsimile.

3 Stripping and burning are both phases in the production of offset printing plates. Stripping refers to the placement of film negatives in orange masking material in order to compose the pages (and placement of various negatives which register on the page) and burning is the actual exposure of the plate. A plate may be exposed any number of times before it is developed in order to layer line-shots, half-tones, and other images onto it — some of the pages in **French Fries** involved up to thirty overlays (done by Philip Zimmermann) so that a wide range of colors was produced in three print runs.

4 As in the case of **I Mean, You Know** in Chapter 10, there is a striking comparison between these works and the **zaum** plays of Ilia Zdanevich discussed in Chapter 3.

5 Spatial mapping onto a cultural terrain is the issue motivating Alfredo Jaar's **Two or three things I imagine about them** (Whitechapel, 1987). Consisting of a Chilean passport rubberbanded together with maps of Brazil, Nigeria, Hong Kong, and the People's Republic of China, this is more a conceptual piece than a book work: the image of the "pasaporte" in its official blue and gold-stamped format is an icon which holds the disparate functions of maps and cultures to a single point of personal reference, but there is little use of exploration of the book form beyond this. I have trouble putting this work into the context of a discussion of artists' books.

6 Robert C. Morgan, "Systemic Books by Artists," **Artists' Books: A Critical Anthology and Sourcebook** (Visual Studies Workshop Press and Peregrine Press, 1984), pp. 207-222.

7 Paul Zelevansky, **The Case for the Burial of Ancestors** (Zartscorp, 1981), intro.

8 Shelley Rice, "Words and Images: Artists' Books as Visual Literature" **Artists' Books: A Critical Anthology and Sourcebook** (Visual Studies Workshop Press and Peregrine Press, 1984), p.80.

9 Among the books I have left out here is General Idea's **The Getting into the Spirits Cocktail Book** (1980) since I only know it through reproductions.

10 For a more developed discussion of this work see Germano Celant, pp.96-97, "Book as Artwork: 1960-72" in **Books by Artists**, Tim Guest and Germano Celant, (Art Metropole, 1981).

11 See Bruce Altschuler, **The Avant-Garde in Exhibition** (Abrams, 1994).

12 This book was co-published by the Kunsthalle in Zurich, the Serpentine Gallery in London, and the Wurrtembergischer Kunstverein in Stuttgart.

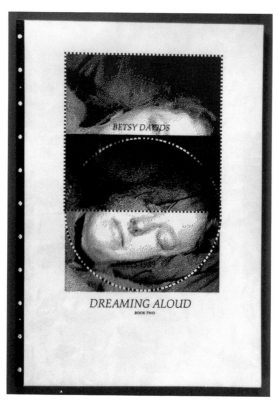

Betsy Davids, **Dreaming Aloud, Book Two**, 1985

13
The Book as Document

The books in this section demonstrate the capacity of artists' books to serve as documents — either reproducing a record of experience and information or serving as the document themselves.1 While the idea of the book as a document is hardly an artistic invention, this ability to serve as a record has extended aspects of conceptual and performance art into book form. As a document, the book becomes a space of information. The standard format of the book serves very well as a place in which an experience, account, or testimonial can be produced. A book can be a document which is not duplicated elsewhere or it can be a reproduction of an already extant piece.2 This use of the book seems almost obvious, something one can take for granted. In fact, the forms which such books take is quite varied, and the formal and structural means by which their presentation is realized ranges from the banal to the extraordinary, as in every other realm of artists' books.

Diaristic and Personal Statements
Sol Lewitt's **Autobiography** (Lois & Michael K. Torf and Multiples, 1980) is in some ways the paradigmatic instance of the artist's book as a personal statement. It is specific, focused entirely on the artist, and uses the book form to reveal and document personal identity. In other ways this work is completely impersonal — or at least, refuses to reveal any intimate information whatsoever in spite of its exhaustive cataloguing of the artist's belongings. Consisting of page after page of small photographs (laid out in a grid) of all of the items in Lewitt's possession at the time, the book is fascinating as an artifact. Art supplies, chairs, lamps, dishes, clothing, family memorabilia and other personal items are presented in the grid. The images ask us to take them as a record but don't reveal their connections to each other or the lived space from which they are extracted. Neither do they reveal much about Lewitt. On the one hand, this is a

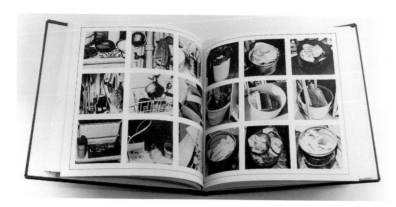

Sol Lewitt, **Autobiography**, 1980, NYPL

detailed and specifc autobiography, and on the other hand, it shows how generic the existence of the middle-class American is in material terms. The funky, eclectic, and functional items in Lewitt's **Autobiography** seem interchangeable with those of many individuals of my acquaintance. Rich in visual information, the autobiography in this photographic catalogue is without a textual exposition — and without any contextualization of the information it provides. Even the threads which more circumstantial photographs would have provided are absent. We are offered these images as information, grouped according to types of things (all towels together) in a way which deprives them of much of their situational information, the invisible quality of their relations to each other and their user. Mute, the images urge their presence on us and then refuse to speak. They do not disclose very much, though they appear to disclose the full extent of the life lived. The individual to which the materials of this life belong are conspicuously absent. Seductive by virtue of its extent, successful on account of its formal means, the book signals the difficulties of an autobiographical statement. Lewitt seems to pose the difficult question of how to locate a "self" in **Autobiography**, or how to project one from it. Lewitt's point seems to be that the autobiography can conceal as much as it reveals about a person. The most replete inventory may provide a demographic profile but not index a voice, manner, or character.

This project is similar to the ongoing project by Christian Boltanski in which he systematically catalogues all of someone else's material goods. Inventory of the **Objects Belonging to an Inhabitant of Oxford** (Westfalischer Kunstverein, 1974) is one of these works, and the curious parallel between this and the Lewitt project show how close to anonymity these revelations remain. The way in which Boltanski presents the belongings of the "inhabitant" is very similar to that of Lewitt, except that instead of using the formal grid, Boltanski adjusts the layout of his pages to accomodate the shapes of the objects in the photographs. Long suits, short shoes, cricket bats, cuff links, etc., merit differently proportioned image blocks. But the fact that Boltanski's premise is that this is "an Inhabitant" — any inhabitant — shows how little the catalogue is considered to violate the anonymity of its object. The sense of who the individual is relies so entirely on circumstantial and superficial information that though an accurate demographic portrait could be easily compiled — height, weight, income, class background, professional interests, and leisure activities all accounted for — the person's character would still escape. Boltanski's work is about this demographic mapping. This sense that person-ness and individuality are inflections of a generic and socially constructed sense of identity is crucial to this work. But from the perspective of providing a sense of what would determine whether one wanted friendship, marriage, business relations, or any other personal contact with the individual, this work shows the impossibility of representing an individual by their possessions alone. In the case of Lewitt and Boltanski the fact that these documents are contained within a book provides the conviction that they are complete. The book's finitude becomes a sign of the catalogue's completion — the question of whether there is more is answered by the pages' being bound within their covers.

Betsy David's **Dreaming Aloud, Book I**, (Rebis Press, 1985) and **Dreaming Aloud, Book Two** (Rebis, 1988-89) reveal the most intimate and personal details of her life through records of dreams and their analysis. Davids has been involved with dream writing for many years. Dreams informed her early poetry and performance texts, as material to be used, transformed, and edited into creative work. In **Dreaming Aloud, Two** the dilemma of more direct revelation is addressed by Davids in her introduction. She states that the process involves overcoming her own barriers and taboos against publishing them — because of what they reveal about her and also the way they might be construed as comments on or processing of her relations to the real people who appear in them, people who are very much part of her life. Davids made the decision not to hide these or her identity, but to allow the dream vocabulary to justify the presentation. The named characters, after all, are not the person, but a version of Davids herself. The two volumes are not identical in design. Both were

Betsy Davids, **Dreaming Aloud, Book Two**, 1985

produced on a Macintosh computer, both use digital images of Davids in various states of sleeping and partial waking, and both use a fairly distinct text/image layout in which the images occupy the borders of the pages, sometimes stretching into them but never really losing their discrete identity. The first book was output with a laser printer, then xeroxed onto a single side only of sheets which were folded and velo-bound — the open end of each fold bound into the spine. In the second volume each page was individually laser printed. The black and white values are striking, sharp, and the cotton-fiber sheets very white. The gently manipulated images have much more variety in the second volume, the distance from earlier to more sophisticated Macintosh and image interface is apparent. The color, tone, and general richness of **Book Two** could even pass for a contemporary interpretation of the visual density of William Morris's ornate borders and complex pages. These are highly personal documents which use the book form to reveal their intimacies through close contact with an individual reader.

If Davids' work invites intimacy and in the process reinforces the sense of the deeply personal aspects of her book, then Frances Butler's **Occult Psychogenic Malfeasance** (Poltroon, 1980) has the opposite effect. The book is composed of letters, photographs, and other documentary evidence collaged together to provide an account of an aborted relationship which Butler had with a man she met through a personals ad. The color-

338

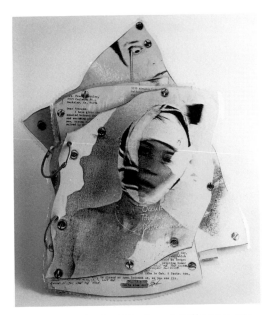

Frances Butler, **Occult Psychogenic Malfeasance,** 1980

xeroxed edition is laminated in plastic, in irregular shaped pages, bound with binder rings almost big enough to be handcuffs. The edges of these irregular pages are trimmed with pinking shears into regular but sharp little points. The images and letters provide a dialogue between Butler and this man. We are presented with his writing but her image, his text response to her and her visual response to him. On the cover she shows herself with a bandana or towel wrapped around her head, her face as tightly bound as a person with a head injury. Her shoulders and upper arms are naked, her face looking outward with an expression of mental agitation, mouth open, eyes staring, slightly unfocused into space. Other images show Butler peeling her eyelid back with a screw driver and lying on the garden grass, her feet raised to the camera, eyes closed. The man's letters condemn Butler, accusing her of being deranged, unbalanced, defensive, and anti-male. They are personal letters — written in anger and frustration. But it is Butler who is revealed here, her own process of purging the events from her mind gave rise to the book and its self-representation, though ironic, is harsh. One feels the intensity of disturbance which provoked this work and still produces it as an effect.

Francesca Woodman's **Some Disordered Interior Geometries** (Synapse Publishers, 1981) is also a disturbing book, if only because she committed suicide so close to the date of the photographs and writing which compose it. Like most of Woodman's photographs, these are self-portraits. The framework, however, is an Italian geometry text which has been used as a foil for the images. The regularity of the text, as well as of the systems, objects, and world it describes is in striking contrast to the blurred, complex, often multiply-exposed images of a body whose identity is disintegrated. A title on a page like "surfaces and volumes with three round forms" reads jarringly against a photograph in which torso, hands, and arms move through space around an empty seeming center. These are not merely formal contrasts. The reproductions of collaged pages make a record of dislocation, the document of (at the least) a body which cannot be stabilized within the geometrical system with which it tries to establish some coordinate points. Woodman, like Butler, shows us herself without giving any explanatory or discursive text. In both cases the women make the book a presentation of that self, a document of her condition whose reading is largely left to the viewer — unlike Davids, whose self-presentation is more clearly framed by directions for its interpretation.

Matthew Geller, **Difficulty Swallowing**, 1981, NYPL

Matthew Geller's **Difficulty Swallowing** (Works Press, 1981) uses documentary evidence to tell the story of his girlfriend's death from leukemia. In an introductory note, Geller explains what the documents and their sources are — from the files of medical personnel, friends, his own records, her diary, and so forth. After this note the materials are reproduced. Geller's own diary serves as the narrative text, but it is continually intercut with other materials and information. The book attempts both an unsentimental and an undesigned effect — subtitled "A Medical Chronicle" it eschews self-consciousness in its presentation. Here the problem of claiming the neutrality of the documentary format is clear: the editing, and selection of the pieces work in spite of their uninflected presentation. The sections of diary, Geller's and his girlfriend's, are much more intimate and compelling than the medical documents. The sheets of doctors' reports or blood tests tend to lose their identity, becoming pages of deferred attention, mere sheets to be turned before going on with the story, rather than contributing elements to its elaboration.

Bill Burke is a photographer who is well aware of the personal subtexts which underly any documentary work. Rather than attempt to conceal this, as Geller does, Burke makes this process of revelation part of his work. In **I Want to Take Picture** (Nexus Press, 1985), Burke overtly synthesizes the presumed objectivity of photographic journalism and the personal motivations which bring it into being. This is a book about a trip Burke made to Southeast Asia in 1982. It is a travel book, a log of a journey, and at the same time, a work in which personal issues inform every collage and photograph. There are certain similarities between his collaged pages of materials (cigarette packages, beer labels, and printed ads for houses of prostitution) and the structure of Betsy Davids's **Sites and Passages** (see Chapter 7). Both use diary pages as texts within these collages, texts which locate the reader in the writer's experience, their handwritten quality mirroring the immediacy of the traveller's response to the scene. But Burke's work also includes large black and white images from his photographic encounter with the people and circumstances of Thailand, Cambodia, and Burma. We are continually aware that it is Burke who is looking out through the lens, and Burke who is being looked back at. There is never a pretense of objectivity, rather the opposite, an attempt to inscribe as much of the subjective, the personal, and specific as possible into every exchange and every image it produces.

The large scale of this book contributes to its effectiveness: the pages are almost tabloid-size, close to 17 by 22 inches opened, which makes the openings enormous. Such an expanse supports a complex page structure. Burke is able to move through his narrative and pastiche significant amounts of supplementary material into the book. The format is never constant. Moving from the cluttered bars of Bangkok, filled with prosti-

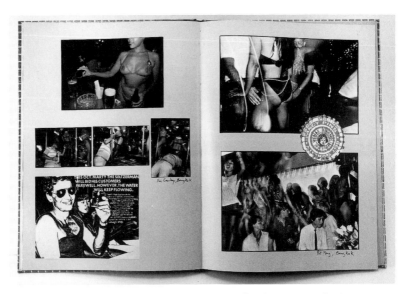

Bill Burke, **I Want to Take Picture**, 1985

Bill Burke, **I Want to Take Picture**, 1985

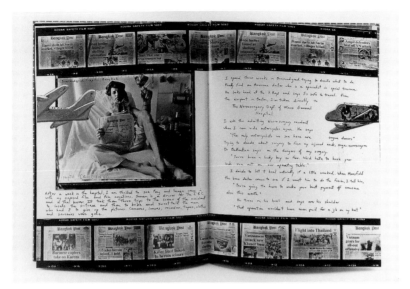

Bill Burke, **I Want to Take Picture**, 1985

tutes, to more remote rural areas, Burke changes his pages from busy lay-outs of group photos filled with fragmented frenetic action to large for-mat images, often with a single figure, holding their own on the page. His encounters with the Khmer Rouge, his records of soldiers, maimed men, and guerilla techniques are framed by his return to Bangkok, his automo-bile accident, and neck injury. At every point this book is located in his own experience. One reads and looks, into the photos, at the medallions, money, and printed ephemera. The newspaper headlines whose official accounts of military actions in the region Burke has just visited seem remote by contrast to the close-up view he has just provided. The full impact of this book comes from the juxtaposition between the scale of an individual consciousness and the scope of events which are produced as history with global repercussions. Burke does not heroicize, this is not a book of glory but of perception. Burke shows the self as a vulnerable and specific site of complex intersections with the world. He reveals the processes of mythification through his own point of view, offers it, and then leaves the reader to decide what use to make of the information.3

Reproduced Records

The concept of the reproduced record forms another approach to artists' books. In some cases, these "records" are fictitious or contrived

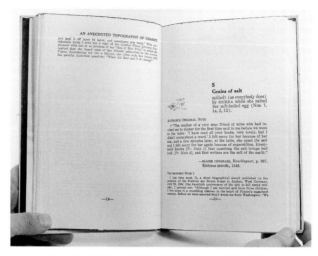

Spoerri and Williams, **An Anecdoted Topography of Chance**, 1966

and it is the documentary appearance which gives the works the appearance of an authenticity they in fact only imitate. In other cases, the book allows a record to be produced which serves as a document of experience, knowledge, or the complex relations of information. Daniel Spoerri and Emmett Williams's **An Anecdoted Topography of Chance** (Something Else Press, 1966), is a curious combination of all of these. The kernel of this book was a catalogue Spoerri had made for an exhibition in 1962 at the Galerie Lawrence in Paris. Spoerri is a sculptor who works with still-life compositions of real objects. Often the remains of a meal, the sculptures imply a scenario of activity of which they are the residue. The idea of recording the changes in the "topography" of such terrains as tabletops and other surfaces formed the basis of the project. Attempting to assess these random or chance events, Spoerri assigns to their placement and displacement all manner of significance through descriptive detail. The work is "anecdoted": stories which describe the objects and their relations to each other or the author are included to expand the mapping into a network of intricately lived relations. The translator, Emmett Williams, has interwoven his own text in an ongoing series of notes which add further commentary to the work since Williams was also a friend and participant in the events. In the introduction, for instance, Spoerri starts with "In my **(Tr. note 1)** room, No.13, on the fifth floor of the Hotel Carcassonne at 24 Rue Mouffetard, to the right of the entrance door, between the stove and the sink, stands a table that VERA painted blue one day to surprise me."

Williams' **Tr. note** 1, on the very next page, is an entry as long as the original. It begins: "My room too, during the author's absence from Paris to prepare an exhibition [...] Thus I begin this my translation [...] only an arm's length away from the principal terrain feature of the topography, the blue table."4 The book includes notes, tiny sketches, bits of information from various sources meant to complement the author's or translator's texts. This is a work of elaborate pastiche which "anecdote's" the authors' interactions with each other through a nuanced exchange. Each comments on the other's selections, information, and materials either directly or with other materials so that the whole is an expanding archive of interrelated notes — a record of its own making, constructing, and the auto-inflationary potential of the book.

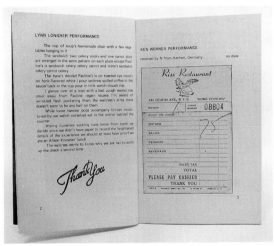

Alison Knowles, **Identical Lunch**, 1971

Several books by Alison Knowles function as documents, for instance, as scripts or scores of performances. However, the two works which will be discussed here are not entirely performance scores, though **Identical Lunch** (Nova Broadcast Press, 1971) is a journalistic account of a series of performances of a single piece. The book begins with a description of "the identical lunch" which consists primarily of "a tunafish sandwich on wheat toast with lettuce and butter, no mayo, and a large glass of buttermilk or a cup of soup." These were eaten "many days of each week at the same place and at about the same time." After this description, and a reproduction of a restaurant check for same (total, with tax, $1.68, for **two**) there follows a series of accounts of the performance of this "identical lunch" by Susan

Hartung, John Giorno, Dick Higgins, Vernon Hinkle, and others. Many of these accounts have dates, some identify the place and circumstances and difficulties or rewards of the performance. The accounts are recorded in different formats — perhaps by the original performers — using typewriter, typesetting, handwriting, and so forth. The book collects records of lunches which both are and are not identical. Knowles' **Gem Duck** (Edizione Pari & Dispari, 1977), in contrast, is a book whose artwork was produced through a xerox of shoes, shoe parts, heels, and lifts. The book is about shoes, its title taken from the trade name of a heavy fabric which is used in shoe construction. The book is offset printed in a rich silvery-grey ink, on coated stock, with a sewn binding, which transforms the original xerox images into finely produced pages. An extensive glossary of manufacturing terms for shoes serves as a textual/pictorial element, and there are other text documents layering typewritten, handwritten, and typset phrases onto the pages, though without any narrative unity. Most of these refer back to the manufacturing process as well, so that this is not a revealing document, rather an amassing of material information around a theme.

Eleanor Antin, **Being Antinova**, 1983, NYPL

Eleanor Antin's **Being Antinova** (Astro Artz, 1983) documents a sustained performance which she staged in 1983 on a trip to New York during which she constructed her public persona as that of "E. Antinova." Making herself into a character who was displaced in historical time as well as cultural time and physical space, Antin "became" a woman who had danced with Sergei Diaghilev's Ballets Russes. She posed herself in costumes and

346

then staged photographs to emphasize the look of the period — Antin's own Russian ancestry serving her well in the images. Exotic, sexual, and charged with a performer's intensity, Antin made a convincing record of these non-existent escapades. She reproduced the "sketchbooks" in which she jotted down reminiscences of various figures around the Ballets Russes — including notes of her encounters with the mythic Isadora Duncan. Interwoven with the "historical" materials are Antin's recollections of her trip to New York and she staged her performance as Antinova. Discussions with her friends, social and professional connections are interspersed with a journal about her anxieties about the project and its reception, and specific information about the mechanics (makeup, dress, accent) of the performance. This is an artist's account, making the various textual and photographic materials available, though its central focus is the actual activity whose details it records. It exists now as a historical document in its own right, and was conceived as such. As an artist's book it relies upon conventions rather than investigating or challenging them and its conceptual investigations take place within the material of her performance and its presentation, rather than through the format of the book.

Mary Kelly's **Post-Partum Document** (Routledge and Kegan Paul, 1983) is a document of an exhibition, the only such work included here. But it works as a book and is as self-sufficient as Barbara Bloom's **The Reign of Narcissism** or Alison Knowles' **Identical Lunch**. More significantly in relation to the other works in this section, it is the record of an exhibition which was conceived of as a documentary project. Kelly recorded the events of the first three years in the life of her son — from his first sounds to his first sentences, his feedings and defecations, his scribblings and every other aspect of activity. Saving shirts, diapers, and all matter of evidence, Kelly used the project as a challenge to certain received notions of maternity, particularly those generated within a Freudian psychoanalytic tradition. Demonstrating that a mother's fetishistic relation to the child was something entirely absent from theories of child development and Oedipal struggles, she articulated a female subject position — that of the mother's experience — as a feminist project. The exhibition generated considerable critical response. There were those who considered the art gallery display of soiled garments offensive — and others who grasped the critical implications of Kelly's art project as a challenge to theoretical writings. The reproduction of the materials from that exhibition are what comprise the book: each page is dedicated to a single one of the about three hundred items which were in the original exhibition. The book works as an exhibition space, reproducing the materials to allow a viewer to experience them as closely as possible to the original gallery situation, and also as a document, one which uses the conventions of book form. This is a highly personal document, but one which makes Kelly's voice typical rather than unique — for all its obsessive record keeping, it reveals very little about her personality or that of her child, instead concentrating on their relation in structural terms.

Joan Lyons, **My Mother's Book,** 1993

Another document which deals with maternity and identity is Joan Lyons' **My Mother's Book** (Visual Studies Workshop Press, 1993). Many aspects of this book belong to the category of the personal document: the text is transcribed and presented "in my mother's voice." These are familiar memoirs for Lyons: "I have heard each frail memory recounted a dozen times. We both pretend it is beng told, or heard, for the first time." Lyons' relation to the book as a form is completely different from that of Kelly — her movement into the work is structured visually and graphically through the page sequences rather than through a blunt straightforwardness. From the silvery cover image of her mother as a young girl in hair ribbons and white dress one turns to the title page; on the inside front cover is the continuation of the image — arms, waist, hands holding roses. The movement through the image becomes a movement through the book. As the book moves forward, pages of text alternate with these extracts of images, and when the centerfold of the first signature opens it displays the full formal family photograph of a Russian Jewish family at the turn of the century, the young girl, Lyons' mother, whose fragmented image we have seen all along is seated in the front at the left — now in context. The book is a double codex: a second signature and set of pages is bound into the cover fold at the end of the book. At the moment of transition from one part of the story to the next photographs dominate: the three-panel opening contains images of Ida Fischman (Lyons' mother) as a young girl, an older woman, and an adult woman. The story is at once unique and generic, its details of shtetl childhood, emigration to the United States, personal and financial struggles, family life, and so forth are interchangeable with those of others whose demographic profiles match Fischman's. But the voice of the individual woman comes through, her particular character and personality, as does Lyons', both in the format of the work and the snippets of text which are in her voice. The double pamphlet book folds up neatly, the presentation of the work integrated with the structure at every turn.

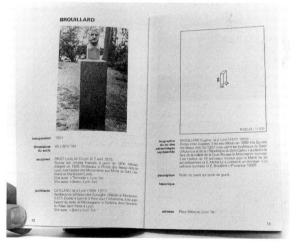

Daniel Buren, **Ponctuations statue/sculpture**, 1980

Daniel Buren's **Ponctuations statue/sculpture** (Nouveau Musée Lyon, 1980) is a handbook on the public monuments of Lyon, France. The book provides the means to "punctuate" these monuments through a proposed application of Buren's characteristic use of bands of alternating color. The book contains an exhaustive display of these monuments — statues, fountains, sculptural works, whose bases are measured in order to indicate the precise site of the suggested intervention. The interventions have not actually been made, instead they are to be made mentally by the reader by moving through the city and following the instructions to envision the transformations indicated on the page. This is the document of a projected work, which only exists conceptually and which would not exist at all without this book. It seems to be a guide to a non-existent exhibition, a catalogue which creates the work. Buren insists that his work "punctuates" the monuments the way they themselves accent the sites in the city in which they stand, the fact is that this context does not come into the book. Instead we are presented with guidebook style information one is accustomed to find in almost any guidebook: the date of inauguration of the sculpture, the name of the sculptor, notes on the person or persons represented, description of the work including its dimensions, materials, and its history. The book is both document and gallery, exhibition and record, its smooth paper, compact size, and finely printed pages quoting the form of the high-quality guidebook.

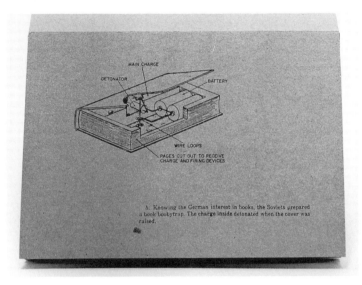

Skuta Helgason, **Boobytraps**, n.d.

Facsimile Documents

Various strategies of appropriation participate in books which function as reproduced documents. Brian Lane's **Fridtjof Nansen's Fog Log** (London, 1978) is a small pamphlet which reproduces pages from a logbook recording atmospheric conditions during a sea journey of several hundred years ago. This is precious imitation of a facsimile — using handwriting, pseudo-parchment paper, small format, and the conventions of nautical dating. The work is neither a document nor a deconstruction of one: it uses appropriated material which has been excised and transformed from its original form — the overt strategies of appropriation which feature strongly in artworks of the 1980s are not at work here. Lane has appropriated the text but presented it in a transformation. But in Skuta Helgason's **Boobytraps** the appropriations are direct. Unsigned, undated, unidentified, the book makes direct use of the 1965 Department of the Army Field Manual on the topic. To a contemporary eye this book reads like a savage parody though it is, in fact, an authentic reproduction: diagrams for the construction of flashlights, irons, bottles and every other conceivable device demonstrate the most effective means of using them to conceal explosives. As a book artist, Helgason clearly could not resist putting the book traps first in this volume. The clear line drawing of battery, detonator, main charge, and wire loops shows the location of these elements within a book whose pages have been "cut out to receive charge and firing devices." The drawing is accompanied by this caption: "Knowing the German interest in books, the Soviets prepared a book boobytrap. The charge inside detonated when the cover was raised." In Helgason's work, the use of found materials becomes a means to a critical end, rather than merely a means of presenting quotations in a thematic book treatment.

Tom Trusky, **Guest Book,** 1992

Tom Trusky's **Guest Book** (Boise State University, 1992) is a genuine fascimile document. The book's format is that of a mass-produced guest book, the sort used to record the public's comments to a gallery exhibition, wedding, or other event. This is precisely what is recorded here: the entries into the guest book record responses to the exhibition "Some Zines." "Zines," journals or magazines produced for a highly specialized group, circulate mainly among the fans or aficiandos of a particular cult-like activity (from Trekkies to Barbie followers, Brad Pitt fans, roller bladers, conspiracy theorists, and so forth). This exhibition generated considerable controversy in Boise, Idaho when it took place. It was also accompanied by a catalogue so that the **Guest Book**, doesn't serve any of the catalogue's functions. It just reproduces the audience's commentary. The book floats free from its context, however. Many people encountering this work won't know the details of the exhibition which generated it — and the comments are not specific enough to provide information about the exhibit. Nor does the work contain enough information to be a book in its own right. Instead, it becomes a facsimile guest book one could use, plant as a performance, in any number of situations. Though the source is acknowledged on the colophon, it is not evident within the work itself. The comments, ranging from "This is totally uncalled for" to "This excellent display expresses issues and feelings prevalent to today's society ..." would function as a comment to almost any exhibition. Trusky has included the ballpoint pen in its swivel holder so that any reader who feels inclined may add a comment to the existing text.

Hanne Darboven, **oo-99 Ein Jahrhundert**, 1976

Information

Some books by artists are structured around the presentation of information as information, which is to say, they are composed of material which is purely denotative. Hanne Darboven's books **Information** and **oo-99 Ein Jahrhundert** (Sost and Company, 1976) and Richard Kostelanetz's **Accounting** (Edizioni Amodulo, n.d.) are concerned with information as counting, a mathematical process which is empty of other content. These are works which contain a form of information which is hard to connect with systems of personal reference or hard to assign any particularly resonant qualities. Darboven's works are deeply personal, since they record the passing of her own time and the experience of its passing. The systems in which she counts and writes out the systemic counting are both a record of the system she is elaborating and a record of the time in which the accounting occurs. In **Ein Jahrhundert** the text consists of writing out the combinations of numbers which describe the progression of the year. Long tabular columns, large white pages, long rows of handwritten lines — all the visual codes of the account book structure the work. The book is purely a document of the account whose visual form was generated exclusively by its process. In **Accounting** Kostelanetz parodies the accumulation of numerical facts in the accounting process: a pyramid of numbers rises from page to page in an ever increasing stack of "information." Here there is no subtextual content to the numbers — they are a concrete element of visual poetics, a literal image of numerical manipulation.

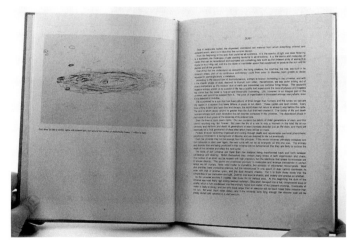

Agnes Denes, **The Book of Dust**, 1989

Agnes Denes's **The Book of Dust** (Visual Studies Workshop Press, 1989) and **Isometric Systems in Isotropic Space** (Visual Studies Workshop Press, 1979) have the look and feel of neutral, scientific presentations of information. If the information itself were not so esoteric, there would be almost no way to distinguish these from textbooks which elaborate on nuclear physics or quantum particle mechanics. In fact, Denes's sources

are often from the scientific community. She researches her books extensively, finding the many esoteric studies and investigations of the topics
she presents. These are like files put together by an obsessive scholar of
arcane areas which are both microscopic in focus and cosmic in their scale
and implications. The subtitle of **The Book of Dust** is "The beginning and
end of time and thereafter." The many minute particles discussed in this
work suggest that the scale which forms galaxies and the scale which
forms dust particles differ merely by a matter of degree — but are structurally similar. Denes's books are visually varied, with reproductions of
charts, diagrams, and elaborate analytical tables. The lines which distinguish the absurd, the trivial, and the profound are often close: the intense
seriousness of Denes's work makes the book a place of studied humility,
in which the documentary material is offered as a means of inquiry into
the abstract and often infinite nature of the world and the schemes of
knowledge by which we define it.

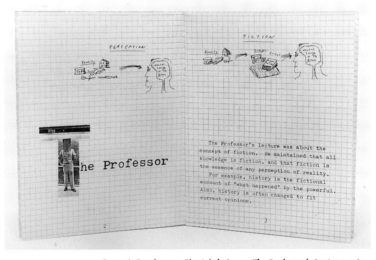

Francois Deschamps, **Einstein's Swan, The Professor's Lecture**, 1989

Francois Deschamps's, **Einstein's Swan, The Professor's Lecture**
(Deschamps, 1989) looks like an imitation school book with the black and
white marbled pattern familiar to American elementary-school children.
Into the line for the "name" the words "Private" and "Secret" are written,
followed by the words "DO NOT OPEN" — all in the same slightly inept
scratchy pen lines. Inside, printed in black ink on graph paper, is the
account of a lecture by "The Professor." Pictured as a man in khakis wear-

ing a brown paper bag on his head into which eye and mouth holes have been cut, the "Professor" delivers a lecture on the idea that "all knowledge is fiction." Topics of politics, physics, war, and color are touched on in a brief lecture which ends with the comment that we "do our best to understand what we cannot see." The small size, pamphlet form, and careful photographic reproduction of the school book all combine to make this parody of didactism successful as a critique of pretentiousness and assertions of expertise.

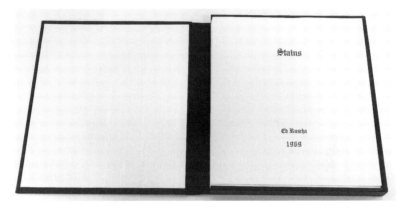

Ed Ruscha, **Stains**, 1969, Spencer Collection, NYPL

Actual Document

The contrast between Robert Morris's **Continuous Project Altered Daily** (1969) and Ed Ruscha's Stains (Heavy Industry Publications, 1969) demonstrates the differences between the book as a reproduced record and the book as an actual document. Morris's work consists of sixteen sepia-toned photographs of a series of items whose relations are altered on a daily basis. The items change each day as part of the continuous project, and the documentation of that process resulted in this work. But the book is a reproduction of the record, neither its actual realization in material form nor a direct production of the recording process. Ruscha's book, Stains, is both product and record: it is very literally a book comprised of sheets of stains. Its pages are embedded with grease, coffee, olive oil, meat, and coca cola. They are the testament and embodiment of the acts of staining. There is, of course, a sense of humor in Ruscha's "real" work — the insignificance and triviality of the occurrences, images, and marks are an antidote to the elaborate presentation and formality of the book itself (boxed portfolio, large pages, thick paper, glassine interleaving sheets).

355

The book contains everything one would not want on the pages of a book — substances whose presence causes reactions over time which threaten the book's longevity. These are the thematic content and the material substance of the book. But they are real, the stains in their actual presence on the page make the book a record of their occurrence, a document which documents itself. It may not be an important record, but it is one which makes the book integral with its material history.

1 These works differ from the documentary texts discussed in Chapter 11 because they do not have an explicit social or political agenda. Many have an implicit one, but the major concerns here are aesthetic.

2 I have tried to avoid works which are reproductions of existing pieces since they tend to fall into the incidental rather than intentional book realm — the only such work I have knowingly included here is Mary Kelly's **Post-Partum Document**.

3 A book which offers an interesting contrast to this is Paul Rutkovsky's **I am Siam** (Visual Studies Workshop Press, 1984). Rutkovsy's photographs, text, and coded meta-critical commentary on the amount of East/West cultural influence in each circumstance erases his presence except as documentalist and evaluator.

4 Daniel Spoerri and Emmett Williams, **An Anecdoted Topography of Chance** (Something Else Press, 1966) pp.xv and xvii respectively.

14

Metaphor and Form: The Artist's Book in the 20th Century

At the beginning of Emily Brontë's novel, **Wuthering Heights** (1847), there is a long description of the narrator Mr. Lockwood's investigation of a pile of mildewed books which he finds in the corner of a room he has been given for the night. It was the room of Catherine Earnshaw, the "Cathy" beloved by Heathcliff, and they are books which were hers since childhood. Inadvertently, Lockwood sets one of these ancient volumes alight with his candle "perfuming the place with an odor of roasted calf-skin." Snuffing out the smoldering binding he opens the book and thus enters unsuspectingly into the young woman's own intimately recorded thoughts. "It was a Testament, in lean type, and smelling dreadfully musty: a fly-leaf bore the inscription — 'Catherine Earnshaw, her book' and a date some quarter of a century back. I shut it and took up another and another, till I had examined all. Catherine's library was select, and its state of dilapidation proved it to have been well used, though not altogether for a legitimate purpose: scarcely one chapter had escaped a pen and ink commentary — at least the appearance of one — covering every morsel of blank that the printer had left. Some were detached sentences; other parts took the form of a regular diary, scrawled in an unformed, childish hand. [...] An immediate interest kindled within me for the unknown Catherine and I began forthwith to decipher her faded hieroglyphics."

The process of intimate discovery described in this passage is fundamental to the experience of the book as a form. From its many daily functions to its metaphoric existence, the book has the potential to provide a private space for communication and exchange across vast spaces of time and geography. Lockwood's first encounters with Catherine feel like a conversation — her presence has an immediacy and strength of personality which comes through in the handwritten entries and the tenacious persistence with which she sought out the space to make the clandestine marginal notations which protest against the conditions of her tormented life.

Lockwood remarks, for instance, on her very full use of an extra blank page in the endsheets saying "quite a treasure, probably, when lighted on." The preciousness to which he refers is not material, but spiritual — it is in these fortuitously encountered spaces which Catherine can find room to express the thoughts which her confining circumstances can't accomodate. She writes into books, not from them, using their private confines as a safe place to deposit the record of her struggles. And the books keep her counsel, until they open by chance to the eyes of this sympathetic reader.

Many artists' books which I have encountered have had this same feeling. They provide a glimpse or the expression of another person's experience suddenly revealed, communicated, across the space of time and with no other thread of connection than the existence of the book itself. They communicate not through an ordinary text or presentation but — as in the case of Catherine Earnshaw's writing — in all the opportune spaces and interstices which a book can provide. But it is also the independent life of these books — their persistence — which extends beyond the life of Catherine herself and gives them a potent autonomy. This life of books and ability to circulate on their own suggests an animate quality to these inert objects, moving them from one set of circumstances to another. Books I've lost, books I've found, books whose provenance is obscure and yet which are now clearly part of my collection — these are all evidence of the capacity of books to be in the world with an independence and mobility unlike that of any other work of art. One doesn't just happen to "find" a Jackson Pollock painting or a Nancy Spero drawing among one's things — or among the haphazardly organized shelves of a first- or second-hand bookstore. There are artists' books which will never have such a free life — precious objects with more sheltered existences. But who knows in what later lifetime even these will find an unexpected place. Books meet each new encounter without any need for their batteries to be recharged, software upgraded, or chips replaced. The durability of the book is part of its demonstrated value, and the elegant simplicity of the codex form is part of that durability. But it is the densely informative immediacy and intimacy of the experience provided by books which is at the heart of their longevity — their capacity to provide the sense which Lockwood has in encountering Cathy's palimpsests that he is in dialogue with the absent young woman, in touch with her spirit, her longings, her yearnings, her humor and wit, her desperation and exuberance, all through the medium of her scrawls and sketches.

Artists' Books as Metaphor and Form

The compelling quality of artists' books is the way in which they call attention to the specific character of a book's identity while they embody the expressive complexity of the book as a communicative form. In the course of my study, I have pointed out various aspects of what constitutes the identity of books in physical, material, and conceptual terms as well as the way they engage with the production of meaning. To a great extent, the material constraints of the codex (its fixed sequence and boundedness) are parameters which are observed — but stretched and extended — in the format of artists' books. Within these parameters the decisions about how to use the self-conscious awareness of the finite limitations of page, openings, turnings and sequence are all manipulated through decisions about layout, material choices concerning paper, ink, collaged or accrued elements, and binding structures. Artists' books take advantage of the efficiency of the codex and its capacity to contain considerable quantities of information (visual, verbal, literal and metaphoric) in a workable form. An artist's book may succeed on the strength of its formal qualities or on the compelling vision of its meaning, but the best artists' books are those which integrate production and content so dynamically that such distinctions are moot.

There are certain important critical tensions inherent in book structures. One of these is the tension between the fixed sequence of the codex form in a material sense and the expansive, non-linear, spatialized effect of reading and viewing. In other words, the tension between its physically finite and determined order and the linearity of the material form is continually counteracted by the experience of associations produced in the work's structure. No single encounter with a successful book closes off its polyvalent possibilities. The sense of limit which an edge, binding, and spine provide is countered by the infinite space of the page and opening, capable of drawing the reader inward in an endlessly expanding experience of sensation and association. There is another critical tension between the apparent conventionality of the book and its capacity to be reinvented anew through creative practice. And finally, there is a tension between the seeming simplicity of that conventional form and the unlimited complexity produced through the relation of elements to each other in a finite arrangement.

As an object, the codex is a form with infinite and inexhaustible possibilities. The page is the primary element of this form — one whose defined

359

edge is its boundary of identity. Permeable edges blur the relations between book and world; highly marked boundaries enclose the book into its hermetic self-definition. We enter the space of the book in the openings which position us in relation to a double spread of pages. Here the manipulated scale of page elements becomes spatialized: we are in a physical relation to the book. The scale of the opening stretches to embrace us, sometimes expanding beyond the comfortable parameters of our field of vision, or at the other extreme narrows our focus to a minute point of intimate inquiry. Enclosure and intimacy are two familiar features of this spatial embrace, and as a personal experience offering itself anew to each viewer, the book is unparallelled for its richness of detail, variety, and repleteness. In a conceptual sense, a page can subdivide infinitely; in a metaphoric sense, the process of looking and reading leads us into the labyrinthine web of associations which a book provides.

These formal features participate in the metaphoric possibilities of the book as an artform. All media have their metaphoric associations — painting, writing, sculpting, film and video — each conjures tropes in which the activity has a symbolic as well as a pragmatic value. These metaphors attach to the book's iconic form as well as its cultural significance in so many ways that it is impossible to invoke the book as a form without some of these many phantoms attaching themselves. The merest hint of red on the fore-edge of a book will invoke its liturgical functions, for instance, while tissue thin paper and miniscule type can hardly ever escape their phone-book identity. Artists' books take up these metaphoric associations from the broader cultural function of the book form, often deliberately turning them into self-conscious gestures or even cliches. The rich cultural history of book formats — from illuminated manuscripts to volumes of pulp fiction — is part of the language available to artists making books while new forms and formats are continually emerging. The sidebar and the pull-down menu, for instance, are recent motifs compared with the older iconography of rubricated letters or double columns of even toned text.

The idea of using books as the material or site of a metaphoric work has developed in tandem to the production of artists' books. Many works which make use of books as objects with metaphoric value use them generically: it is the general category of "book" rather than a particular book which serves to indicate "book-ness" within a sculptural work or assemblage. An early practitioner of such work was the English conceptual artist John Latham who made a series of infamous "SKOOB" sculptures in the 1960s called "book event structures."1 One of these consisted of a "skoob tower" (a pile of books) which he set afire in a ritual ceremony near the British Museum and its library. Latham says his intention was "not in any degree a gesture of contempt [for] the books as literature" but meant "to put the proposition into mind that perhap the cultural base has been burnt out." Given the continued production of books thirty years later, not to mention the persistent scholarly and spiritual traditions in which books preserve cultural memory, such a gesture seems naively premature, even inaccurate. Many contemporary works which call attention to the "end" of the book as a viable form seem oblivious to the continued vitality of print media in an age of electronic production. More importantly, however, Latham's piece shows the contradictions of such work — it tends to denigrate real books in the name of their metaphoric image.

Latham's work is most interesting in its relation to the specific art historical moment in which he produced it, such as his 1965 transformation of Clement Greenberg's **Art and Culture**. In this piece, titled "Still and Chew," Latham checked Greenberg's book out from the library of St. Martin's School of Art, invited a group of friends over, and proceeded to have them rip pages out of the book, chew them, and drop the masticated sheets into a bottle of acid. After this had fermented for some time the book was recalled. Latham returned the contents of the bottle to the library — where it was summarily rejected. Latham was then served with a notice terminating his appointment as lecturer. The bottle, its contents, the letter — all housed in a leather case — are now in the permanent collection of a major modern museum. The radically aggressive anti-formalism of this piece served to open a space for Conceptual art practice in opposition to the formalist aesthetics of high modernism then dominant in the artworld. Clement Greenberg's work, associated then and now with the high modernist position, had a genuine symbolic value which gives this piece a certain charge. Latham did other book mutilation sculptures and his work participates in a significant moment in the development of contemporary art — the abandonment of the investigation of form in favor of emphasis on the conceptual basis of art production.

Latham's work provides one historical precedent for those contemporary artists for whom books are used as material components of projects rather than a form in themselves. There are others: book-like objects, sculptural book works, and books transformed to the point where they lose their identity are part of the history of art since mid-century. But such pieces have little to do with artists' books: these are sculptural pieces which reference the book as a cultural icon rather than explore the potential and identity of book form. Their legitimate identity is in the realm of sculpture where the book-like object loses its functional identity as a book and becomes a formal and metaphoric icon serving a distinct — and different — aesthetic agenda.2 As such they are outside the parameters of my study and should not, in my opinion, be conflated with the category of artists' books. The confusion arises because of the presence of book elements in both cases — but every aspect of the experience of these works — spatial, temporal, and aesthetic — is posed in very different terms than those which serve as the basis of artists' books.

The Twentieth-Century Art Form

But it is with a return to my very first point of departure that I want to close my discussion: the idea that artists' books really are the quintessential 20th-century artform, one obviously fated to continue into the next century. In the course of this last hundred years, artists' books have acquired an identity which synthesizes the traditions of the craft of the book, the visions of the fine press and independent publishing, and the conceptual artistic idea of the multiple in all its variations into a form which did not exist before. Unlike sculpture or painting, printmaking or even photography, each of which has a longer history as an artform with its own identity, the artist's book is a new hybrid whose identity is continually emerging as distinct from any of these contributing antecedents. The form did not precede the 20th century in any significant way, and it is only at the end of the century that its full scope as an artistic activity is beginning to be recognized. In this regard it is similar to film and video, but with the exception that it builds upon very old traditions.

In looking over the history of the book in the 20th century, it is interesting to realize the extent to which books have managed to play a role in so many diverse movements. Books have participated in aesthetics as varied as Russian Futurism, Conceptual Art, Performance work, and Pop; they have expressed feminist concerns and been the repository of masculinist fantasy; they have found venues in museums, galleries, bookstores, and through hand to hand circulation. Books have demonstrated their capacity to play a flexible role in more forms of artistic thought than any other single medium or genre. Where painting or traditional sculpture have recently been perceived as moribund signs of the outmoded artisanal tradition, books remain viable, expressive, and transformable. In his 1965 essay "Intermedia," Dick Higgins pointed out that with all the varied modes of representation entering in the artworld, books were the one form which had the capacity to contain drawings, writings, performance and musical scores, photographs, transcriptions, and even material records and documents. This has proved to be true. In addition, because books are largely a reproductive artform, they make use of the expansion of art into the realm of mechanical reproduction, the multiple, the non-unique and non-auratic object in a way which was not conceptually legitimate in the art world before the 20th century. Rare, affordable, unique, or banal, books are a major staple of the artworld — as yet uncanonized and marginal, but omnipresent.

It is curious that the book as an artistic form has been considered largely incidental — as if its use were somehow not significant as a fact in its own right, merely a convenience. And yet, within each moment of the book's century-long interaction with the arts, books have mutated, expanded, transformed, and been reinvented to serve particular aesthetic sensibilities. Though my account of these interactions has been brief, the case has been made for the artist's book as an artform which will leave the 20th century with a very different identity than that with which it entered. And the arts, especially in the latter half of the century, would not have been the same without artists' books as a component. The legacy of this century-long investigation will be a rich one — once it is fully recognized.

The Future of the Book

In closing, it seems appropriate to reflect once more on the imaginative scope of the concept of the book in all its symbolic richness. Somewhere between the book as the world (the complete universe of human experience metaphorized into a representation) and the world as a book (a bound object so replete one is lost in its complex field forever) are real books. A book is an inhabitable universe of image and thought and language, a mute space of unrealizable dreams and manifest desire for form. The book is a passage of time, an expandable space, a fluid sequence of elements whose discrete identity becomes absorbed into the reality of a seamless experience, a static set of units whose unresolvable differences return the viewer to the cells of its interior spaces in a contradictory act of engagement and transcendence. A book is a received form endlessly reconceived to serve the vision and function of its new author, a form in which we all participate, reshaping its identity in the search for our own, experiencing its specificity in our desire for communicative exchange, working through its finitude in our need for a mortal expression of our own bid for immortality. At a point in time when there is much discussion of the end of print culture, the hype of new media and new technology burgeoning forth new forms, more books — and certainly more artists' books — are being produced than ever before in human history. It would be a mistake to see this as a last gasp bid for existence in the face of threatened annihilation. Quite the contrary. The culture of the book is our future, our continued work a legacy across time and space, a continuation of an ongoing tradition. Paper may become precious, printing technology transform, and production methods expand — but the potential of the book as a creative form will remain available for exploration. There are no limits to what artists' books can be and no rules for their construction — and fortunately there is no end of their production in sight.

1 Daniel Wheeler, **Art at Mid-Century** (Prentice-Hall, 1991), p. 171.

2 Tom Vogler, **Books as Objects**, (Comus Gallery, Portland, OR, 1994) exhibition catalogue.

INDEX